Psychobabble

A straight forward, plain English

guide to the Benefits of NLP

Donna Blinston

ISBN13 9781904312826

Published in the UK by

MX Publishing, 335, Princess Park Manor,

Royal Drive, London, N11 3GX

www.mxpublishing.co.uk

Cover Design by www.staunch.com

Donna Blinston is a certified trainer of Neuro Linguistic Programming (NLP) and the founder of Inspirational Solutions in your hands consultancy, trained by the only recognised trainers of NLP accredited by Kingston University. Inspirational Solutions started out as a one on one life coaching consultancy service. As the business has progressed additional partners with Business, HR and ICT backgrounds have been enlisted to develop Inspirational Solutions into the bespoke training and consultancy organisation it is today.

"I have always been passionate about developing myself and others. I love learning and feel privileged to be a part of helping others to learn and develop. I first found out about NLP in January 2005 when I did the NLP diploma. This changed my life in so many ways, I discovered what was important to me and more importantly, focused on what I wanted out of life. I was able to appreciate other people's point of view and build better personal and professional relationships. My professional life developed profoundly, which only increased my passion for finding out more about NLP".

By background Donna Blinston is a professional staff nurse in an ICU-Intensive Care Unit and intends to bring NLP techniques into common practice in the NHS. After dealing with a range of clients she has realized that the realms of NLP are limitless, with different techniques and practices lending themselves to benefit professionals from other professional backgrounds. Each course has been specifically designed for their target audience and will enable professionals to reach their full potential, get what they want out of their career and enjoy their work.

To my brother Jack Sheehan. For everything he has done, bringing my dreams to life.

1

Psychobabble: A straight forward, plain English guide to the Benefits of NLP

As a NLP trainer, I spend a lot of time speaking with students and found the one common trend in their misunderstandings was that they found the books available on Neuro Linguistic Programming (NLP) were too hard to read and understand, or didn't understand how they could transfer the skills into their everyday life. After researching the books available on the subject, I found that half of them were heavily academically referenced and theoretical, making them almost unreadable, while the other half only focused upon a specific audience, be that a key demographic or focusing on applying NLP to a certain profession.

Furthermore the main drawback of NLP is that it has lots of needless fancy/overcomplicated names that can put people off further. Through experience of working with clients from both business and healthcare backgrounds, to say; today we shall be studying "Anchoring" often leads to people looking with blank faces or worse, instantly shut off. Once the technique is described in real life terms asking "how would you feel if you had a confidence switch that you could just turn on whenever you choose?", then the whole room is at least interested in what I have to say, before making their judgments on whether or not it is appropriate to them.

So I went about writing; *Psychobabble: A straight forward, plain English guide to the Benefits of NLP*, a practical text book written in plain English so that all readers can follow and utilize the techniques of NLP up to Diploma level. After introducing what NLP is and how it originated, the NLP Diploma is then broken down into techniques organized by chapter. Each chapter then follows the same layout, further broken down giving a real world definition, the benefits, the history and/or science, a reference structure and real life examples of the technique. The chapter finishes with examples of when and how to use the techniques and practical exercises for the reader to learn and develop the technique

3

further for themselves. The purpose behind using the same chapter structure is to create familiarity and an easy reference structure to the reader, giving them the full range of information available, broken down into bite size chunks, allowing the reader to go straight to what they wish to read, without being force fed pages of theory if they do not wish to read it.

Moreover this textbook shows the practical benefits NLP can bring to a wide audience, making it ideal as recommended reading for students studying this subject, or supplementary reading for most Business & Management Degrees, Healthcare courses or simply for professionals in managerial positions.

Who am I? Well I am a certified trainer of NLP and the founder of *Inspirational Solutions - in your hands consultancy*. I was trained by the only recognized trainers of NLP who are accredited by Kingston University. Inspirational Solutions deals with clients from business and healthcare backgrounds and so a lot of the examples in this book relate to these industries. However I would like to stress that this is only down to my professional experience and due to its very nature NLP lends itself to be applied to any field, profession or background, for example you would use the same confidence exercise to build confidence in your abilities for sales as you would for patient care or in sport.

Due to its widespread application, NLP being a relatively new practice and due to the uniqueness in its methods and techniques, NLP could be viewed negatively, further disadvantaged by the field presently being unregulated. Inspirational Solutions is working with the appropriate bodies to get NLP academically recognized and the field more regulated, but for now simply wishes to show that NLP is simply an established set of principles for teaching, learning and personal development that provide you with a variety of strategies for maximizing both your professional performance and business potential. *"Psychobabble: A straight forward, plain English guide to the Benefits of NLP"* has been designed as an informative tool kit to enable you to navigate the jargon of NLP and realise the practical techniques this new science can bring you. Each technique has been organised by chapter so that it is easy to find for future reference. It is recommended that you first read the book from front to back, so that you understand the basics which are needed to utilise the techniques in the later chapters.

Each technique can be applied to your own needs and used at your own pace, as you start implementing these tools and techniques you will find they lend themselves to be used time and time again in different contexts, a few of which we have outlined in their respective chapters.

Even though you may see the benefits of using these techniques straight away, you may want to return to this book several times in the next few months. It is no good just reading, it is vitally important that you do the exercises in order to apply the techniques correctly for them to be beneficial to you. No single technique is a magic pill for success, by practicing the techniques again and again will allow them to become second nature to you, this is when you will start to realise the practical benefits they bring.

Despite its alien name, NLP offers a range of useful practices and techniques that lend themselves to benefit you in a whole range of situations. As the old saying goes: if you keep doing what you've always done you'll just get more of what you've already got. If you

> *"When you pick up one end of the stick, you pick up the other"* Dr Stephen R. Covey

decide to take responsibility for your circumstances, you automatically tap into the power to change them.

Chapter 1 defines NLP, looking at its benefits, where it originated and its history.

Chapter 2 shows the founding principles of NLP. These are easy to grasp concepts which are applied and expanded upon in the respective later chapters. The areas covered are:

1. Communication model
2. Presuppositions of NLP
3. Cause and Effect
4. Feedback Sandwich
5. Ecology
6. Principles of success
7. The stages of learning
8. Taking responsibility for your results

Chapter 3 introduces Sensory Acuity or what is more commonly known as sensory awareness. It is the ability to gain awareness of another person's unconscious responses to deduce whether what you have said has been understood correctly. Sensory acuity allows you to gather a whole host of new information about another person and is most effectively used to prevent misunderstandings or breakdowns in communications. By becoming more sensory aware you enhance your interpersonal skills, enabling you to communicate even more effectively.

Chapter 4 expands on sensory acuity moving into Rapport. Rapport is commonly known as being "in sync" with, or being "on the same wavelength" as the person with whom you are talking. Moreover it is the ability to relate to others in a way that creates a climate of trust and understanding. It is the capability to see each other's point of view and to appreciate each other's feelings. The aim is to be able to establish rapport with any person at any one time. When people are like each other, they like each other and are open to the other person's suggestions. It is important to stress that rapport is not just "liking", but more about being comfortable in the other person's presence and surroundings. Rapport is not manipulating another person to agree with your views, it is a way of allowing them to be more comfortable in your surroundings so that they broaden their horizons and acquire the ability to see where you are coming from, which makes it an essential skill in negotiations.

Chapter 5 continues to apply previous theory to make and achieve Goals and well formed Outcomes, which can be applied on a personal, professional or organizational basis. This chapter looks into what makes goals successful, highlighting potential reasons why goals have not been met previously. Comparing where you are now with where you to want to be, to ensure that when you get there; you have more beneficial opportunities open to you and realise the positive by-products of your goal.

Chapter 6 looks into our Representational Systems: how the human mind processes information. This is one of the more well known techniques as it has many similarities to the different learning style indicator tests carried out in high schools and produced by the likes of Honey & Mumford. Representational systems are also known as sensory modalities, the 4-tuple, and abbreviated to VAKOG. It states that for practical purposes, information can be treated *as if* it is processed through our senses and is the way we represent, code, store and give meaning to our experience. Understanding someone's preferred representational system enables you to communicate to them more effectively.

Chapter 7 assesses the Power of Language and looks at language as a set of tools to increase your awareness of the language you use and the impact it could have on another person. Language is one of our most powerful filters and often beyond our conscious awareness. Words communicate much more than we can consciously process. By taking responsibility for our language and utilizing language effectively, we are able to gather much more information than was presently available from a situation.

Therefore language is a huge topic which we have broken down into the following subchapters to help navigate through and to serve as easy to find techniques for future reference.

Subchapter 7.1 introduces the foundations of the language chapter: Linguistic Presuppositions, which are what we assume to be true in a sentence in order for it to make sense. The power of linguistic change presupposes that the unconscious mind has to accept the presuppositions inherent in the sentence in order for the unconscious mind to make sense of the sentence.

Think of the statement "The window is broken", what do you presume for this statement to be true? We can assume that it's cracked, it's shattered, it does not open, hinge has gone, needs fixing, it's been smashed. The truth is simply: there is a window, it's broken. The thing about Linguistic Presuppositions is that it aims to distinguish between the truth (there is a window, its broken) and a mind read (someone has smashed it, the hinges have gone). Paying attention to the presuppositions someone uses will allow you to help them explore where they are limiting themselves and to find out the strategies that they are using to achieve their current results, so that you can question that linguistic presupposition to show them other strategies.

Subchapter 7.2 contrasts the Milton Model and the Meta Model. The Milton Model is a set of language patterns that are ambiguous and artfully vague. By being artfully vague in our language we can induce trance states enabling individuals to overcome their problems and discover new resources that they were previously not aware of. The use of language is essential in directing a person's experience and focus of attention. The Milton Model lists the key patterns of speech that are useful to subtly and effectively direct another person's line of thinking. The principle behind the Milton Model is that the general use of language can lead to more rapport, where specific language is more limiting and has a greater chance of excluding concepts from a person's experience.

In contrast the Meta Model is the language of specificity. The Meta Model was developed to recover information about how the client has created their model of reality, through a framework for the reconstruction of what someone has deleted, distorted or generalised about an external event. The principles of the Meta Model are based on the presupposition: the map is not the territory, the words we use are just the words we have chosen to explain the event and the meaning that event had for us. By using language specifically; we can obtain additional true information relating to the event, allowing new choices to become actualized.

Subchapter 7.3 continues looking at the Hierarchy of Ideas technique as an order of thinking. By being flexible in our language, we can pace a client's model of the world and influence them to higher or lower levels of abstraction or specificity. The Hierarchy of Ideas technique utilises the concept of chunks of information and our ability to take such a chunk and '*chunk up*' to a higher level of abstraction or '*chunk down*' to a lower level of specificity and even '*chunk sideways*' or laterally between two chunks at the same level of abstraction.

As we get more and more abstract, we deal with larger and larger (Picture/Mission/Purpose) chunks of data. As we get more specific, we deal with smaller and smaller chunks of data. Imagine being on top of the Eiffel tower, from the top you have a lovely overview of Paris, seeing for miles and miles in all directions. However you cannot see what is going on in the streets, houses and shops below you until you come down the tower and walk from its base. When we "chunk up," we move up the Hierarchy of Ideas to the more abstract, when we "chunk down," we get more and more specific.

There are many examples of when we can utilise chunking up or down, one example of how we use this Hierarchy of Ideas technique is in a meeting or during a discussion, to get back on track with the agenda by chunking up and then chunking down a different way, back to the topic that was being questioned and resulted in the meeting going off piste. We tend to differ less on the bigger-chunk items as most people in a meeting could agree on

9

such sweeping statements as "We want the company to succeed." So when there is disagreement, chunking up to a place where people agree can help remove personal agendas and emotion to defuse the tension and give everyone the same context. You can then carefully chunk down, preserving agreement, to ensure the agenda is met and to develop the details that you require.

Subchapter 7.4 finishes the language section, looking at the Logical Levels within language, which assume that human processes can be described along a ladder of categories that represent the cause of the problem. This ladder suggests a natural hierarchy, the levels influence each other in both directions, where a change on a higher level will have a greater impact on the lower levels, whereas a change on the lower levels will not necessarily affect the higher levels. The Logical Levels model can help you align your environment, behaviours, competencies, beliefs/values, identity and purpose, to make you aware of any in-congruency. Why? An example would be to ensure your behaviours represent your overall identity, so that every part of you is working towards achieving your personal mission.

Chapter 8 is about Submodalities, which are the finer distinctions of our representational systems of visual, auditory and kinaesthetic, covered in chapter 6. They are how we code, order and give meaning to our experiences, therefore having a great impact upon how we perceive what goes on around us. By changing these finer details we can make positive memories more empowering and negative memories less restricting, e.g. enabling us to change attitudes towards activities/foods we like & dislike and to empower our goals and future.

Chapter 9; Anchoring is a stimulus that creates a response in you or another person. Therefore the process of anchoring is using a memory (Visual, Auditory, Kinaesthetic, Olfactory or Gustatory) of a positive resource to produce a positive state of mind and change your behaviour. A Psychotherapist might anchor positive states like calmness and relaxation, or confidence in the treatment of anxiety, such as in public speaking

Chapter 10 builds upon all you have learnt so far and teaches you the technique of Perceptual Positions: the skill of adopting more points of view in an experientially rich and organized way, therefore allowing you to have multiple perspectives in a situation so that you can have a greater influence and be more flexible. The technique is commonly used in problem solving, conflict resolution, creativity, career planning, departmental realignment and new product/service development. Perceptual Positions, enables you to gain insights not only into situations but also into yourself and how you are being perceived by other people. You start to see things from another person's point of view, respecting their model of the world, enriching your leadership and management skills.

Chapter 11 concludes the NLP Diploma, explaining the concepts of Framing and Reframing, a further expansion of perceptual positions. Firstly looking at how to put different 'frames' around what you are saying to give maximum impact and change the perceptions (the way you think about or see things) of whom you are communicating to. The frame you set reflects the way you perceive, providing a context, focus or guidance for your thoughts and actions. Frames provide focus on our activities and a context in which we can assess our progress, to explore other possibilities and ensure common understanding. The meaning of all experience is dependent upon the frame we put around the experience or the context of the experience.

Reframing is the process whereby an element of communication is presented to transform an individual's perception of the meanings or "frames" attributed to words, phrases and events. Changing the way the event is perceived allows responses and behaviours to also change. When you are reframing you are asking people to notice where else this 'behaviour' would be useful, or what else could this 'behaviour' mean, the answer of which can completely transform the problem.

Chapter 12 goes beyond the NLP Diploma syllabus and introduces the concept of Values. Values are the primary source of motivation in people's lives where when met or matched, people feel a sense of satisfaction, harmony and rapport. But when values are not met people often feel dissatisfied, incongruent or violated. Values are a powerful perceptual filter that we use to assess situations to basically gauge what we do and don't desire. Values affect all the outcomes that we set for ourselves and the decisions we make.

In short they steer our lives, completely motivating our actions, determining what we achieve, what we perceive ourselves and how we develop as individuals. I have included Values in this book because having your values elicited gives you great insights into what is truly important to you, so that you can evaluate and align the different areas of your life to your values, to have all parts of you working towards the same goals. These principles and techniques can also be applied in an organizational context, realigning the company values to ensure the company's mission is portrayed in each and every department.

Chapter 13 is simply a glossary of terms: all the "psychobabbly" words, phrases and terms which have been used in this book are additionally defined here. (I would like to stress these terms have been explained throughout the book in their respective chapters and it is not the case that when the reader comes across the term they have to flip to the back of the book. This glossary is just an additional easy navigational resource!)

I would like to take this opportunity to acknowledge the many teachers and developers of Neuro Linguistic Programming. The NLP tools and techniques written within this book reflect the work of those who have developed it. This book intends to put the techniques into easy manageable chunks, providing the underpinning knowledge and principles of how and why these techniques are so successful.

Connirae Andreas

Steve Andreas

Gregory Bateson

Richard Bandler

Robert Dilts

Charles Faulkner

John Grinder

Tad James

Judith De Lozier

Henrietta Laitt

Ian McDermott

Bill O'Hanlon

Anthony Robbins

Shelle Rose Charvet

John Overdurf

David Shepard

Robert Smith

Dr Wyatt Woodsmall

I would like to give an additional special mention to Jeremy Lazarus, who has taught me more than he will ever know, especially Lisa Wake, my inspiration and Suzanne Henwood for introducing me to this subject.

I am greatly indebted to all these teachers for their knowledge, understanding and their commitment to ensuring the power of NLP is available to all who want the personal and professional development it enables. My mission is to bring NLP into healthcare, bringing the tools and techniques alive so that the readers easily understand and can reference the usability of the techniques to enhance their current practice. I also want to thank my students, who have prompted the production of this book and enhanced the depth of my own learning and understanding of NLP, it is for them that this book has been written.

13

Chapter 1:

NLP Defined - NL What?!

"Whether you think you can or you think you can't, you're probably right" Henry Ford

What has NLP got to offer?

There are many applications of Neuro Linguistic Programming (NLP), I specifically deal with NLP in business, healthcare and on a personal one to one level, however these techniques can be universally used and applied to the fields of sport, education, training and coaching. In this book I want to leave out as much of the psychobabble as I can, giving just the practical techniques that I have found most beneficial. I have however given explanations and history behind each technique (for those of you who are interested) and real life examples of where you would use it, leaving in a just a few of the key terms and phrases for those of you who are studying this subject.

Success requires courage, commitment and focus. When applied appropriately to your needs, or those of your organisation, NLP can significantly contribute to your success through;

- Increased sales & revenue.
- Improved personal performance.
- Improved leadership, management and teaching skills
- More focused & effective change initiatives.
- Better personal communication & influencing skills.
- Enhanced staff motivation
- Business vision and goal setting.
- Ability to create stronger patient/staff relationships.
- Resolution of ward conflicts.

"Until one is committed, there is hesitancy, the chance to draw back and always ineffectiveness. Concerning all acts of initiative, there is one elementary truth the ignorance of which kills countless ideas and splendid plans: that the moment one definitely commits oneself then providence moves too. A whole stream of events issues from the decision, raising in one's favour all manner of unforeseen incidents, meetings and material assistance, which no man could have dreamt would have come his way" W H Murray

15

- Empower and motivate your colleagues and patients.
- Develop greater team work, creativity and problem solving skills

NLP Defined

There are many definitions of NLP, from the illustrious and vague: *"How we use the language of the mind to consistently achieve our specific and desired outcomes"* (Richard Bandler) to the more plain English and accessible: *"A model of interpersonal communication chiefly concerned with the relationship between successful patterns of behaviour and the subjective experiences (esp. patterns of thought) underlying them" and "a system of alternative therapy based on this which seeks to educate people in self-awareness and effective communication, and to change their patterns of mental and emotional behaviour"* (Oxford English Dictionary)

We shall start with Richard Bandler, the Godfather of NLP if you like, who we shall also discuss later in the history of NLP.

Richard Bandler (thankfully!) also describes Neuro-Linguistic programming (NLP) as *"An attitude and methodology that leaves behind a trail of techniques"*, explaining that an attitude of wanton curiosity and a willingness to experiment to understand how things work leaves behind (gives the user) an increased range of skills and techniques that benefit their daily life. This hunger to understand how things work leads to discovering and taking on the beliefs, values and behaviours found in people who are outstanding in their respective fields, to utilise and benefit yourself and others.

Knight (2002) reinforces this statement in her definition that NLP is *"The study of what works in thinking, language and behaviour. It is a way of coding and reproducing excellence that enables you to consistently achieve the results that you want both for yourself, for your business and for your life"*

To me NLP is simply an established set of principles for teaching, learning and personal development that provide you with a variety of strategies for maximising both your professional performance and business/career potential.

Why would we want to learn NLP?

We live in a world of unpredictable, complex and continuous change. The more we learn the more that unravels itself in which to seek. We need skills and attitudes to help us learn how to make sense of this evolving change and more importantly, we need to know how to communicate with people of vastly different cultures and understand others' perceptions, regardless whether they are similar to or poles apart from our own.

NLP aims to overcome this, preparing us to anticipate and welcome change and to use language effectively with all the people we meet.

So why the silly name?

Let's break Neuro Linguistic Programming down; Neuro is understanding the patterns in our thinking. By understanding we can learn how these patterns influence the results we are getting in our work and personal life. Therefore the key to finding personal and business success comes primarily from within ourselves and learning about how we think enables us to utilise our inner resources.

Linguistic is appreciating that what we say is what we think we can (and can't) do. Learning to understand and master the structure of our language is essential in a world where we trade increasingly through our ability to communicate.

> *"Argue for your limitations, and sure enough they're yours"*
> Richard Bach

Finally, Programming; we run our lives by having strategies/goals/objectives, very similar to how a computer uses a program to achieve a specific result. By realising and understanding the strategies we use to run our lives we give ourselves greater choice: choice to do more of the same or choice to enhance our potential and our individual excellence.

In essence, NLP is the study of our thinking, behaviour and language patterns so that we can build sets of successful strategies that work for us in making decisions. NLP can be described as the study of the mind and body link and the direct effect they have on each other. If you believe that you can achieve something then your positive state will enable you to find the resources to achieve it.

History

NLP stands for Neuro-linguistic programming and was developed in the early 1970's when John Grinder and Richard Bandler (the founders of NLP if you like) began working on the theory of modelling (Modelling is discovering and taking on the strategies, beliefs, values and behaviours found in individuals who were exceptional in their respective fields and utilising these values and behaviours to benefit yourself and others). As I see it they came up with the crazy name from their respective backgrounds; Bandler was a mathematician, therapist and computer programmer (programming) and met John Grinder at the University of California at Santa Cruz, where Grinder was a language professor and a world-renowned linguist (linguistic) and began to study the field of human change and the study of the mind, (neuro).

They studied experts in this field (of human change and the study of the mind) and noticed some very interesting, if not conflicting, patterns. When studying Viginia Satir, a successful family therapist based in Palo Alto, California, they discovered that she affected and changed the behaviour in her clients by being very specific. While in contrast, when they studied Milton H. Erickson, commonly known as the father of hypnotherapy, they discovered that he achieved behavioural change by being extremely ambiguous with his use of language.

From this Bandler and Grinder devised the Meta Model and the Milton model (which we shall look at in Language subchapter 7.2) the Meta model being very specific while the latter is vague and ambiguous. This was the start of Neuro Linguistic Programming: through the application of their discoveries Bandler and Grinder modelled these techniques and created a process for learning them, the "how to" of getting into rapport (covered in chapter 4) for example.

Bandler and Grinder continued to study the techniques of people who were the leaders in their field, they then modelled and organised these techniques so that they could be learnt and replicated by others to achieve their desired success. NLP has expanded throughout the years, being taken up and expanded upon by other NLP practitioners and academics; in addition to therapy NLP has been applied to business, education, the arts and many other vocations.

References

- Bandler, Richard; Grinder, John. (1979) *Frogs Into Princes.* Real People Press, Moab, Utah,
- Bandler, Richard; Grinder, John. (1975) *Patterns of the Hypnotic Techniques of Milton H. Erickson, Vol. I.* Meta Publications, Cupertino, California,
- Bandler, Richard; Grinder, John. (1975) *The Structure of Magic, Vol. I.* Science and Behavior Books, Palo Alto, California,
- Bandler, Richard; Grinder, John. (1976) *The Structure of Magic, Vol. II.* Science and Behavior Books, Palo Alto, California,.
- Bandler, Richard; Grinder, John; Delozier, Judith. (1977) *Patterns of the Hypnotic Techniques of Milton H. Erickson, Vol. II.* Meta Publications, Cupertino, California.
- Knight, Sue. NLP at work. (2002) Nicholas Brealey publishing, London
- nlpuniversitypress.com
- Wake, Lisa. (2008) *Neurolingustic Psychotherapy*, Routledge.

Chapter 2:

Foundations of NLP

"For a tree to become tall it must grow tough roots among the rocks." Friedrich Nietzsche

In this chapter we shall be learning the fundamental principles of NLP, which need to be learnt and understood to grasp how to effectively use the techniques in the following chapters.

1. Communication model
2. Presuppositions of NLP
3. Cause and Effect
4. Feedback sandwich
5. Ecology
6. Principles of success
7. The stages of learning.
8. Summary: Taking responsibility for your results

NLP Communication Model

To understand how we take information into our neurology and how that affects our behaviour, there is the NLP "model of communication". It is based on the notion that our five senses; sight, hearing, touch, taste and smell, take in two million bits of information at any one moment. Our conscious mind however, is only able take in approximately 126 bits of information during this same time period.

In order to compensate for this vast difference the mind filters the events our senses take in by deleting, distorting and generalising the information through our language, memories, attitudes, values, beliefs, decisions, etc. We then make an internal representation of the world we are taking in, with pictures, sounds and feeling. That puts us in a state of mind, which can change our physiology, that affects our behaviour. All this happens in a fraction of a second and none of it has to happen in any particular order. We are in a constant state of flux, where our physiology can affect our attitudes just as easily as our behaviour can affect our language.

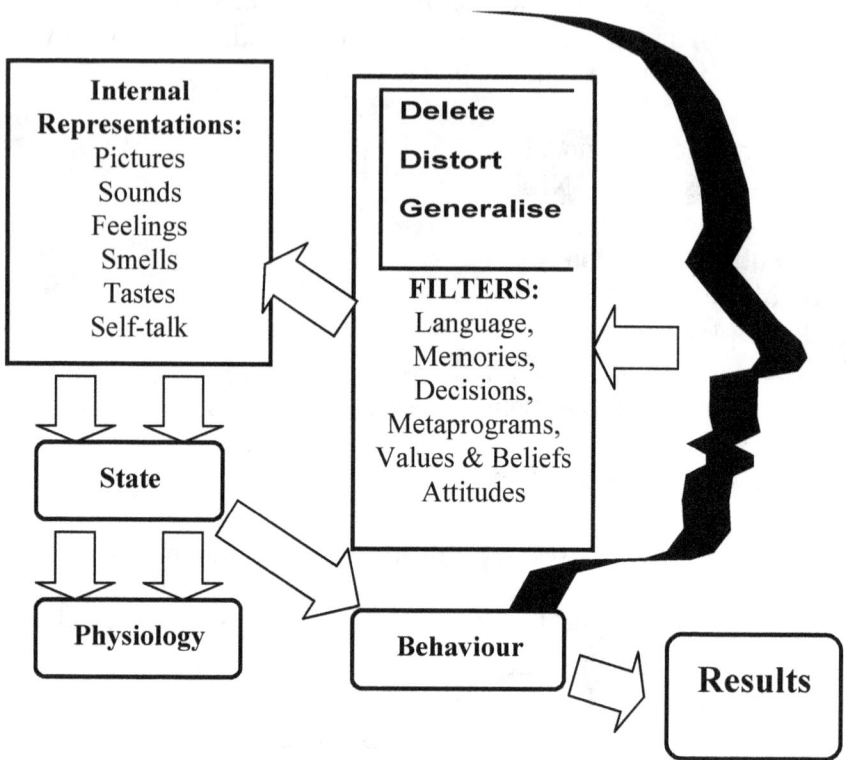

The communication model shows how we as humans interpret the world differently. Boyes (2006) explains that we are all unique individuals that have our own set of rules, which govern how we interact with people, how we talk to ourselves and how we choose what we focus on and achieve. At any one time during your waking experience, you are being bombarded by over 2 million bits of sensory (light, sound, feeling, tastes & smells.) information. We unconsciously filter out the information which is irrelevant to our cause. We leave out the unnecessary so that we can reduce the incoming information to what matters to us at that time.

Boyes (2006) states that these filters do the job of deleting, distorting and generalising according to our model of the world. Each second these 2 million bits of information come in through our senses and are filtered through our memories, beliefs and values, decisions, meta-programs (how you react to information given to you due to your personality traits i.e. how you conceptualise, perceive and comprehend information) and your idea of time/ space, matter & energy. At the end of this process you're left with your perception. This perception is your internal representation (re-presentation) of the external information around you when it is reduced down from 2 million bits to 126 bits. All internal representations are made up of images, sounds and sensations that constitute our model or image (belief) of the world. These are instantly translated through the nervous system (neurology) and expressed as chemicals in the body (emotion) which then influence our actions (behaviour). Because of this process how we perceive reality can be completely different to the person stood next to us, who generalises this information down to another set of 126 bits of information and experiences their own version of reality, therefore reality is not "out there" but how we filter it to be.

> "What we see and hear is what we think about. What we think about is what we feel. What we feel influences our reactions. Reactions become habits and it is our habits that determine our destiny." Bob Gass

The encyclopaedia of NLP developed by Dilts and DeLozier (2000) expands on the communication model stating that the world is far from the passive act it appears to be, for when we look at something we see it coloured by our own set of unique experiences. If I am looking at a sunset, and feel depressed, my mood seeps into the sunset, making the whole appearance of the scenery sad. If I am joyful, the same sunset reflects my joy back to me. This fusing of "me" and things "out there" is what makes our experience "subjective". Just by listening, looking smelling, tasting, and feeling, I can turn the world into my world.

The only reality for each of us is our own individual subjective (sensory) experience of it. Human reality depends heavily on the unconscious (94-96%) and conscious (4-6%) beliefs we hold, which act as the glue of interpretation. This holds a notion which relates back to work done by Freud and later by Jung where they looked into the concept of "perception is projection"; that we all have differing perceptions of reality, and it's these perceptions that we project into the outside world. According to Charvet (1995) the words we use are not actually the event or the item they represent, they just describe the event we have chosen them to represent; the words themselves are not the actual event itself.

Robert Dilts goes onto say that subjective experience relates to our own unique perception and understanding of the world within and around us. This encompasses all our sensations, emotions, beliefs and knowledge base that have been developed through our life time. These accumulated personal life experiences are made from our filters, which influence our perception of the world and the way we choose to interact with the world. We create our own reality based on our past experience. Our language becomes a 'map' of the 'territory' of our constructed reality, through the information we have obtained through our five senses.

Going back to the NLP communication model, which states that we Delete, Distort and Generalise the external event through our set of filters (Language, Memories, Decisions, Metaprograms (in short; what we do and don't pay attention to), Values & Beliefs and Attitudes) that directly influence our internal representation of the external world. We can start to appreciate that basically what you believe is your result – the same event can, depending on your beliefs and values, give different internal representations. We delete portions of experience determined by our ability to handle abstract data and a preference for absorbing data into more manageable chunks, we then further generalise the event on past learned experiences and behavioural responses and finally distort the event by interpreting it in a way that best fits our internal world. If we did not delete, distort and generalise the events we take in, consciously we would be in sensory overload: the sensation of more things happening than you can handle, which can be quite overwhelming, can't it?

<u>Deleting, Distorting and Generalising explained.</u>

Delete - This is when we omit data or selectively pay attention to certain experiences and not to others. Think of a time when you were so engaged in a conversion that you were unaware of the other events going on around you, i.e. in a restaurant. Have you walked down the street with a friend of the opposite sex and later that day when you are back at home they ask you your views on the new phone/game/computer/electrical shop, which you didn't even see! You then talk about the girl with the bright green hair, or new clothes/handbag shop which they didn't notice.

A further example of this would be right now as you are reading this book you won't have been aware of the feeling of your back in the chair or of the feeling of the socks on your feet until I mentioned it.

Distort – Distortions are when we misrepresent our reality. A distortion is the alteration of the original shape of an object, image, sound, or other form of information or representation. This is when you distort reality, i.e. can you imagine this room in red? Another example of distorting reality is when you and another person both go to see the same film or to the same meeting but you both have a different interpretation of what you saw/heard.

Generalise – Stereotyping generalisations are ideas or conclusions that have a general application/thing in common. It is putting ideas, people or things into a convenient group or category, or drawing global conclusions. This is why you don't have to re-learn how to drink from a different glass as you have generalised that it would be the same as drinking from any other glass you have used.

Watch out for the filters you place in your world, for the world is never what we think it to be. If we are taking in 2 million bits of information and only aware of around 126 bits, there is much data we are missing. The words we use are not actually the event or the item they represent: although they describe the event we have chosen them to represent the words themselves are not the actual event itself. We create our own reality based on our past experience. Our language becomes a 'map' of the 'territory' of our constructed reality, through the information we have obtained through our five senses. We code, order and give meaning (through deletion, distortion and generalisation) to our experience in words, sounds, pictures, feelings, tastes and smells. Five different people might all experience the same event, but each will take a different experience away from it depending on their own beliefs and values.

Presuppositions of NLP – Convenient assumptions

These are the founding principles of NLP which, when utilised, will provide you with a framework for learning and understanding the techniques in the following chapters. Some of these principles are going to be alien to you, try not to dismiss them out of hand; we have all lived a good life by our own principles, so what harm will come of trying new ones? An unfortunate example of this is after 10 years of playing squash an old man tapped on the gallery window and told me I was holding my racket wrong. Rubbish I thought, my serves are powerful and returns are low. The old man kindly (rudely!) took my racket and explained where my thumb and forefingers were meant to be placed and then went on to say I had the hardest job of all, as I had been playing for so long I had to put my old technique aside and will have to adopt this new technique. I will be truthful and say at first it was not easy, and sometimes I slipped into my old habits. But by staying firm and practicing, I am happy to say I have become a better squash player. The bad news I'm afraid is that this applies to you adopting these principles below;

a. **Respect for the other persons "Model of the World".** In order to create change effectively in another person, you do not have to believe what they believe, but simply respect and seek to understand it, and then you can seek to be understood. Talking in a way and using examples that appeal to their values and beliefs. Think back to the communication model; we all see the world differently because we all delete, distort and generalise differently dependant on our background and personal makeup. The other person's model of the world is right for them.

b. **The meaning and outcome of communication is in the response you get.** Again all about taking responsibility for your results. We are taught by communicating our thoughts and feelings clearly that the other person should understand our meaning. In truth; that other person will only respond to what they think you have said. You can only determine how effectively you are communicating by the response you get. By taking responsibility for your communication you can stress the importance of what you are saying, gauging on the other persons response as to whether they have actually completely understood it. If you do not receive the response you were expecting, then what is it about your communication that they have not understood?

c. **The mind and the body affect each other.** Very *"Matrix-esque"*?! The mind and the body are one interconnected unit and so it is not possible to make changes in one without the other being affected. If you believe you can, or you believe you can't, you are most probably right. When you set about a task with a negative mindset that you cannot do it then you will struggle and/or fail. Changing your mindset will increase your opportunities for success. One example of the mind-body link is the feel good factor after exercise.

d. **The map is not the territory.** The words we use are not actually the event or the item they represent. Although they describe the event we have chosen them to represent the words themselves are not the actual event itself. We create our own reality based on our past experience. Our language becomes a 'map' of the 'territory' of our constructed reality, through the information we have obtained through our five senses. We code, order and give meaning (through deletion, distortion and generalisation) to our experience in words, sounds, pictures, feelings, tastes and smells. Five different people might all experience the same event but each will take a different experience away from it depending on their own beliefs and values. NLP is the art of changing our map to create more choices.

e. **People are doing the best they can with the resources they have available.** A person's behaviour is adaptable to the situation, their present behaviour is simply the best choice available to them with the resources they have available at that time and their behaviour has a positive intent for them. Their behaviour is not who they are; by accepting the person you can support and assist them to change their behaviour into a more positive resourceful state.

Just as "Bob" who is given 5 minutes to prepare a presentation, Bob's presentation will be the best he can deliver with the resources he has available to him, drawing on his current level of knowledge and the examples/experience that he has had. Another person, "Tom" who is more experienced than Bob may give a better presentation. Just as Bob would if he had been given more notice and time to prepare, research more data, and acquire and use props.

f. **Behaviour is geared towards adaption.** A person's behaviour is their response towards a situation; it is their level of understanding. Presenting the behaviour of confusion is done to find and gain understanding. Their behaviour is not the person themselves, it is simply just the way the person can represent their feelings/understanding. For example, by knowing that their behaviour is due to a lack of understanding enables you to support that person by giving them the additional information that they need to change. This links back to the presupposition: that people are doing their best with the resources they have available. When realised people can change their behaviour and make it more appropriate to who they have become or who they wish to be, their behaviour is adaptable as new resources are available.

g. **Pay attention to behaviour.** Actions speak louder than words, behaviour is the truest and best quality information people can give to you. Notice the incongruence between what a person says and what their body language says, and get curious, ask

> *"Nothing is more revealing than behaviour"*
> Martha Graham

questions like: *Are you sure that that is ok? Do you want me to go over that again? Do you understand?* Remember we all delete, distort and generalise differently through our own unique set of filters. So maybe you were explaining it in a way that prevented it going through. Once you start to see congruence you will know that they have understood.

h. **Behaviour and change are to be evaluated in terms of context and ecology.** All meaning is context dependant, however most of what is said is taken out of context and so it is important for information to be placed back into its original context to understand its true meaning. Behaviour is created specifically to the context and the reality currently being experienced, whether this behaviour is good, bad, useful or un-useful it was adapted to the situation in which it was created. When doing change work with another, ensure it is ecological to that person. Because if it is not, then not only are you going to struggle but these changes will be short lived and the negative consequences will outweigh the positive intention. Evaluate behaviour and change in terms of what the person is capable of becoming, and the impact it will have on the person's life overall.

i. **People have all the resources they need to make the changes they want**. People themselves are not un-resourceful, they are simply experiencing un-resourceful states, which when changed allows them to access all the resources within them to accomplish whatever they choose.

j. **Possible in the world and possible for me is only a matter of how**. There are no limitations in a person's ability to learn. If another person in broadly similar circumstances to me is capable of performing a behaviour/task, then it is possible for me too, or at least improve my own performance by learning.

k. **The system (person) with the most flexibility (choices) of behaviour will have the most influence on the system**. For those of you who study NLP, you will recognise this as the law of requisite variety. Basically the more options you have available to you the greater the chance of change and success.

l. **There is no failure, only feedback.** If a person does not succeed in something, this does not mean they have failed, it just means they have not succeeded yet. It took Edison over 700 attempts to create the light bulb, and like him we can all vary our behaviour and be more positive to find a different way to achieve our outcome. We can all learn from our mistakes, by having this mindset we are able

> *"I have learnt more from my failures than my successes"*
> Richard Branson

to pick ourselves up and get on with it. Simply put: if what you are doing is not getting the results you want, try something different.

m. **There are no resistant clients, only inflexible communicators**. This resistance is a sign of a lack of rapport and can be broken down by being more flexible with your communication to appeal to the client's beliefs and values to create a climate of trust and cooperation. How can I explain this differently in order for the other person to understand what I have said?

n. **All procedures should increase choice and develop greater personal flexibility**. Your goal being to increase the choices you have available to you now, opening more doors, giving you more options for your future/ the situation you are in. For example; going on a particular course could enable you to develop professionally. Your learning will be increased if this course opens more doors for you both personally and professionally by increasing your flexibility; a goal beyond a goal.

o. **All procedures should increase wholeness**. Fewer parts mean more congruence and less conflict.

p. **Change can be quick, easy and lasting** as long as you are clear on what and why you want to make the change, ensuring that it is ecological for you and those around you.

q. **We are in charge of our mind and therefore our results**. If we are not getting the results we want then it is up to us to change the way we are going about it until we get the results we want. If we do not achieve something then it's only ever our fault and our responsibility to change in order to achieve what we want as other people will not change for you.

31

Now that you have understood the communication model and the presuppositions of NLP, I wish to introduce the concept of Cause and Effect, which is about taking responsibility for everything within your life.

Cause and effect – take responsibility for everything

How responsible are you for your life? Are you the cause in your life? Or the effect of things that occur in your life? You always have the choice of how to respond to actions/situations/events.

> "One Man with Courage makes a majority."
> President Andrew Jackson

In all situations you have a choice about how you respond. You can make excuses and blame others so that any possible solutions will need to be the responsibility of other people. This response will mean that you are powerless; you will make it appear that there is nothing you can do. Alternatively you can take responsibility to respond to the situation in the most resourceful way you can and so empower yourself and allow yourself to be part of the solution. You have a choice about how you respond to every event in your life, understanding that gives you the power to constantly influence and direct your results.

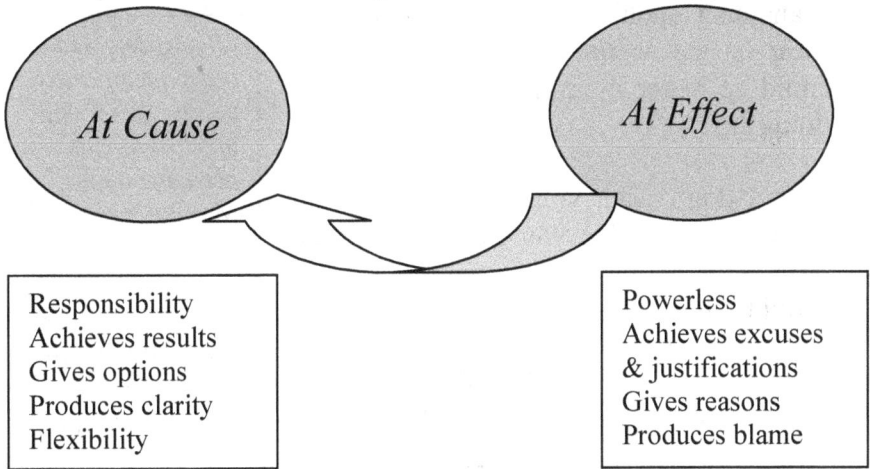

At Cause

At Effect

Responsibility	Powerless
Achieves results	Achieves excuses
Gives options	& justifications
Produces clarity	Gives reasons
Flexibility	Produces blame

How RESPONSIBLE are you for your life?

Taking responsibility for situations not only moves away from the unhelpful and inefficient practice of looking for something (or

> *"Example has more followers than reason"* John Christian Bovee

someone!) to blame, but allows you to effectively review why you did not achieve the desired outcome, teaching lessons that will allow for you to succeed next time.

Another person's behaviour can course direct inconveniences to you: allowing that behaviour to inconvenience you or being a result of that inconvenience is being at Effect, as you are the result of someone else's behaviour. An example would be Jimmy Boyle, a well known villain and convict. Once released from jail he found it hard to find employment, due to his lack of employment skills and secondly others people's attitude towards him. Yet he managed to turn his life around, rather than being 'who' he was perceived to be, he turned his energy into helping young offenders see the wrong in their ways and teach them additional skills to help them fit into society. What is it that Mahatma Gandhi says? *"Be the change you want to see in the world"*. If something could be better by doing X then go about doing X.

> *"Being defeated is often a temporary condition. Giving up is what makes it permanent"* Marilyn Vos Savant

Now I don't want you to take what I am saying to mean that you can no longer get upset/angry/annoyed, as you can and should when appropriate as there are many nasty, evil things that happen in the world and sad, horrible things that can happen to each and every one of us. What Cause and Effect means is how long are you going to stay at effect for being upset/angry/annoyed? How long will you let X affect your life and prevent you from doing things?

You will remember Steven Laurence the young black British teenager who was killed in a racist attack by a group of white youths. I cannot even possibly imagine what his family went through and by rights they could go through that for the rest of their lives and nobody could ever question their behaviour. Yet they are at Cause; they set up the Steven Laurence Foundation Trust to promote racial awareness and prevent things like that from happening again.

A final example is of Victor Frankl, a Jewish survivor of the Holocaust. He has written an inspirational book called *Man's Search for Meaning*, in which he explains how seeing his fellow prisoners sharing their last piece of bread taught him that no matter what happened they could not take away their human right. How can a man after experiencing what he has gone through, be so at peace and insightful? Because he was at Cause, taking responsibility for his situation rather than being the result (Effect) of another's behaviour.

Take the example of a project failing due to running out of funds before it is completed. In such situations the manager either looks for reasons and who's to blame, or they can shoulder the negative emotional burden of the team. Your team members are already sad, annoyed, frustrated, etc. that the project was not a success, saying a simple statement such as *"I appreciate that this task was difficult due to the limited resources, in the past we found that being more diligent and negotiating on all costs facilitated for our operations to stay within budget, which is something I know we can all achieve"* not only removes these inhibiting negative emotions, but gives them a clear strategy on how to do what you want them to do, getting them rallied up and motivated to solve the problem and to be successful. A useful combination of the three layer sandwich technique; praise, task, praise explained utilising influencing words.

Feedback Sandwich:

Ever noticed that when you tell a child off their head goes down and you can tell they are not really listening? This is because they are so caught in the emotions of being told off that they are not hearing the words you are saying. The same goes for your colleagues! Only now they have learnt they have to defend themselves, and so results in an ineffective shouting match where both colleagues learn nothing and simply get more frustrated and angry.

Illustration

The feedback sandwich aims to resolve this, by simply starting off telling your colleague what they did well will make them more open to listening to what you have to say and be receptive to it. Then you can go on and tell them one or two things that they could do even better, which assumes it was already good in the first place, using influencing language for them to want to achieve it. Then you give them an overall final positive comment as you are leaving, so that their mood is lifted and they feel empowered to achieve it.

What they did well

1 or 2 things they could do to make it even better

Overall positive comment

And the sauce! What are they going to do differently next time?

According to Dilts and DeLozier (2000) the role of feedback is to guide an individual toward their desired goal by indicating how close they are to it. Learners need feedback from the trainer in order to confirm improvement in their development, just as the trainer needs feedback from the

> *Feedback is what sets apart the "good" from the "great."* McCullagh and WrightGood

students on their teaching skills and abilities. Feedback can be used to encourage the achievement of the learners goal or the improvement in the quality of a skill and emphasises the students and the trainer's perception of their own personal development and effectiveness in relation to the skill being learnt. Feedback is probably the primary strategic feature of effective teaching. The friendlier we are toward feedback, the more likely we will achieve mastery and fulfilment in whatever we seek.

> *"Failure is an attitude, not an outcome"* Harvey McKay

One of the presuppositions of NLP is that; "There is no such thing as failure, only feedback." If the trainer takes on this principle they will not only support their own personal development through the feedback that they receive, but they will greater improve their students learning and development.

The feedback sandwich technique is best done within 5 minutes of the event/situation taking place, as the persons involved will already be feeling negative emotions, which not only prevents them from being ineffective and un-resourceful for the next couple of hours but actually motivates them to analyse and resolve the problem.

To check whether your advice has been taken on board, check back after an hour asking that person to tell you how they are progressing, their course of action or what they plan to do differently. Effective feedback serves two major functions; instruction and motivation, as it clarifies deviations between preferred and actual behaviour and increases staffs' desire to perform well.

We have looked so far into different thoughts and approaches to change and now I want to introduce you to ecology, which aims to look at the bigger picture in the context of change.

Ecology - Does what you are planning comply with your values?

One day, a wealthy businessman hired a fishing boat to take him out to sea for a day of relaxation. The sun was shining, and the wealthy man took a liking to the happy young fisherman who guided the fishing boat through the waters of the harbour.

"Young man" called the wealthy businessman. *"I can teach you the secrets of success, if you would only listen carefully".*

"Ok" said the young fisherman, smiling as he cleaned the mornings catch.

Although he was a bit taken back by the young man's casual manner, the businessman began his lesson.

"First off, double your prices. You run a good clean boat and you know where the fish are plentiful".

"Why would I do that?" replied the young fisherman, distracted by a small crab playing in the waves by the shore.

The businessman could feel the irritation rising as he replied; *"because then you will be able to buy a second boat, then a third, and you will be able to take more tourists and catch more fish. If you work hard, you will earn enough to buy a whole fleet of boats".*

"But why would I want to do that?" the young fisherman asked as he rolled over onto his back to soak up the last gentle rays of the afternoon sun.

By now the wealthy businessman was becoming furious.

"Because then you will become rich, and you can hire people to do your work for you while you spend your days fishing and relaxing in the sun!"

"Ah" said the young fisherman, nodding sagely. *"That sounds wonderful!"*

In NLP, ecology deals with the relationships between a client and his or her natural, social and created environments and how a proposed goal or change might affect his or her relationships and environment. It is a frame within which the desired outcome is checked against the potential consequences in the client's life. It treats the client's relationship with self as a system and his or her relationship with others as subsystems that all interact.

When someone considers a change it is important therefore to take into account the consequences of this change on the system as a whole. One of the main goals and intentions of NLP is to help the client choose goals and make changes that achieve a sense of personal congruency and integrity with personal and other aspects of the client's life. If a change is proposed that is not ecological it will either not work, only be short lasting, or the negative consequences outweigh the positive intention of the change, therefore it becomes negative.

Ecology is the study of consequences and the impact of your action on the wider system. When you are setting an outcome you will want to consider what effect that outcome will have, not only on yourself, but on other people and the environment in which you operate. For example, if you change the way you work, that change may have an impact on your manager, your team, your customers, your suppliers and/or your family. Whether you are setting outcomes for yourself or helping someone else set one, carrying out an ecology check lets the person set outcomes that will fit all aspects of their life.

In setting outcomes, we need to consider very carefully the consequences of achieving that outcome. Ecology is having an awareness of the overall system and an Ecology Check is tracking the consequences of the change made in all aspects of that system. An ecology check on any outcome, assists us to recognise the impact of that change in all systems of which we are a part, ranging from people very close to us, quickly zooming out to the society of which you are a apart, the country you reside in to the planet generally!

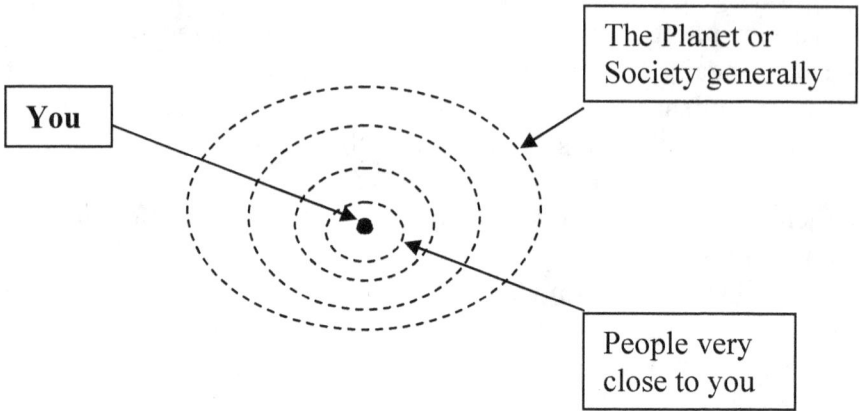

You

The Planet or Society generally

People very close to you

Ecology is a huge topic which is further expanded upon in NLP practitioner and master practitioner levels. It is fair to say it simply cannot be covered in a summary foundation chapter. However in the context of this book we are simply using it to make you aware how important it is to consider how the plans or any change you make will impact on you, your family, career, time available, money, etc. This book simply wishes to make you aware of whether the outcome which you are planning conflicts with your beliefs and values.

Because if the outcome does conflict with your values and beliefs, then no matter how strenuously and articulately you plan, you shall never achieve your true outcome.

Ecology is explained further in chapter 3; Goals and Outcomes. For reference sake I have listed the ecology questions below (self check questions) but for now I want you to consider the situation of either taking a big order, or going for a new job which means more money yet working more hours at work. Now for a family man/woman who likes to spend all his/her time with their family do you think this is an ecological move for them? Or do you think it needs to be redefined so that it takes into account that they would have to give up a lot of their free time in taking on the order/job?

Ecological self check questions;

- For what purpose do you want this?
- What will you gain or lose if you have it?
- What will happen if you get it?
- What won't happen if you get it?
- What will happen if you don't get it?
- What won't happen if you don't get it?

Most importantly: Are there any negative consequences in achieving this goal?

Looking at all options/questions/goals and opportunities in this way allows you to increase your own personal success, ensuring you are clear about what you want - and what you want is clear. It is an awful situation to be in a year down the line when you realise that this goal/target/decision is not right for you, aren't you better finding this out at the beginning? Ecology is a way to be successful in everything that you do, which is why it is one of the pillars of success.

Principles for success

These principles are behaviours that once adapted can produce success.

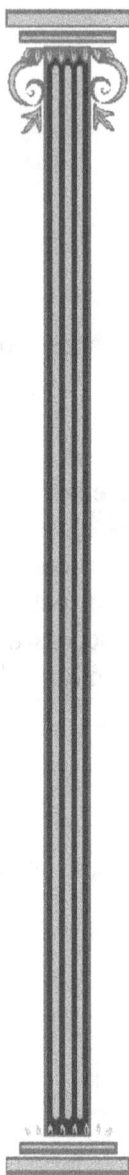

Outcome Orientated-Knowing & having a well defined outcome that is continuously in your mind will keep you focused on the goal making it more achievable. If you don't know where you are going then how will you know when you get there?

Sensory Acuity- (chapter 4) See and sense what is going on in your life as you proceed to your goal. What changes are you noticing in yourself and others? By reviewing and taking continual feedback you can effectively evaluate if you are on track and whether your outcome actually aligns with your values and beliefs.

Behavioural Flexibility- Having noticed the results of your actions tells you whether what you are doing is working or not. Being flexible in your behaviour means giving yourself more choices and using as many ways as you need to achieve your outcome. . Have behavioural flexibility. Be hungry and determined to do whatever it takes to achieve success, if something is not working evaluate why not and if appropriate do it differently.

Take Action- Do it! Without actions there are no results: however well-formed your outcome may be you need to take action to achieve it.

Rapport-To build and maintain rapport (creating a climate of trust and co-operation) to develop and teach understanding.

Psychology and Physiology of Excellence-Operate from a Psychology of Excellence, this is when you are in a totally resourceful state, where you are at Cause, taking 100% responsibility for your communication and results, incorporating the presuppositions of NLP.

The Stages of Learning

Despite us "learning" everyday, the topic itself is rarely covered. Learning is a process that happens over a period of time and over a number of stages. The conscious competence model below explains the process and stages of learning a new skill (or behaviour, ability, technique, etc.) It is most commonly known as the 'conscious competence learning model', or sometimes 'conscious competence ladder' or 'conscious competence matrix'. Whatever you call it, the 'conscious competence' model is a simple explanation of how we learn, and a useful reminder of the need to train people in stages.

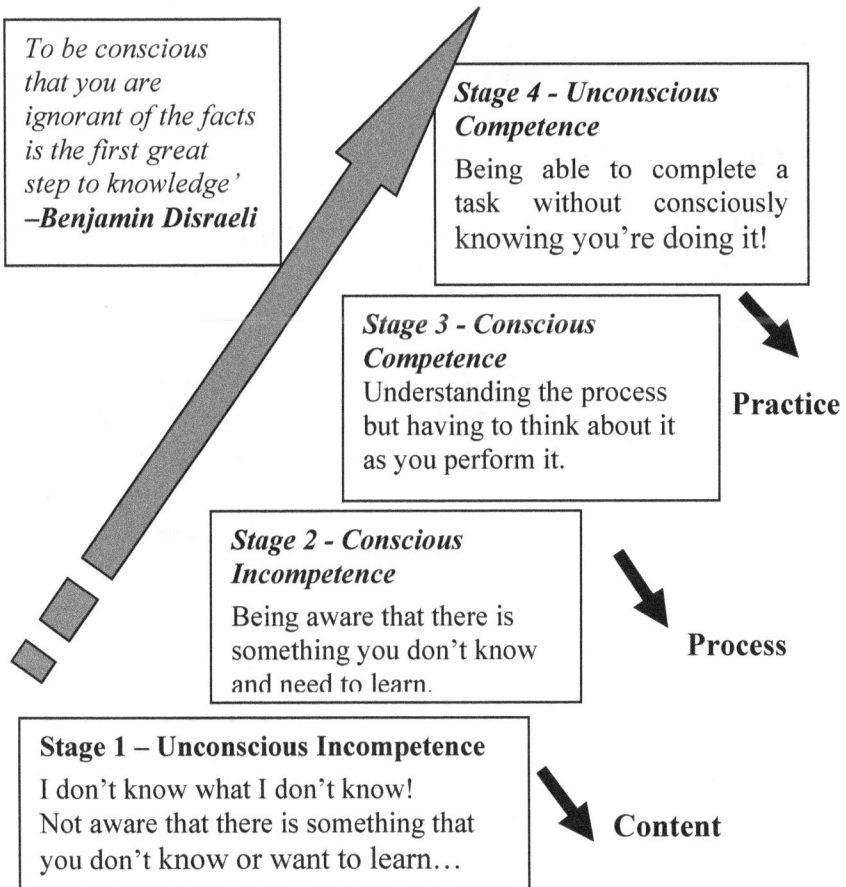

To be conscious that you are ignorant of the facts is the first great step to knowledge'
–Benjamin Disraeli

Stage 4 - Unconscious Competence
Being able to complete a task without consciously knowing you're doing it!

Stage 3 - Conscious Competence
Understanding the process but having to think about it as you perform it.

Practice

Stage 2 - Conscious Incompetence
Being aware that there is something you don't know and need to learn.

Process

Stage 1 – Unconscious Incompetence
I don't know what I don't know!
Not aware that there is something that you don't know or want to learn…

Content

The learner or trainee always begins at stage 1 - 'unconscious incompetence', and ends at stage 4 - 'unconscious competence', having passed through stage 2 - 'conscious incompetence' and - 3 'conscious competence'.

Teachers and trainers commonly assume trainees to be at stage 2, and focus effort towards achieving stage 3, when often trainees are still at stage 1. The trainer assumes the trainee is aware of the skill existence, nature, relevance, deficiency, and benefit offered from the acquisition of the new skill. Whereas trainees at stage 1 have none of these things in place, and will not be able to address achieving conscious competence until they've become consciously and fully aware of their own incompetence.

This is the fundamental reason for failing a training or teaching course. If the learner is not aware of the skill they will simply not see the need for learning it. It's essential to establish awareness of a weakness or training need (conscious incompetence) prior to attempting to impart or arrange training or skills necessary to move trainees from stage 2 to 3. People only respond to training when they are aware of their own need for it, and the personal benefit they will derive from achieving it.

The progression is from quadrant 1 through 2 and 3 to 4. It is not possible to jump stages. For some skills, especially advanced ones, people can regress to previous stages, particularly from 4 to 3, or from 3 to 2, if they fail to practice and exercise their new skills. A person regressing from 4, back through 3, to 2, will need to develop again through 3 to achieve stage 4 - unconscious competence again. For the majority of skills stage 3 conscious competence is perfectly adequate.

Progression from stage to stage is often accompanied by a feeling of awakening - 'the penny drops' - things 'click' into place for the learner - the person feels like they've made a big step forward, which of course they have. One thing to remember is that people only develop competence after they recognise the relevance of their own incompetence in the skill concerned.

Stage 1 – Unconscious Incompetence

- The learner is not aware of the existence or relevance of the skill area
- The learner is not aware that they have a particular deficiency in the area concerned
- The learner might deny the relevance or usefulness of the new skill
- The learner must become conscious of their incompetence before development of the new skill or learning can begin
- The aim of the trainee or learner and the trainer or teacher is to move the learner into the 'conscious incompetence' stage, by demonstrating the skill or ability and the benefit that it will bring to the person's effectiveness

Stage 2 - Conscious Incompetence

- The learner is aware of their deficiency in this area, ideally by attempting or trying to use the skill
- The learner realises that by improving their skill or ability in this area their effectiveness will improve
- Ideally the learner has a measure of the extent of their deficiency in the relevant skill, and a measure of what level of skill is required for their own competence
- The learner becomes aware of the existence and relevance of the skill
- The learner ideally makes a commitment to learn and practice the new skill, and to move to the 'conscious competence' stage

Stage 3 - Conscious Competence

- The learner achieves 'conscious competence' in a skill when they can perform it reliably at will
- The learner will need to concentrate and think in order to perform the skill
- The learner can perform the skill without assistance
- The learner will not reliably perform the skill unless thinking about it - the skill is not yet 'second nature' or 'automatic'
- The learner should be able to demonstrate the skill to another, but is unlikely to be able to teach it well to another person
- The learner should ideally continue to practise the new skill, and if appropriate commit to becoming 'unconsciously competent' at the new skill
- Practise is the single most effective way to move from stage 3-4.

Stage 4 - Unconscious Competence

- The skill becomes so practised that it enters the unconscious parts of the brain - it becomes 'second nature'
- Common examples are driving, sports activities, typing, manual dexterity tasks, listening and communicating
- It becomes possible for certain skills to be performed while doing something else, for example, knitting while watching TV
- The person might now be able to teach others in the skill concerned, although after some time of being unconsciously competent the person might actually have difficulty in explaining exactly how they do it - the skill has become largely instinctual
- This arguably gives rise to the need for long-standing unconscious competence to be checked periodically against new standards.

As touched on the previous page driving is an example of the 4 stages of learning as described below:

Stage 1 – Unconscious Incompetence:

This is before you have started or even thought about driving. You are not confused about how to drive as you have never tried.

Stage 2 - Conscious Incompetence:
This is when you start to learn how to drive, you get confused as to what pedal does what, which indicator is for the left or right or the window wipers. You question why on earth anyone would want to learn how to reverse around a corner when they could simply drive around the block.

Stage 3 - Conscious Competence:
You have passed your test, legally competent to drive. You still have to pay a lot of attention and concentrate, logically processing mirror-signal-manoeuvre.

Stage 4 - Unconscious Competence:
This is when you have been driving for a good while, having arrived at your destination without realising the length of the car journey.

By understanding the learning process not only can we support our students/junior staff/children to learn and develop but also enhance their ability to recognise their own learning needs.

Summary

This chapter looked at the underpinning theory and principles of NLP which will serve as a stepping stone aiding you to grasp the techniques and concepts in the later chapters. The foundations essentially promote you to take responsibility for your own results and the following chapters give you the tools and techniques to enable you to do that even more effectively.

The basis of this book is too provide a plain English guide to NLP, and introduce people to the power of NLP, so that all who read it can replicate that same level of success and fulfilment in their personal and professional lives as the successful people that NLP was modelled on. This book gives you a number of techniques for you to take responsibility for your results to achieve the outcomes you desire and deserve.

References

- Boyes, C. (2006) *Need to Know? NLP Achieve Success with Positive Thinking*, London: Harper Collins.
- Charvet, S.R. (1995) *Words That Change Minds*, Dubuque, IA: Kendall Hunt
- Dilts, R. B. and DeLozier, J. (2000*) Encyclopaedia of Systemic NLP and NLP New Coding*, Scotts Valley, CA: NLP University Press. Available online at http://NLPuniversitypress.com
- Csikszentmihalyi, M. (1990). *Flow: The Psychology of Optimal Experience.* New York: Harper and Row
- RF Baumeister, K Dale, KL Sommer, (1998) *Journal of Personality* - sunysuffolk.edu
- Freud S, (1925) *International Journal of Psycho-Analysis*, PEP Web
- Frankl Viktor, (1946) *Man's Search for Meaning,* Washington Square Press

Chapter 3

<u>Sensory Acuity</u> (Awareness) – broaden your horizons through a heightened sense of awareness.

"What we see depends mainly on what we look for"
Sir John Lubbock

Concept

This technique is based on the presupposition "Pay attention to behaviour"; actions speak louder than words; a person's behaviour is the truest and best quality information they can give you.

Benefits

- Enables you to communicate even more effectively – talking in a way that appeals to another person's representational systems.
- Know whether the other person understands or has misunderstood what you have said.
- Sensory acuity ensures congruence between your verbal and none verbal communication. This enables you to spot in-congruency in yourself and more importantly in other people.
- In selling; you will be able to notice when the client is eager and ready to make a decision to buy to prevent you missing that sale window.
- In coaching and therapy; to know when the client is achieving the changes they want or perhaps to know if the client is not quite ready yet and searching for more answers.
- As a progress gauge to check whether you are on track with a goal.

> "*If you are unable to make progress it is just that you do not yet have sufficient awareness*" David Hemery

What is Sensory Acuity

The conscious mind controls voluntary movements and the unconscious mind controls involuntary movements.

Sensory Acuity is the ability to gain awareness of another person's unconscious responses; we are rarely trained to perceive another person's unconscious feedback, and hardly ever taught to perceive our own. By observing closely through our visual (sight), auditory (sound) and kinaesthetic (feeling) senses, we begin to notice responses that indicate a tremendous amount of new information relating to what the other person has perceived from your communication.

Sensory - relating to sensation, to the perception of a stimulus and the voyage made by incoming nerve impulses from the sense organs to the nerve centres. **Acuity** - the level of sharpness of a sense and its usefulness in resolving fine levels of detail.

Sight, sound, touch, smell and taste are the tools we use to perceive what is going on in the world - both within our own body and outside of it. It stands to reason therefore that the most effective use of our senses will yield the highest quality information. Higher quality information in turn improves our chances of enhancing our performance.

Our major aim in the practice of sensory acuity is not necessarily to improve the senses themselves, but to improve our use of them by increasing and enhancing our awareness of the information provided to us by our senses and to improve our abilities to make even finer distinctions in that information.

For example how is it that when you walk into work and take one look at a colleague you know exactly what kind of day you're going to have, or when you phone your boss, the way they answer the phone makes you decide today isn't the best day to ask for a project budget increase, likewise the saying *"you can cut the atmosphere in here with a knife"*. What is it that makes you know something isn't right?? This is your sensory acuity. By fine tuning your sensory awareness it will enable you to notice moment to moment changes and pick up on in-congruence in a person's communication (verbal & non verbal).

Remember back to the presupposition, the meaning of a communication is in the response you get; you can use your sensory acuity to gauge whether what you are saying is having the desired effect/response in the other person, and thus be able to change direction to achieve your outcome.

Sensory acuity is one of the Principles of Success covered in the foundation chapter; what changes are you noticing in yourself and other people? What is going on in your life as you proceed towards your goal? In personal goal setting terms you can keep a check on your progress and determine through your senses whether you are on or off track and correct, or do what is required to reach your goal.

Sharply focusing our sensory awareness to accurately and fully measure the responses that we are getting to our communication and thus verify if we're communicating effectively is one very important use of sensory acuity. Remember the meaning of communication is in the response you get. The non-verbal elements of inter-personal communication can often give us insights about the communication that are not provided by the words being spoken, which in turn guide us in how to modify our communication in order to get our desired outcome.

History

Now on some level we all use this technique, whether it is a gut reaction, picking up on your partner's feelings, or simply noticing when a colleague is annoyed. The key to sensory acuity is that it is a step by step technique to pick up on the subtle changes from clients/colleagues/friends who aren't forward with their views and don't wish to tell you what they are thinking for whatever reason, i.e. simply being scared or embarrassed to do so.

Sensory Acuity was modelled from Milton Erickson, who had polio and was wheel-chair bound. As he could not always mimic his client's body posture he concentrated on noticing the minute changes his clients made from moment to moment and the meanings that were associated with those changes, to gauge whether his clients were progressing and to enable him to develop the high level of rapport he desired.

As Robert Dilts puts it "Sensory acuity essentially relates to the degree of sensitivity one has as an observer. Increased sensory acuity allows one to make more comprehensive and accurate observations" Sensory acuity therefore is not "a mind read", interpretation, guess or assumption of what the other person is meaning.

How to do it! – Keys

Linking back to the communication model, another person's internal representation of what you have said affects their state and their state affects their physiology, this physiology is what we pick up by being sensory aware. We all already have the ability to pick up on the unconscious responses of our friends and family, i.e. people who we have seen when they are happy/sad/angry/excited/anxious and have noticed and become used to how they express these emotions.

> "There can be no knowledge without emotion" Arnold Bennett

Therefore we can become sensory aware by realising subtle changes in another that are different to their normal selves or noticing how their behaviour is in contrast to the words they are saying. The way that we do this is through "Calibration", simply comparing what the person is like now to how they behave or act normally (i.e. when they are in a positive mood or how they act when they feel good about performing a task)

The importance here is to observe that other person: people make minor changes through all of their senses, in their facial expressions, body posture, skin tone and colour, etc. Noticing the changes they make when they are thinking of something positive or negative or that they like or dislike and if they understand or don't understand something.

What is Calibration?

Calibration is the ability to notice changes that occur from moment to moment in another person using your sensory acuity. It is hugely important to calibrate the person against themselves not generalise them against other people. People cannot be stereotyped or put in box's, stereotyping or "mind reading" does not enlighten you to what is actually happening in the person. For example a person's breathing rate increasing, this could mean that they are anxious or it could mean they're excited, two very different emotions!

Visual Modes of Calibration

LOWER LIP SIZE
Lines...........No Lines

EYES
Focused........Defocused
Pupil   Dilation:
Constricted........Dilated

BREATHING
Rate:
Fast .... Slow
Location:
High.......………Low

SKIN
The tone of the muscles;
Shiny.............…....Not Shiny
Colour:
Light..............…....Dark

Many physiological changes do occur from moment to moment during conversation. Noticing these changes against a client's normal physiology and checking with them, asking them if they are OK? Do they understand? Do they want you to expand further on this? Are all appropriate questions to ensure your communication is effective.

Some examples are:-

Lower lip size - a person's lower lip size changes from fatter and fuller (look for lines) to thinner and more drawn out (no lines).

The eyes - are they focused or defocused? Are the pupils dilated or constricted? Do they have to really concentrate and search for understanding to what you have said?

Breathing - an individual will change their breathing from moment to moment and what we are most interested in is the rate and the location of their breathing.

By watching the torso rising and falling we look to detect if the breathing is fast or slow and whether it is high in the chest or low in the stomach. Generally a person's breathing rate will increase as they get worried, anxious, stressed, upset, just as they could if they were excited or in anticipation. It is important not to try and interpret or guess what it means, notice the changes in their breathing against how they were previously (calibration), during conversation and if different check if the person is OK and whether they have understood what you have said.

Skin Colour - The shift is usually from a lighter colour to a redder colour from their normal skin colour.

The easiest way to look for this is to imagine the person in black-and-white and look for changes from light to dark. This may sound odd but it's a useful way to monitor the shift from paler shades to redder shades by measuring it in terms of a shift from light to dark.

What we must avoid here is applying our own meaning to that colour shift based on that shift alone - we must stick to sensory based descriptions.

We may look at a person with a red face and assume that they are embarrassed and of course we could be completely wrong - they could equally be angry, or be hot from exercising, or the shift could be due to a shift from sympathetic to parasympathetic functioning. The moment we ascribe meaning to a physiological shift we are guilty of mind reading. We must stick to sensory based descriptions in order to use our sensory inputs cleanly.

Skin tonus - the tone of the muscles underlying the skin, particularly of the face, is another useful indicator of physiology and non-verbal communication. We are looking to detect if the skin of the face is tight or loose. Tight skin will tend to look shinier than loose skin, again you will notice this as you calibrate the other person against their normal.

Auditory Modes of Calibration

Beneficial if you deal with clients mainly by phone: being able to notice subtle changes in the client's voice will tell you what they really think about what you just said.

What to listen out for;
1.   Listen to the pitch of their voice, is it: Higher or Lower than when you first started the conversation?

2.   Listen to the tone of their voice, is it: Sharper or Flatter

3.   Listen to how the sentence ends, is it a command, statement or question
   - Command→pitch of last word goes down
   - Statement→pitch of last word stays the same
   - Question→pitch of last word goes up

56

This subtle ending could mean that they need more information from you, yet unsure or uncomfortable to ask, or feel that they should know the answer; this occurs regularly when senior staff give instruction or teach junior staff. The junior staff might agree and respond with a statement to confirm their understanding. Acknowledging this and either extending the information or repeating it will reinforce their learning.

The more time you spend practicing sensory acuity the more skilful you will become. Often it is useful to focus on one element each day and observe a number of people, i.e. on day one: observe skin colour, on day two: skin tonus or breathing and so on.

Remember at all times that the map is not the territory. Keep your sensory input channels clean by describing your observations purely in sensory based terms.

As you practice sensory acuity you will become increasingly aware of things that you have just never noticed before. You will become increasingly and automatically aware of all of the subtle moment to moment changes that people make in their physiology. This in turn will assist you in becoming a master of inter-personal communications as you learn to read just where the other person is and how your communication is getting through.

Exercises

All of the exercises below involve two people – Person A is the 'client', Person B is the NLPer carrying out the exercise.

Exercise 1- Visual Calibration

1. Sit facing each other: Person A thinks of someone/something they like, for example football. Person B calibrates Person A.
2. Person A then clears the screen and thinks of someone/something they don't like, for example football! Person B calibrates Person A
3. Person A thinks of one of them, without saying which one, and Person B calibrates and works out which one it is.
4. Repeat as required until Person B has got it right and then swap over so Person A has the opportunity to practice the technique.

Exercise 2 - Auditory Calibration

1. Person B has their back to Person A. Person A thinks of someone/something they like and counts out loud 1 to 10. Person B calibrates Person A.
2. Person A then clears the screen and thinks of someone/something they don't like and counts out loud 1 to 10. Person B calibrates Person A
3. Person A thinks of one of them, (without saying which one) and counts out loud 1 to 10, Person B calibrates and works out which one it is.
4. Repeat as required until Person B has got it right.
5. Repeat steps 1-4 again only this time Person A says a short sentence, such as "Good morning, how are you?" rather than counting.
6. Swap over so Person A has the opportunity to practice the technique.

Exercise 3 - Auditory Calibration - Over the phone

1. Person B has their back to Person A.
2. Person A pretends to be on the telephone, about to tell Person B that they did not get the job which you have just interviewed them for.
3. Person B calibrates Person A's voice; tone, pitch and tempo...
4. Person B how do you feel when they are talking before they have even told you that you have not got the job?
5. Person A how are you feeling as you tell them?
6. Now repeat, but this time Person B has got the job, again Person A "rings" and Person B calibrates Person A's voice and calibrates their feeling.
7. Person B, can you feel what Person A is going to say?
8. Person A rings again, choosing whether Person B has got the job or not. Person A starts informing Person B of the interview outcome and stops just short of telling them whether they have got or not got the job. Person B has to guess the outcome.
9. Repeat as required until Person B has got it right.
10. Swap over so Person A has the opportunity to practice the technique.

Summary

In inter-personal communication sensory acuity enables us to notice subtle physiological shifts in those who we are communicating with, which in turn provides us with an idea about how our communication is being received, to know if our communication is going in. During inter-personal communication people constantly make very subtle shifts in their physiology from moment to moment, which we often do not consciously notice since the verbal part of the communication takes the focus of our attention.

Sensory acuity allows you to calibrate changes in another persons physiology against their 'normal', enabling you to communicate even more effectively and pick up on the other persons unconscious responses, so you can deduce how they really feel about what you have said and/or so you know whether what you have explained has been understood.

Whether you are coaching, training, negotiating or reassuring it is important to understand how people experience the world around them in order to more clearly express your ideas so that they can see (visual), or hear (auditory) or get in touch with (kinaesthetic) your message.

Sensory acuity is not guessing what is going on in the other person's model of the world. By aiming to understand and. more importantly, demonstrating that you understand where they are coming from (what they mean) will enable you to build a level of trust and co-operation as they will appreciate that they are being listened to.

References

- Henwood, S., Lister, J. (2007) *NLP and Coaching for Healthcare Professionals*. Chichester, John Wiley & Sons, Ltd.
- Druckman (1988), *Enhancing Human Performance: Issues, Theories, and Techniques*
- Dilts, R. (2000) *Encyclopaedia of NLP,*CA: NLP University Press. Available online at http://NLPuniversitypress.com
- Elich, M., Thompson, R. W., & Miller, L. (1985). *Mental imagery as revealed by eye movement and spoken predicates: A test of neuro linguistic programming.* Journal of Counseling Psychology, 32(4), 622-625. note: "psychological fad"p.625

Chapter 4

Rapport – having the trust and co-operation of a friend, with a stranger.

"When people honor each other, there is a trust established that leads to synergy, interdependence, and deep respect. Both parties make decisions and choices based on what is right, what is best, what is valued most highly."
Blaine Lee

Concept

This technique is based on the presuppositions; The meaning and outcome of communication is in the response you get. We are taught by communicating our thoughts and feelings clearly that the other person should understand our meaning. In truth that other person will respond to what they think you have said and you can only determine how effectively you are communicating by the response you get. By being at cause

> *"Just because you are making a noise in my direction, don't think you are communicating"*
> David Gordon

for your communication you can stress the importance of what you are saying, gauging on their response as to whether they have actually completely understood it.

Benefits:

Rapport is important for job interviews, social networking, board room meeting and meeting with clients.
- Creating trust and co-operation.
- Conflict resolution – when people are very angry, upset and defensive.
- Finding a mutual agreement in an otherwise conflicting situation.
- Respectfully contradicting and changing someone else's viewpoint.
- Leave a (positive!) lasting impression and/or stand out from the crowd, when going for job interviews, carrying out sales pitches or in business meetings.
- Negotiate win-win deals – most business decisions are made on the basis of rapport rather than technical merit. (Either rapport made relatively quickly or over a period of time). Individuals more likely to buy, agree, support someone they're in rapport with than someone they are not, as they have a feeling of trust and commonality with them.
- Rapport is an essential Principle of Success!

What is Rapport?

Bandler and Grinder say that '*Rapport means you demonstrate understanding of the other person's model of the world*'. Ellerton goes on to say "*Rapport is the basis of any meaningful interaction between two or more people, that rapport is about establishing an environment of trust, understanding, respect and safety which gives a person the freedom to fully express their ideas and concerns and to know that they will be respected by the other person.*"

Thus rapport is the ability to relate to another in a way that creates a climate of trust and understanding. It is the capability to see each other's point of view and to appreciate each other's feelings. The aim is to be able to establish rapport with any person at any time. When people are like each other, they like each other and are open to the other person's suggestions.

There is a common misunderstanding that rapport is all about getting the other person to like you. While that is often a nice *effect* of having rapport, it is not the core purpose of rapport at all. It is important to stress that rapport is not just "liking", but more being comfortable in the other person's presence and surroundings.

Rapport is one of the most important features of unconscious human interaction. It is commonly known as being "in sync" with, or being "on the same wavelength" as the person with whom you are talking. Have you ever met someone for the first time and just clicked, you have a positive chemistry that just feels right? You feel like you have known them all your life? You see things from the same point of view; whether it's ideas, thoughts, or the same taste in material goods such as clothes, you listen to the same music, or often find you finish each other's sentences. Have you ever talked to a good friend about something dear to you and end up frustrated because they didn't get it? You're obviously still friends, so what's up? At the same time, don't you love it when you meet someone for the very first time and you just click, with them understanding every single thing you say?

Building understanding and demonstrating it is the essence of rapport, and being liked for it is the reward. Notice that it's not only about *saying* you understand the other person's model of the world; it is *demonstrating* that you do to.

When teaching rapport many students often say "*What if someone says something that you don't agree with? Are you telling me to lie by agreeing with him?*" No, this is not what rapport is about, I am not telling you to lie, I am however suggesting to you to be willing enough to expand your model of the world to include theirs and see, hear and feel things from their position. Your Map is in my Territory remember? If you do that, does your own point of view disappear? No, it's still there! and when you do choose to come back to your own point of view, you'll have expanded and enriched your own model of the world with an additional viewpoint.

Below is a model of the communication wheel which further explains the building of rapport and why your physiology and body language are so important.

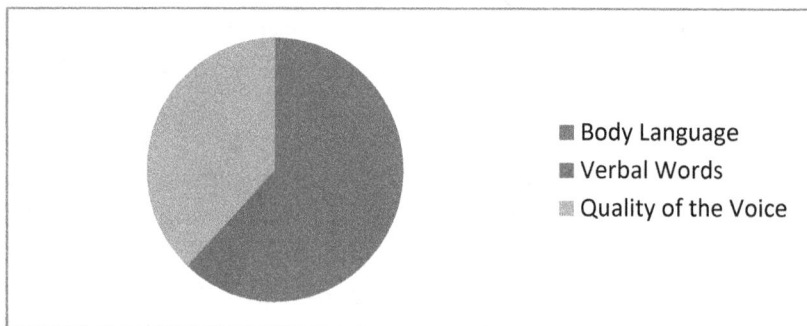

Albert Mehrabian (1972) looked at how live communication was received and responded to. His figures suggested that your impact depends on three factors — how you look, how you sound, and what you say. His research broke it down as illustrated in the communication wheel above: 55 per cent body language, 38 per cent quality of the voice and 7 per cent actual words spoken.

Furthermore that this 93 % beyond the words you use mostly determines the response you get from your communication.

Through this knowledge Bandler and Grindler developed a model to maximise how you use this 93% beyond the words you use, this model in NLP is called rapport.

Now we have all heard the expression: First impressions count. Do you arrive for meetings and appointments hot and harassed or cool and collected? When you begin to talk, do you mumble your words in a low whisper to the floor or gaze directly and confidently at your audience before speaking out loud and clear?

In terms of building rapport — *you* are the message. And you need all parts of you working in harmony: words, pictures, and sounds. If you don't look confident — as if you believe in your message — people will not listen to what you are saying.

Rapport involves being able to see eye-to-eye with other people, connecting on their wavelength. So much (93 per cent) of the perception of your sincerity comes not from what you say but how you say it and how you show an appreciation for the other person's thoughts, views and feelings.

When you are in rapport with someone, you can disagree with what they say and still relate respectfully with them. The important point to remember is to respect the other person's point of view. For example, you may well have different political or religious views to your colleagues or clients, but there's no need to fall out about it. Hold on to the fact that you simply wish to differ with their opinion and this is no reflection on the person. "*A person is more than what they say, do, or believe*" (Myers-Briggs 1962).

History

Rapport itself has always been around, people have always been able to get into rapport with each other, it is just that they have not realized that it is a technique that they are doing. Think back to all the excellent communicators who made you feel that they were talking personally to you, even though you were in a crowd of 'X' amount of people. Think about your life, your family and your friends, the times when you have gone out and behaved the same way as each other or the photos where you are all sitting or posing in the same way. These are examples of rapport which was known previously as just getting on with or "clicking" with another person.

Early in NLP history Bandler and Grinder noticed how Milton Erikson was able to connect with clients so easily and willingly that they were willing to go into trance for change work within moments of meeting him. Bandler and Grinder modelled Milton Erikson's behaviour and became curious as to how he was able to get people who he had never met before to not only completely relax, but feel comfortable and trust him to a level that they would divulge all the necessary information about themselves in order to change. They modelled the techniques that he and other successful therapists used, their ability to connect with people and called it rapport.

Rapport is not manipulating another person. At the end of the day it depends on your opinion of manipulative, if your desired outcome is simply to improve communication, or be more influential, then surely there is no issue; it is just the same as dressing smartly to impress. It is not agreement and nor does it necessarily come from agreement; it is possible to agree with someone and not have rapport, just as it is possible to disagree with someone and be in rapport.

Principles

The important thing to remember with rapport is it needs to be subtle; a little goes a long way, by replicating some of the aspects of a person's behaviour back to them they will start being more open and prone to suggestions. For example tapping your finger in time to their breathing, leaning forward if they are leaning forward, adapting the same hand positions and / or word phrases will help create a sense of coming from the same view point.

> "*A jug fills drop by drop*" Prince Gautama Siddharta

There are a number of techniques that are beneficial in building rapport such as: matching your body language (i.e., posture, gesture, and so forth); maintaining eye contact; and matching breathing rhythm. Think back to the presupposition; The mind and the body affect each other. If you are doing the same gestures as the other person or have the same body posture, at an unconscious level, you will be in rapport, which will create a climate of trust and commonality.

Think back to sensory acuity and the communication model. In sensory acuity you are paying attention to someone's physiology. With rapport you are matching this physiology and through pacing and leading (covered later in this chapter) you change this physiology, which impacts on their state, which impacts on their internal representation of the external event allowing them to have a broader view of that event and the ability to see where you are coming from.

How to do it!

How we get into rapport is by matching/mirroring and then pacing & leading, we **Match** (match their physiology with the same physiology in yourself, e.g. both cross right leg over the left; this is less intense and makes you seem 'similar' so they can decide to separate from you e.g. in sales to avoid buyer's remorse); **Mirror** (match their physiology with the mirror image in yours, e.g. their right leg over their left; your left leg over your right; this is more intense, it makes you seem like a 'reflection' of their own experience); or **Crossover** (match their behaviour with a different behaviour of yours, e.g. move your foot in time with their breathing, use this when it is unsafe to match the other person).

Matching

You match a variable of the other person's physiology until you have gained a sufficient level of rapport that allows you to slowly change what you are doing (pacing and leading) and have the individual following your lead, not only in their body movements but also in their views and line of thought.

When using matching to build rapport there are multiple physiological variables you can match;

- Posture
  - Body posture
  - Angle of body
  - Direction body is facing

- Blinking
  - Speed of blinking (not appropriate if they rarely/don't blink, especially if you blink frequently as this could look like you are staring)

- Breathing
    - The rate of their breathing. (Use common sense and be aware of conditions such as asthma!)
    - Copy when they take deep breaths (very supportive when working on a one to one basis, a deep breath or sigh could mean that it was something 'big' for them)

- Voice tonality
    - Tone of the voice
    - Tempo of the voice is referring to the speed/pace or rhythm of the voice
    - Pitch of their voice
    - The Timbre of your voice its quality and characteristics of the voice

- Speed
    - Speed they are talking
    - Speed they are moving

- Gestures
    - Only match their gestures when it's your turn to speak

- Words:
    - Key words and phrases
    - Predicates (covered further in chapter 7.1): are they visual, auditory or kinaesthetic?
    - Common experiences and interests
    - Chunk size (covered in chapter 7.3) - basically give them the overview of the...... or the specific details of the...... depending on how they process information

As previously discussed, we tend to like people who are like ourselves, as we get on better with them and so communicate more effectively with them. Therefore to build rapport involves matching and as you will have noticed, people who are in rapport tend to act like each other. Matching to build rapport builds upon what you have learnt in sensory acuity as you need to use your sensory awareness of the other person as well as of yourself, to match the other person subtly. If you directly match everything that they do it will not only be obvious but will also be annoying. For example; matching their gestures used when they are talking, doing this at the same time will be obvious, so you would only match when you are communicating and rather than doing exactly the same you would tone them down or just do it occasionally.

This also applies to their body posture, if you were to move when they move it would be obvious & just plain weird, yet waiting until you talk would appear that you are just getting comfortable before you start talking. You are also able to match their breathing, if they are breathing fast or slow, as long as this is medically alright for you, then you breathe at the same rate and depth as them. Voice is another thing you can match, this being the speed of their voice, tempo, pitch and the words they use (not their accent!) This is highly beneficial in conflict resolution; matching their tempo, pitch and speed at the start of an argument, pacing them till you have reached an understanding/agreement at some level, then lead them, decreasing your tempo, pitch and speed so that you can discuss what needs discussing in a calm manner.

You need to use your common sense to build rapport through matching; don't abruptly change your posture or voice and don't mimic them, they are their own person just as you are yours. Matching happens gradually; for example with posture, rather than lean back, cross legs, cupping hands and tilting head to right all at once, gradually lean back then cross your legs, while they are speaking you could tilt your head in a curious way, listening to what they are saying and just have your hands cupped on your lap.

Once similar postures have been comfortably achieved (like lent back, arms or legs crossed) and you are in rapport your interests should focus on the content of the conversation, rather than physiology, as the physiological matching has provided the foundation of rapport.

Mirroring

This is similar to matching, only you aim to be the mirror image of the other person rather than doing the same. For example: posture, if a person has their legs crossed to the left, you would cross your legs to the right so that they see themselves in you (mirror image). If they lean to the left you lean to the right and so on. As with matching; use your sensory awareness and common sense, this is to be subtle and gradual. Breathing would be at the same pace as their breathing, likewise voice tonality, speed and words used, which is really matching but if you spoke into a mirror then the reflection would be: you... speaking slowly. So we move onto mirroring their gestures, for example if they rotate their right arm at the wrist when explaining something then you would rotate your left. A note here would be to do it subtly on a smaller scale; if their hand is freely in the air then you would have yours just off your knee.

Crossover Matching/Mirroring

This is the most practical and preferred way to subtly build rapport, especially when giving a presentation, whether in a meeting, interview or teaching environment, as if you are stood up (most likely) it is not always possible to cross your legs or fold your arms. Crossover matching/mirroring is when you match part of your physiology with another person. If you had your arms crossed in front of an audience you could be presenting yourself as being authoritative or unapproachable, sat on a high chair at the front with your lower legs crossed however gives the opposite impression. If you are standing then have one arm across your body and the other up towards your chin, you could use this arm for gestures whilst looking thoughtful due to your position.

This is also appropriate in a one to one meeting, if you are both leaning back with your arms crossed it could suggest that you're not interested and with you both being so far apart there is a potential for you not to be able to click. In this situation you would sit up part way forward (not all the way as this could be intimidating) with your arms open (interested) and your legs crossed (if not over the knee then at the lower legs).

Parents often use cross over matching with their children, especially with babies; they will rock the baby in time with its breathing or tap its back in rhythm with its crying, rocking at the same time. When they have paced the baby for long enough they will start to slow down, leading the baby to a calm and gentle sleep. If someone is bouncing their leg or tapping their foot then tap your finger or pen in time with them. Cross over matching is particularly useful if you are in a situation where you are physically unable to match the person's physiology. Milton Erickson had polio and was wheelchair bound, limiting his movement, hence cross over matching was modelled as he had the ability to build exquisite rapport quickly with all of his clients.

Pacing and leading.

Pacing and leading has been mentioned several times through this chapter, basically you go along with whatever the person is doing at the time, matching where they are at. If they are bored, match their boredom; if they are full of energy, be full of energy; if they are talking slowly, talk slowly. You don't have to do exactly the same, and often it would be unhealthy for you to do exactly the same. But you can always match something about you with something of theirs. If you do this smoothly you will both feel that you understand each other to a certain degree.

Pacing and leading is the real magic of rapport. Firstly you pace somebody by adjusting your voice tonality, breathing patterns, body language, and gestures etc. to match theirs. Then choose a desired state where you would like to lead the client to and make the necessary changes. If the rapport building - pacing exercise has gone well, as we change our posture and gestures the client will follow. You can lead a client to any state that you desire by using these invaluable techniques! This method is very useful for motivating a depressed person. Saying 'cheer up!' in a cheery tone does nothing to break their state, but pacing their experience, gaining rapport and leading them, you are able to make huge changes to a person's emotional state in seconds!

Leading is whatever you say or do that is intended to get the client to change their state of mind, get access to different information, find out something new, or see things differently. Usually it is something you say, you might ask questions, or you might give directions, or you might explain something. You might also just change the way you talk about something and see if the client goes along with it.

If the client goes along with the change you are introducing, then they are following your lead. Like, if you ask them to see an issue from different viewpoints, and they starts answering, then they have already gone along with the idea of there being several different viewpoints, a sense of rapport helps to ease an interaction. Some people are able to gain a natural rapport from the outset due to similarities that already exist between them. These may be similar likes or dislikes, giving a workable direction to small talk, or, on a more fundamental level, two people may be using the same representation system as each other (this is discussed further in chapter 6 on representational systems).

If you cast your mind back to Principles for Success you will remember that one of those principles was have sensory awareness to know if you are being effective. This is where your sensory acuity really comes into play as it is the building block to rapport. If you pay close attention to your senses, in particular to what you see, hear and feel, you will recognize the rapport state when you achieve it.

Indicators of Rapport; (as per Tad James 1996)

1. You get a feeling inside of warmth towards or familiarity with the other person, a feeling of understanding and conformity.

2. The clients colour shifts; a blushing or a flushing of the skin in the other person - a shift from light to dark, from a lighter shade to a redder shade. This is indicative of their autonomic nervous system switching from sympathetic (fight-or-flight) to parasympathetic (rest-and-digest) functioning. In other words, the skin colour change is an unconscious indicator of relaxation.

3. The other person will commonly say something to indicate that they are in rapport i.e. *Do I know you? Haven't we met somewhere before? Are you an Aries?* Verbally indicates a sense of recognition.

4. You switch from **pacing** to **leading** and they follow. Until now you have been **pacing** the other person - matching and mirroring their physiology, tonality, key words etc. When you have rapport you should be able to **lead** - when you move, they move. Try crossing or uncrossing your legs and within a matter of moments they should match or mirror you, lean back in your chair and they should do the same. As long as you maintain rapport you should be able to continue leading as you have achieved unconscious compliance and physiological replication.

By establishing good rapport at the outset we can gain commitment from the other party, conscious or unconscious, to trust the process even when they do not fully understand how the process works and what the ultimate outcome will be.

Key points:

- To build rapport you don't have to like or agree to the other person's model of the world, but you have to at least understand it.
- Take a genuine interest in getting to know what's important to the other person. Start to understand them rather than expecting them to understand you first.
- Pick up on the key words, favourite phrases and ways of speaking that someone uses and build these subtly into your own conversation.
- Notice how someone likes to handle information. Do they like lots of details or just the big picture? As you speak feed back information in this same portion size.
- Breathe in unison with them.
- Look out for the other person's intention — their underlying aim — rather than what they do or say. They may not always get it right, but expect their heart to lie in the right place.
- Adopt a similar stance to them in terms of your body language, gestures, voice tone and speed.
- Respect the other person's time, energy, favourite people and money. They will be important resources for them.

Exercises

Exercise 1 – Observe Physiology

1. This exercise involves three people – Person A is the 'client', Person B & C are the NLPer's carrying out the exercise.
2. Person A tells a story (e.g. about a holiday, their hobbies) for about 5 minutes. If person A runs out of material, start again! (The content of the story is irrelevant!).
3. Persons B & C observe and notice physiology i.e. gestures, posture, blinking, facial expressions, breathing.

4. B & C spend 1 minute comparing what they noticed about person A's physiology and what they could match if they needed to do so.

5. Change round twice so that each person tells a story and each person has the chance to observe twice.

Exercise 2 – Matching/Mirroring Exercise

1. This exercise involves two people – Person A is the 'client', Person B is the NLPer carrying out the exercise.
2. Person A picks a <u>mildly</u> controversial topic to talk about.
3. Person B, whatever their personal views, **disagree** and **match** physiology.
4. After 2-3 minutes, person B then **agrees** with A and **mis-matches** physiology.
5. After 1-2 minutes, person B **matches** A and have the conversation continue for about 2 minutes.
6. Person A, notice at which point(s) you felt comfortable with person B, and which point(s) you didn't.
7. Swap round and repeat the exercise.

Exercise 3 – Auditory Matching

1. This exercise below involves three people – Person A is the 'client', Person B is the NLPer's carrying out the exercise and Person C is the observer.
2. Person A and Person B are facing away from each other, either seated or standing. Person C stands so that he/she can observe and hear both A & B.
3. Person A says a short phrase. Person B repeats it, matching tone/volume/intonation/speed.

4. Person A says whether they felt that person B had matched them. If not, and after another attempt or two, person C can coach person B to match person A.
5. When person B has successfully matched person A, person A gradually increases the length of the sentence for B to repeat.
6. Finally, once B has established Rapport with A, have a conversation with B still matching A, with person C only providing 'coaching' if needed.
7. Swap over twice so that everyone gets to play each role once.

Summary

Rapport is the ability to relate to others in a way that creates a climate of trust and understanding. To build rapport you don't have to like or agree to the other person's model of the world, but you have to at least understand it, by taking a genuine interest in getting to know what's important to the other person. Start to understand them rather than expecting them to understand you first.

Rapport is not manipulating another person to agree with your views, it is a way of allowing them to be more comfortable in your surroundings so that they broaden their horizons and acquire the ability to see where you are coming from. Through picking up on the key words and phrases someone uses and building these subtly into your own conversation, you will be able take rapport even further; these are known as predicates.

When listening to the person's language you will notice whether they prefer to have an overview, the big picture of the discussion, or if they need the specific details. You will have noticed that the people you click with like the same 'chunk' size information as you and are able to relate to you instantly. Likewise the people who have the opposite say big chunk/picture people will get overwhelm or lose interest in what you are saying if you give them loads of details. In these situations you will notice the discomfort as you seem to 'miss' each other's intentions. This is the same for detailed people - if they need all the specifics about the topic and you just give them the overview, then you will appear as being vague and ambiguous, they will not 'get' what you are saying. Being aware of this will not only enable you to build effective rapport but it will also ensure you are communicating effectively.

There is a lot of research into having folded arms which apparently suggests that this means the other person is cold, not interested and closed off from you. In my personal experience this is not true; in fact it just means that they are comfortable with their arms crossed, to suggest anything else is mind reading. Use your sensory acuity and notice what else is happening with the other person, if their arms are crossed and you are concerned first establish rapport then pace and lead them. Have your arms also crossed maybe looser or cross over and have your legs crossed.

Rapport is a hugely powerful tool that enables you to communicate even more effectively, as it removes the barriers in conversation. There will be areas that are new to you and may feel strange at first but as you practice and start to learn the skill of rapport you will find that you are unconsciously building rapport and your communication and interpersonal skills have improved tenfold.

References

- M. Argyle, et al. *British journal of Social and Clinical Psychology, Vol. 5 1970 pages 222-231*
- Allan Pease *Body Language,* page 9.
- Bandler, R. & Grinder, J. (1979) Frogs into Princes. Utah: Real People Press
- Laborde, G. (1985) *Rapport on the Telephone.* Syntony Publishing's Co.
- Ellerton; www.renewal.ca

Chapter 5

Goals & Well Formed Outcomes – the importance of saying it the way you want it

"A goal is nothing more than a dream with a deadline"
Joe L. Griffith

Concept

This technique is based the presupposition; Possible in the world and possible for me is only a matter of how. There are no limitations in a

> *"What is now proved, was once impossible"*
> William Blake

person's ability to learn. If another person in broadly similar circumstances to me is capable of performing a behaviour, then it is possible for me too, or at least improve my own performance through learning.

Benefits:

- Allows you to make S.M.A.R.T goals: Smarter.
- Broadens your horizons to view the goal from multiple perspectives.
- Compare where you are now with where you to want to be, to ensure that when you get there you have more beneficial opportunities open to you and realise the positive by-products of your goal.
- To create purpose and so make your outcome even more compelling; empowering yourself to move towards a solution.
- Breaks the goal down into manageable chunks; enabling you to assess your progress and establish when you have achieved your outcome.
- You get to "try your goal on" to ensure the goal is ecological and agrees with your values and beliefs.
- Ability to see a goal "As if" you already have it, allowing you to realise the additional unexpected steps you carried out to achieve it and what other methods were available in obtaining it.
- Create a "goal beyond a goal" to help prevent you from slipping back into your old ways once you have achieved it.

What is a Goal/Outcome?

The Oxford English dictionary defines a Goal as a "broad statement of what the program or person hopes to accomplish". In NLP that simply is not good enough! A Goal is a specific outcome stated in the positive. A lot of you will have already heard of "S.M.A.R.T" outcomes, NLP takes this further reviewing the power of the words we say and whether or not they conflict with our pre-existing values, beliefs and ecology.

> "Don't wait for your ship to come in; swim out to it." Anon.

It is important to think back to ecology when creating goals because if someone's main value is spending time with their family then "having a higher positioned job with a higher salary" is not going to be an appropriate goal, if it means they are going to be working 24 hours a day 7 days a week to achieve it. However if they stated "It is 1st January 20XX and I have £X amount of my own money in my bank account. I spend time with my family and I am happily married to a partner I adore and who adores and supports me."

Then the goal is specific to them and their circumstances, it has a deadline and an end figure. It takes into account the conflicting value (not having as much time with family if you achieve this goal) as a positive; that your family will help and support you to reach this goal.

For me john F Kennedy describes goals the best; *"We choose to go to the moon in this decade, and do the other things not because they are easy, but because they are hard – because the goal will serve to organise and measure the best of our energies and skill. Because that challenge is one we are willing to accept, one we are unwilling to postpone, and one we intend to win"* In setting outcomes, we create a direction and purpose in life by which we can "programme" ourselves to consistently achieve what we want. By achieving our

> "The purpose of life is a life of purpose" Robert Bryne.

outcomes and continually reviewing and setting new outcomes, short and long term, we create the success we desire and deserve in all aspects of our life.

The difference between an outcome and a goal is that an outcome goes beyond a goal; it is the goal beyond a goal. For example competing in a 100 m local race, the goal is to come first and win, then what? An outcome on the other hand looks at the beneficial opportunities that come from achieving that goal, they are the stepping stones into your future. What avenues does achieving that goal open up? What will achieving that goal enable you to do? Going back to our race example, winning the race opens doors to represent your town in the county race, and then you could enter as a junior athlete and represent your country competing for gold at the Olympics. Then you can even become the fastest person to have ever run a 100m race, the list goes on. Outcome orientation gives direction and purpose; *"Start with the end in mind"* (Steven Covey 1990) if your "end" is to just win the race then your goal has been achieved, but if it is to achieve your personal best at the Olympics then this is the goal beyond a goal. Remember the presupposition; All procedures should increase choice and develop greater personal flexibility, your goal being to increase choices through having a choice of techniques facilitating flexibility.

> *"How do you eat an Elephant? One bite at a time"* Bill Hogan

Another example is weight loss; anyone can reduce their weight if they are determined enough, but then what? The temptation to slip back into your old ways after this goal has been achieved usually results in this weight just being put back on; and there you have the classic Yo-Yo diet. But if you set the outcome "Walk 500 meters a day" that is specific to your circumstances, has a deadline and a detailed end result, then the chances of you keeping the weight off have just significantly increased.

History

In Bandler and Grinder's earliest modelling experience of Satir and Erickson, they discovered the basic premise of modelling excellence. One of the key differences that made Satir and Erickson excellent in their respective fields was that they were outcome oriented in their client work, specifically to the outcomes that the client wanted.

Bandler and Grinder realised that by setting a specific positive outcome we become aware of the difference between what we have currently and what we want instead. By focusing on what we want to achieve we pay attention to the opportunities which will assist us in achieving our desired outcome.

It is important to take into account external influences, both positive and negative, as a well formed outcome is not a given. Going back to our Olympics example; you can achieve your goal (achieve your personal best at the Olympics) but not necessarily win the Gold medal as you are also competing against other athletes who are striving to achieve their personal best, which I am afraid is outside your control.

Think back to the presupposition; The mind and the body affect each other. The mind and the body are one interconnected unit and so it is not possible to make changes in one without the other being affected. Likewise in the communication model, we delete, distort and generalise through our unique set of filters, the important filter here is values and beliefs. If the goal (external event) is not important to us and/or we don't believe we can do it then you're most possibly right. We create our own internal representation of the external event; our internal representation affects our state and therefore our behaviour which ultimately affects our results.

> *To accomplish great things, we must not only act, but also dream; not only plan, but also believe.* Anatole France

84

An example of this is Roger Bannister. Roger Bannister was determined to complete the 4 minute mile, believing it was possible against the beliefs of his doctors who said it simply was not, declaring the heart would simply combust under the strain! However in 1954 Roger had done it! With 37 more athletes breaking the 4 minute barrier over the course of the next year and this time is now the standard for all professional middle distance runners. As one of our filters; our beliefs and values have a great effect on whether or not we can achieve our goals.

> *"Enjoyment appears at the boundary between boredom and anxiety, when the challenges are just balanced with the person's capacity to act"* Mihaly Csikszentmihalyi

While going about setting your own goal use your sensory acuity to gauge whether this goal is congruent for you (with your beliefs, values and ecology). When assisting somebody else to achieve their outcome use your sensory acuity to deduce whether the outcome is what they truly want and whether it is congruent for them, whilst being in rapport at all times.

It is important to remember the presupposition; The person with the most choices of behaviour will have the most influence on the system (in this case, on their future). For those of you who study NLP you will recognise this as the law of requisite variety. Having multiple ways to achieve a goal will increase your chances of success because you will not give up just because you have got into difficulties. Basically the more options you have available to achieve your goal the greater the chance of change and success.

Motivation

One other important aspect to setting goals is the motivation required to achieve them. We as humans can be categorised into being "towards" or "away from" motivated, which relates to our meta-programmes covered in linguistic presuppositions (Language subchapter 7.1). If you think back to the communication model of NLP you will see that we delete, distort and generalise information through our meta-programmes, which are our personality traits (how you react to information given to you due to your personality traits i.e. how you conceptualise, perceive and comprehend information). The direction filter is one of these traits, it's the trigger that puts a person into action, whether they move towards an object/goal, or away from a problem/negative consequence means that person is either towards or away from motivated.

According to Shelle Rose Charvet (1997) people with a 'towards' pattern are motivated to achieve, attain, to get, to have, whereas 'away from' people are motivated by moving away from what they don't want, to avoid, by deadlines, problems to be solved. By knowing what direction focuses you/your client, you can attain their full attention, establish a deeper rapport and avoid misunderstandings.

Carolyn Boyes (2006) expands on this, explaining that we are motivated by two types of values; a value that pull us towards something, or values that push us away from something - carrots to tempt us or sticks to punish. By being aware of this and asking yourself/the client what is important to them about achieving their goal, you can attain by which direction they are motivated. With this knowledge you can structure your language to motivate them to focus on getting what you/they want, by either assigning tasks/setting goals, or by telling them what they would avoid if they do it. That is people are motivated "towards" achieving a goal or motivated "away from" what they have now.

It is also important to realise that a goal or an outcome can never be "to find happiness" as this is a state which can be recalled at any time from past experiences. The following chart describes the differences between Goals & Outcomes verses States further. Through a goal you can achieve a state but for the goal to be a state will not have enough drive to achieve a goal, as states are achievable through multiple other means.

State versus Goal

Value or State (Confidence)	Goal or Outcome (£1m, be married, weigh 12 stone)
Stated ambiguously	Stated specifically
Write affirmations	Write goals / outcomes
You can have it now	Time is involved
No steps	Steps are needed to get there (get final step and work backwards)
Infinite	Measurable
Stated for self and/or others	Stated for self only

Ok, I get outcomes, were does the "Well formed" bit come in?

This is the term used in NLP to describe a process of systematically refining goals, objectives or targets so that they fulfil the criteria. The process is similar but more thorough than that of the more widely-known process called SMART goals. When our wants, dreams or wishes are refined using this process they become more believable and realisable. This is why they are then described as being 'well-formed' outcomes

The term 'well-formed' has been around in NLP for over 35 years and, as with many of the rather strange NLP terms, this name can get in the way of understanding the simplicity of the model. Some people, to make things even more obtuse, even refer to it as the 'well-formedness conditions for an outcome'. Simply put, what the term really means is that the outcome has been refined or checked against eight tests and once it has 'passed' these tests it is well-designed (well-formed!) You can use this process to clarify your own wishes so that they are more realistic and action - focused - and to assist others in doing the same.

Well-formedness Conditions *(Adapted From Ian McDermott)*

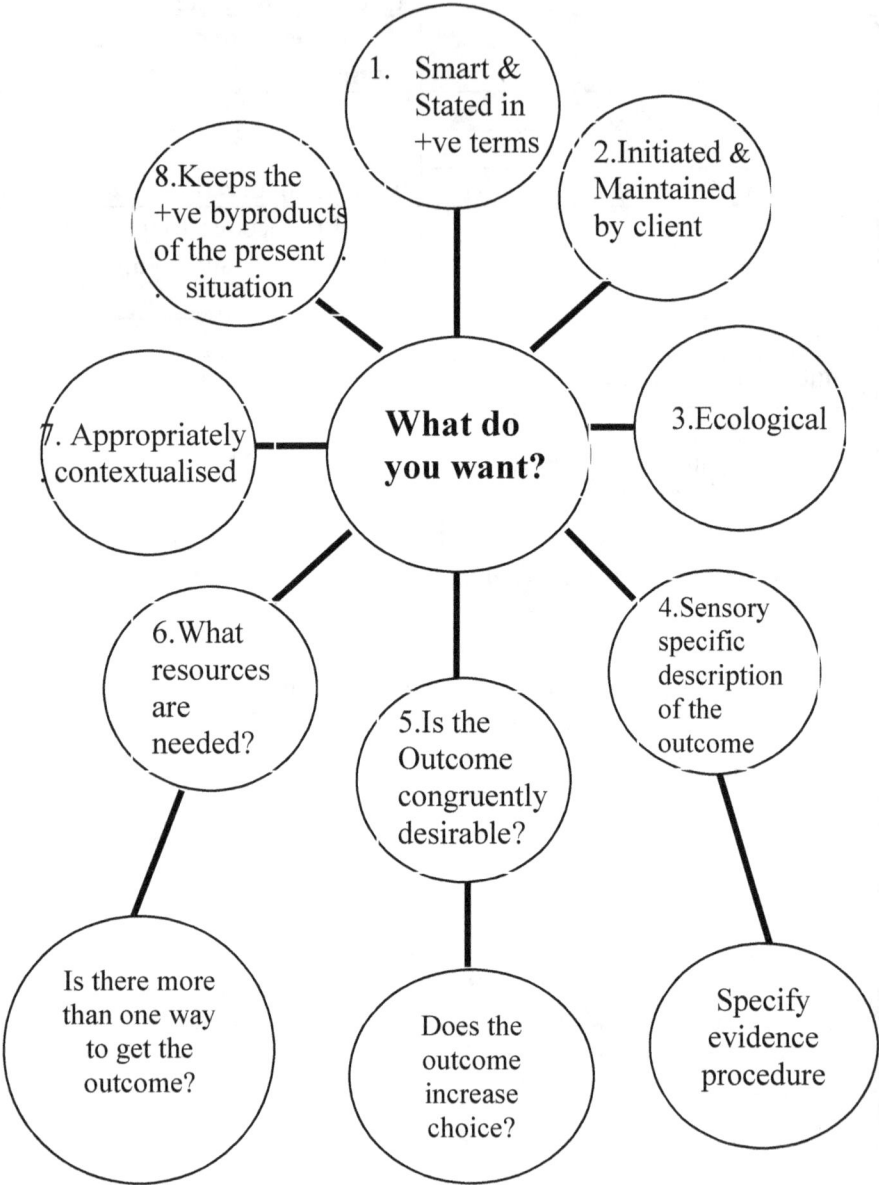

1. Smart & Stated in +ve terms

2. Initiated & Maintained by client

8. Keeps the +ve byproducts of the present situation

What do you want?

3. Ecological

7. Appropriately contextualised

4. Sensory specific description of the outcome

6. What resources are needed?

5. Is the Outcome congruently desirable?

Is there more than one way to get the outcome?

Does the outcome increase choice?

Specify evidence procedure

S.M.A.R.T Outcomes

S	Short Specific Simple
M	Measurable Meaningful to you More than one way to achieve it
A	As if now, in present tense Achievable All areas of your life
R	Realistic Responsible / Ecological Right for you
T	Timed Toward What You Want, Positive (no negations & no comparatives)

Specific

Goals should be straightforward and emphasize what you want to happen. Specifics help us to focus our efforts and clearly define what we are going to do.

The specifics are the What, Why and How of the **S.M.A.R.T** model.
WHAT are you going to do?
WHY is this important to do at this time? What do you want to ultimately accomplish?
HOW are you going to do it?

Ensure the goal you set is very specific and clear rather than setting a goal like "*to lose weight*" or "*be healthier*", set a specific goal "*to lose 2cm off your waistline"* or *"to walk 500 meters a day"* or *"to drink 1.5l of water a day"*.

Measurable

In the broadest sense, if you can't measure it, you can't manage it. The goal statement is a measure for the project itself; if the goal is accomplished, how will you know? Choose a goal with measurable progress, so you can see the change occur and the process of the achievement. What will you see, hear, feel or be doing? How will you see the success when you reach your goal? Be specific! *"I will fit into size 12 clothes before my birthday"* shows the specific target to be measured. *"I want to fit into my old clothes"* is not as measurable.

> *"I never ran 1000 miles. I could have never done that. I ran one mile 1000 times"*
> Stu Mittleman

Make sure you have established concrete criteria for measuring progress toward the achievement of each goal you set. When you measure your progress, you stay on track, reach your target dates, and experience the exhilaration of achievement that spurs you on to continued effort required to reach your goals.

Achievable

When you identify goals that are most important to you, you begin to figure out ways you can make them come true. You develop the attitudes, abilities, skills, and financial capacity to reach them because you are focused on your goal, noticing the opportunities that previously you had not seen. Goals that you set which are too far out of your reach, you probably won't commit to doing or will be half prepared to fail even though you may start with the best of intentions, the knowledge that it's too much for you means your subconscious will keep reminding you of this fact and will stop you from giving it your best.

A goal does need to stretch you slightly as this is what will spur you on as you feel the sense of achievement when you manage it, you feel you can do it and it will need a real commitment from you. For instance, if you aim to lose 20lbs in one week, we all know that isn't achievable. But setting a goal to lose 1lb and when you've achieved that, aiming to lose a further 1lb, will keep it achievable for you. The feeling of success which this brings helps you to remain motivated.

Realistic

This is not a synonym for 'easy.' Realistic, in this case, means 'do-able.' It means that the learning curve is not a vertical slope; that the skills needed to do the work are available; that the project fits with the overall strategy and goals of the organisation. A realistic project may push the skills and knowledge of the people working on it but it shouldn't break them.

Start by planning a way to get there which makes the goal realistic: the goal needs to be realistic for you and where you are at the moment. A goal of "Never eating sweets, cakes, crisps and chocolate again" is not exactly realistic for someone who really enjoys these foods. A more realistic goal would be to eat a piece of fruit each day instead of one sweet item. You can then choose to work towards reducing the amount of sweet products gradually as and when this feels realistic for you. Be sure to set goals that you can achieve with some effort! Too difficult and you set the stage for failure, but too low sends the message that you aren't very capable. Set the bar high enough for a satisfying achievement!

Timely

Set a timeframe for the goal: for next week, in three months, by fifth grade. Putting an end point on your goal gives you a clear target to work towards a dead-line. If you don't set a time, the commitment is too vague. It tends not to happen because you feel you can start at any time. Without a time limit, there's no urgency to start taking action now, this time must be measurable, achievable and realistic.

Examples of an **S.M.A.R.T** outcome:

"It is 1ˢᵗ January 20XX and I own a 4 bedroom house with a ½ acre garden and a garage, within 20 minutes of my office in Wembley."

"It is 1ˢᵗ January 20XX and I weigh 70kg. I feel fit, strong and healthy, and have exercised for more than 1 hour at a time, more than 3 times per week for the past 6 months and enjoy it."

The PACER model by Francis Wardle (2007); The steps towards a well formed outcome:

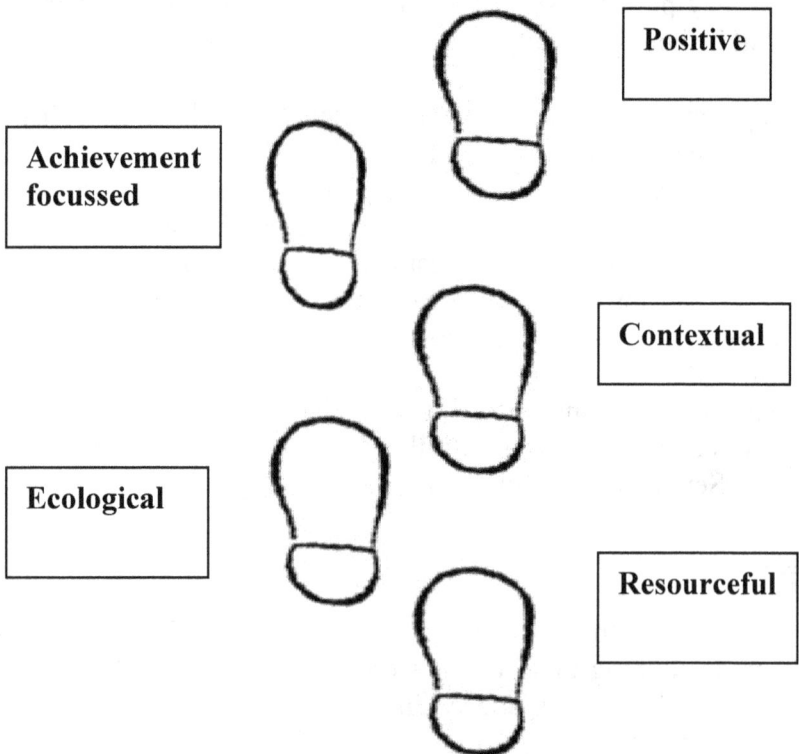

Achievement focussed	**Positive**
Ecological	**Contextual**
	Resourceful

Positive. Positive means stated in terms of something you want rather than something you want to avoid. To turn a negative outcome into a positive one, ask;

- What do you want?
- What will that bring you?
- What else?

Achievement focussed. It is important to think about how you will know you are succeeding and how you will know you have succeeded, so that you can assess your progress. What type of feedback will give you this information? What will you hear, see and feel when you have succeeded? Make sure you know what the first steps towards your outcome will be and that they are achievable.
- How will you know when you have got it?
- How will someone else know you have got it?

Contextual. You will want to think about the contexts in which you want or don't want this outcome. There may be some situations in which the outcome is inappropriate.
- When, where and with whom do you want it/not want it?
- How long for?

Ecological. You will want to consider how achieving the outcome will affect the wider system. It may have an impact on resources such as finance and time. It may have an impact on other people, on other roles you play in your life and on the choices it gives you.
- Are there any negative consequences?
- How OK is it for you to achieve this goal?

Resourceful. Can you start and maintain the outcome? This condition is about how much direct control the person setting it has over the achievement of the outcome and how much other people will be involved.
- What resources have you got already?
- What resources do you need?

<u>Positive By-products</u> (From Ian McDermott)

In all behaviour there is a positive intention otherwise you wouldn't do it. When you are helping yourself or others bring about change there will be positive aspects of the old behaviour that the person may want to keep. Spending sometime identifying what those by-products are will enable you to make sure you can keep the positive elements and so make it easier to change. This also ensures that the change is appropriate and ecological for the person/organisation, because if it loses those positive by-products it could impair the achievement of the goal.

Whether it is individual or organisational change you wish to bring about you can identify the positive by-products by asking the following questions:

Personal	**Organisational**
What is this behaviour doing for me?	What functions / purpose does this behaviour or practice perform?
What are the positive by-products of my present behaviour?	What are the positive by-products of the present behaviour or practice for the individuals doing it and for the larger system?
What else happens – directly or indirectly – when I do this?	What else happens – directly or indirectly – as a result of this behaviour or practice?
What do I get out of doing this?	What do they get out of doing this?
What else do I get out of doing this?	What else do they or others get out of doing this?
What of this is worth keeping?	What of this – in their opinion – is valuable and worth keeping?

How to do it! – Keys to an achievable outcome

The below exercise can be carried out by you when making goals for yourself, or with another when making goals for them;

> *Our ideals resemble the stars, which illuminate the night. No one will ever be able to touch them. But the men who, like the sailors on the ocean, take them for guides will undoubtedly reach their goal.* Carl Schurz

1. Establish where you/the client is now; describe the current situation in your/ their own words.

2. Get the scores on the doors, (a convincer, if you will, of the increased possibility of you/ them achieving the goal) score out of 10 the current possibility of them achieving this goal (1 being no possibility, 10 being "I can achieve this goal").

3. Make the outcome S.M.A.R.T and stated as a positive. Avoid using negative words such as lose, don't, unwell. For example: in relation to weight loss use; *"To weigh 12 stone by 1ˢᵗ December 20xx"*, rather than *"To lose 2 stone by 1ˢᵗ December 20xx"*.

4. Ensure the goal is initiated and maintained by yourself/ the client; ask questions like do you need other people to do it for you? (If so their contribution is out of the clients control and will affect the outcome.) Outcomes ideally need to be set up and carried out by yourself/ the client.

5. Is the goal ecological?
   - For what purpose do you want this?
   - What will you gain or lose if you have it?
   - What will happen if you get it?
   - What won't happen if you get it?
   - What will happen if you don't get it?
   - What won't happen if you don't get it?

- Are there any negative consequences in achieving this goal?

6. Specific sensory-based description of the outcome.
   - What will you see?
   - What will you hear?
   - What will you feel?
     - Specify evidence procedure.
   - How will you know when you have it?
   - Make it compelling.
   - Make it as if you have it now.

7. Is the outcome congruently desirable?
   - What will the outcome get for you?
   - What will the outcome allow you to do?
     - Does the outcome increase choice?
   - What other options are there available to you?

8. What resources are needed?
   - What resources do you have now and what do you need to achieve your outcome?
   - Have you ever done this before?
     - Is there more than one way to achieve the outcome?
   - What other avenues are there available to you?
   - Do you know anyone who has done this before who can advise you?

9. Is it appropriately contextualised?
   - Where, when, how and with whom do you want it?
   - What will you gain or lose if you have it?
   - What will happen if you get it?
   - What won't happen if you get it?

10. Keeps the positive by-products of the present situation
    - Do you lose anything from achieving this outcome?

11. Read/ show the client all you have written down and ask:

-"Out of 10, how possible is it to achieve this goal?"

You are looking for a 10/10; if this is not the answer get curious and ask yourself/the client:
"What would need to happen for it to be a 10/10?" and/or
"What is stopping it from being a 10/10?"

This answer may mean that the goal needs to be redefined or that a process goal needs to be established first. If this is the case then design the goal in the same way, using steps 1-10 keeping the original goal, just checking that the timings are appropriate.

Then check again *"Out of 10, how possible is it to achieve this goal?"*

N.B this is for both goals.

Exercises

Exercise 1 – define you!

The most important things in the world to me are:
1.
2.
3.
4.
5.

If I could be/ do anything in the world I would:

_____

_____

I know I am succeeding when:

_____

_____

My skills, qualities, gifts, talents:

_____

_____

Exercise 2 – Write yourself a S.M.A.R.T goal

As outlined in the exercise above, for example: *"It is 1 January 20XX and I own a 4 bedroom house with a ½ acre garden and a garage, within 20 minutes of my office in Wembley."*

Exercise 3 – Write yourself a Well formed outcome

Rewrite your goal above following the keys to an achievable outcome on page 95, this can either be done individually, or in pairs, where Person A is the 'client' and Person B is the NLPer carrying out the exercise.

Summary

A Goal is a specific target you want to achieve within a given context.

An Outcome is the future benefit of achieving the goal within the given contexts; it is the goal beyond a goal.

Goals and Outcomes are not states, they may result in a state but they are not the achievement of a state.

When it comes to well formed outcomes it is important to state them in the positive, basically: Say It the Way You Want It!

By making outcomes sensory specific it asks you to see what you will see, feel what you will feel and hear what you will hear when you have this outcome in the future, making that outcome much more real, compelling and achievable.

Outcomes direct a person's thoughts and actions. Use them for your goals, dreams, and wishes - and watch what happens. The 11 well formed outcome questions distinguish between those factors which are relevant to getting what you want and those which are in the realm of history, complaint, etc.

Using this process improves your rapport with other people. If you have a joint project using the well-formed outcome process to match and align your objectives adds to the rapport already existing between you – since you now have a joint commitment to the outcome towards which you are both moving. And when you use it to assist someone in clarifying what they want for themselves they are likely to appreciate your concern and interest.

It provides a means of evaluating progress. Having a well-formed outcome makes it more likely that you will quickly recognise when you are thinking or acting in ways that are at variance with your well-formed outcome, giving you a signal to stop and re-evaluate your activities.

When used to clarify formal discussions work-related discussions or meetings the outcome steps provide a framework that keeps discussions and activity on course.

Use the questions. It may not be necessary to go through all of the questions for every objective. Use your discretion and apply the questions that are appropriate at the time. When using the questions with other people first establish a very good quality of rapport and then either introduce the process formally or use the process in a conversational manner

References

- Boyes, C. (2006) Need to Know? NLP Achieve Success with Positive Thinking, London: Harper Collins.
- Andreas, S., Andreas, C. (1987) Change Your Mind and Keep The Change. Utah, Real People Press
- Bandler, R. (1985) Using Your Brain for A Change. Real People Press
- Bandler, R., Macdonald, W. (1989) An Insiders Guide to Submodalities. Utah, Real People Press
- http://www.businessballs.com/sevenhabitsstevencovey.htm Bill Hogun
- Charvet, S.R. (1997) Words That Change Minds, Dubuque, IA: Kendall Hunt
- http://twm.co.nz/hologram.html
- http://www.nlpu.com/Articles/artic25.htm

Chapter 6

Representational systems – how we experience the world around us

"We don't see things as they are,
but rather as we are"
Anais Nin

Concept

This technique is based on the presupposition; There are no resistant clients, only inflexible communicators. This resistance is a sign of a lack of rapport (chapter 4) and can be broken down by being more flexible with your communication, using language that appeals to your audience's preferred learning and listening styles.

Benefits

- Matching your audience's (boss, client, or colleague) preferred learning style allows them to more easily understand and connect with what you are saying.
- Allows you to speak in a way that triggers intrigue and maintains interest in what you are saying.
- By identifying a person's sensory preference you can match it, create rapport and communicate even better.
- Describing your viewpoint through a person's preferred listening style, reduces barriers and allows you to influence their views.

What are Representational systems?

Representational systems (also known as sensory modalities, the 4-tuple and abbreviated to VAKOG) examine how the human mind processes information. It states that for practical purposes, information can be treated as if it is processed through our senses and is the way we represent, code, store and give meaning/ language to our experience.

There is a representational system for each of our 5 senses; this is the way we experience the world. We all continually make use of all of the representational systems, switching from one to another for different reasons throughout our day. What we actually perceive are representations of what each sensory organ transmits to us.

These representational systems are;

👁 **Visual** (V)	Ve – Visual external – What you see outside
	Vi – Visual internal – What you visualise inside

🎧 **Auditory** (A)	Ae– Auditory external – What you hear outside
	Ai – Auditory internal – Sounds you remember
	Ad – Auditory digital – How you talk to yourself

✋ **Kinaesthetic** (K)	Ke – Kinaesthetic external – Tactile – Touch, temperature, moisture, texture

	Ki – Kinaesthetic internal
	  Visceral – emotions and internal feeling
	  Proprioceptive – muscle memory

👃 **Olfactory** (O)	O - Smells

👅 **Gustatory** (G)	G - Tastes

Which leads us to the last representation system; Auditory Digital (AD), this is different to the others as it is not related to any specific sensory organ. It is the voice inside our head; the internal dialogue we use to make logic of a situation and which we tell ourselves off with.

<u>So why would you want to learn this?</u>

Well, the Primary Representational System is the one someone uses the most. We mainly work with the four representational systems of Visual, Audio and Kinaesthetic and Auditory Digital. Olfactory and Gustatory do not play a major roll as they are often included within kinaesthetic (unless you are in a profession such as a chef or work with fragrances, as you would use these to a large degree).

Furthermore most people tend to favour one representational system over the others and process most communication in this manner. Some people even adversely dislike using one! If you think back to your school revision days I am sure you can all remember your revision technique, reading, re-writing or speaking verses out loud, well this is the same principle. If you were unable to learn in such a way, i.e. just being told something out loud (auditory) and like me you had to write everything down (kinaesthetic) then chances are now you have grown up you still don't like using your auditory processors and prefer written reports instead of being simply told something.

For some people it is very easy to deduce what representational system they prefer by looking at their profession, for example photographers/designers are very visual people, obviously musicians are auditory, athletes and fabric designers tend to be kinaesthetic and mathematicians and scientists are auditory digital. So let's have a look at which system you prefer:

<u>Exercise</u>

For each of the following statements, place a number next to every phrase using the following system to indicate your preferences:

4 = Closest to describing you   **3 = Next best description**
2 = Next best   **1 = Least descriptive of you**

1. I make important decisions based on:
____ gut feelings.
____ what sounds best.
____ what looks best.
____ after a precise review of all the issues.

2. During an argument, I am most likely to be influenced by:
____ the other person's tone of voice.
____ whether I can see the other person's argument.
____ the logic of the other person's argument.
____ whether I feel in touch with other person's true feelings.

3. I most easily communicate what is going on with me by:
____ the way I dress and look.
____ the feelings I share.
____ the words I choose.
____ my voice tones.

4. It is easiest for me to:
____ find the ideal tuning and volume on a stereo system.
____ select the most intellectually relevant point in an interesting subject.
____ select the most comfortable furniture.
____ select attractive colour combinations.

5. I
____ am attuned to the sounds in my surroundings.
____ am very adept at making sense of new facts and data.
____ am very sensitive to the way articles of clothing feel on my body.
____ have a strong response to colours and to the way a room looks.

105

Now Copy your answers in the same order from the test to the lines below.

1.___K	2.___A	3.___V	4.___A	5.__A
___A	___V	___K	___Ad	___Ad
___V	___Ad	___Ad	___K	___K
___Ad	___K	___A	___V	___V

Finally, Add the numbers associated with each letter in the grid on the below. There will be five entries for each letter.

	V	A	Ad	K
1				
2				
3				
4				
5				
TOTALS				

The comparison of the totalled scores gives your relative preference for each of the four major representational systems.

Now, I know you are thinking that this is all very well and good for me but how do I find which system other people like to use? I can't go out and ask them to fill in this form can I?! Well no, but thinking back to sensory acuity and picking up on the physiology and predicates words and phrases used by the other person whilst communicating (predicates - covered later in this chapter) highlights their preferred representational system. Now I appreciate there can never really be a "one size fits all" but physiological indicators and predicates go a long way in aiding us to distinguish and categorise how people prefer to communicate and learn.

As previously covered, physiological indicators include:

1. Eye movements
2. Voice tone and tempo
3. Rate and position of breathing
4. Postures and gestures

So let's look at how we can detect someone's preferred representational system, so that we can appreciate and get the best out of our communication with them in a work context.

Visual: The process of translating communication into pictures.

How to detect visual people

♦ They will be breathing from the top of their lungs and their upper shoulders and breathe fairly rapidly.
♦ Tend to speak rapidly with a high clear tone.
♦ They often sit forward in their chair and tend to be organised, neat, well groomed and orderly. Appearance is important to them.
♦ Use picture descriptions during conversation.
♦ Use gestures that may be high & quick.

How to get the best out of your communication with visual people:

♦ Visual people memorise by seeing pictures, and are less distracted by noise. So show them plenty of pictures, graphs and diagrams as they are interested in how things look about your program.
♦ They often have trouble remembering verbal instructions because their minds tend to wander, especially if you speak slowly, so speed up your conversation and aim to be efficient with your words.
♦ Use phrases like: "A picture paints a thousand words".
♦ Must see things to understand them, so show them how to do it.
♦ Like visually based feedback.

Auditory: The process of translating communication into sounds.

How to detect auditory people:

♦ They will be breathing from the middle of their chest and breathe evenly in pace.
♦ Tend to speak at a medium pace and melodious.
♦ Will move their eyes sideways.
♦ Excellent at repeating back instructions.
♦ Use auditory descriptions during conversation

How to get the best out of your communication with auditory people:

♦ They are easily distracted by noise so talk in a quiet room.
♦ They memorise by steps, procedures, and sequences (sequentially).
♦ The auditory person likes to be TOLD how they're doing.
♦ Responds to a certain tone of voice or set of words rather than what you are actually saying.
♦ They will be interested in what you have to say about your programme.

Kinaesthetic: The process of checking communication with our feelings.

How to detect kinaesthetic people:

♦ They breathe from the bottom of their lungs, so you may see their stomach go in and out when they breathe.
♦ They often move and talk very slowly, with a low deep tone.
♦ They like to stand close to people.
♦ Very physical people, like to touch during conversation.
♦ Uses gestures that are low and smooth.

How to get the best out of your communication with kinaesthetic people:

♦ They respond to physical rewards and touching.
♦ They memorise by doing or walking through something.
♦ They will be interested in your programme if it "feels right".

Auditory digital: The process of internally checking communication by talking to ourselves.

How to detect auditory digital people:

♦ The auditory digital person can exhibit characteristics of the other major representational systems.
♦ Speaks in a clipped, crisp monotone.
♦ Breathing patterns like an auditory person, higher up in the chest.

How to get the best out of your communication with auditory digital people:

♦ They will want to know if your programme "makes sense" so tell them how it is practical and makes "common sense".
♦ Dissociated from feelings.

I believe it is important to stress that as human beings, the *one size fits all* technique is never going to truly work. Representational systems are not stereotyping people, as people work from more than one representational system, particularly professionals in high profile jobs. Representational systems simply show how people like to communicate and learn. Furthermore by being aware of a representational system that you don't like using allows you to develop this skill further.

History

Modern day examples are 'Student Learning Styles', very much like the exercise you carried out above. Representational systems, however, have been around for a very long time and link back to neuro-science, in particular the work done by William Sheldon in 1942 on somatotype-personality hypothesis and habitual electroencephalography (EEG) patterns: patterns along the scalp produced by the firing of neurons within the brain. Work from this postulated that by noticing patterns of posture, voice tone and breathing enables you to establish someone's preferred representational system. It went on to show that the basis for the relation of eye movements to representational systems rests on the assumption about laterality of brain function and use of language in particular the words that they use.

Think back to the communication model: we delete, distort and generalise information we receive through our filters, in this instance the filter of language. If the information given to us is not in our preferred representational system then we are more likely to distort and generalise its meaning, or worse delete it altogether. This is why people end up with completely different meanings/interpretations (internal representation) of the information given (external event). Have you ever had a conversation with someone and they have just simply not grasped what you are trying to say? Or where two people have read a global work email and interpreted different instructions from what it said? The presupposition; The meaning of communication is in the response you get, helps to explain this point further, as the words you have chosen to use might be from that person's undesired representational system, therefore they do not see, hear, feel, sense the same view (internal representation) as you and hence the misunderstanding.

Additionally think back to sensory acuity and rapport: how do you know when communication is effective or not? By noticing this response you can change the representational system from which you are communicating to better suit the person you are communicating with.

How to do it! – Predicates

Listening to and understanding the way a person talks allows you to pick up on verbs, adverbs and adjectives that show a pattern of preference which highlights a representational system. It indicates what type of sensory based stimulus that person is most likely going to notice and respond to, so that you can communicate to them (be this verbally or in written form) using words in a manner that is most appealing to them.

Representational systems not only indicate the process by which people formally create their model of the world, they also provide us with a format by which we can understand how and what they experience. By being able to understand and speak to people in their own representational system, you heighten the sense of rapport between you.

Predicate Phrases & Words

Examples of certain phrases that are associated with a particular representational system.

Visual	Auditory	Kinaesthetic
An eyeful	Afterthought	All washed up
Appears to me	Blabbermouth	Boils down to
A shadow of a doubt	Clearly expressed	Chip off the old block
Bird's eye view	Lend me your ear	Hold it!
Get a perspective on	Get a grip!	Keep your shirt on!
Clear-cut	Hold your tongue	Hothead
In view of	Loud and clear	Pain in the neck
Looks like	Well informed	Stiff upper lip
Mental picture	To tell the truth	Get a load of this
Paint a picture	Tongue-tied	Get in touch with

Examples of certain words that are associated with a particular representational system. You can use the Auditory Digital words when you wish to give the person a choice of thinking, i.e. so that they can express themselves more freely and not be limited to one representational system.

Visual	Auditory	Kinaesthetic	Auditory Digital
look	hear	feel	sense
view	listen	touch	proceed
vivid	tell	get hold of	understand
show	tune in/out	hard	learn
illuminate	I'm all ears	concrete	process
imagine	rings	experience	logical
clear	resonate	handle(ing)	consider
attractive	deaf	solid	obtain
crystal	quiet	impression	require
picture	announce	sensation	arrange

<u>Examples of predicates in work</u>

Visual

If I could <u>show</u> you an <u>attractive</u> way in which you could achieve the deal you want, you would at least want to <u>look</u> at it, wouldn't you?

If this <u>looks good</u> to you we will go ahead and <u>focus</u> on getting the paperwork done.

Auditory

If I could <u>tell</u> you about this month's deals, you would at least want to <u>listen</u> to them, wouldn't you?

If this <u>sounds good</u> to you we will go ahead and <u>discuss</u> how to set up an account.

Kinaesthetic

If I could help you <u>get hold of</u> a <u>concrete</u> way in which you <u>sense</u> you are getting the best deal, you would at least want to <u>get a feel for it</u>, wouldn't you?

If this <u>feels good</u> to you we will go ahead and set up an account by <u>handling the paperwork</u>.

Auditory Digital

If I could <u>arrange</u> for you to <u>obtain</u> what you <u>require</u>, you'd want to <u>consider</u> it, wouldn't you?

If it <u>makes sense</u> and is <u>logical</u>, we'll <u>proceed</u> and <u>process</u> the account-opening.

Exercises

Exercise 1

1. This technique can be carried out in groups of 2 or 3.
2. Each person writes a business/work-related letter/email as they normally would, and then repeat it but this time using predicates from various representational systems. Read the two letters to the other person(s) in the group, receiving feedback on which is better and why.

Exercise 2 – Predicates

1. This exercise involves three people – Person A and Person C are the 'clients', Person B is the NLPer carrying out the exercise.
2. Person A states a problem using one representational system predicates only.
3. Person C responds to the statement using only predicates of a different rep system.
4. Person B translates Person A's statement to Person C using the predicates of the rep system that Person C has used, and translates Person C's statement to Person A using the predicates of the rep system that Person A has used.
5. Repeat at least 3 times, then swap over and swap again so that everyone plays each role.

For example:

Person B says to Person A: "The way (Person C) *looks* at it, it *appears* that she has a *clear picture* of the argument'
Person B says to Person C: "(Person A's) *impression* is that there are still some aspects of the situation *kicking about* which you haven't *grasped* yet"

Exercise 3

In groups of 2, 3 or 4 consisting of people who have the same 'least preferred rep system'. Each group has to make up an advert for a product e.g. a bottle of mineral water, using only the rep system they favour the least!

Summary

Representational systems mainly relate to the preferred communication style people like to converse and learn in. You identify and converse in someone's preferred representational systems by using predicates.

If you communicate with people using their preferred representational system and predicates, you will much more rapidly develop understanding with them and build rapport than if you cross-communicate. Indeed, when communicating with a large group of people, such as in a presentation or report, it is better to mix up your own representational systems so as to make sure that you hit the button for all the people in your audience, rather than just the ones that are on the same wavelength as you.

People use their preferred representation system to code, order and give meaning to what has been said as it allows them to store and reference that event/memory. If visual is someone's preferred representational system then they will store information as pictures (a picture paints a thousand words), if they prefer auditory then they will store sounds, if they are kinaesthetic then they store it as a feeling. Recognising this in your staff, colleague, friend or loved one will enable you to empower them as they will analysis and remove the negative emotions that they have attached to their problems.

References

- Skinner, H. and Stephens, P. (2003). "Speaking the Same Language: Exploring the relevance of Neuro-Linguistic Programming to Marketing Communications". *Journal of Marketing Communications* Volume 9, Number 3 / September: 177–192.
- Sharpley, C. F. (1984). Predicate matching in NLP: A review of research on the preferred representational system. Journal of Counselling Psychology, 31(2), 238-248.
- Elich, M., Thompson, R. W., & Miller, L. (1985). Mental imagery as revealed by eye movement and spoken predicates: A test of neurolinguistic

programming. Journal of Counselling Psychology, 32(4), 622-625. Note: "psychological fad"p.625
- http://www.andrew-fogg.com/representational-systems-and-eye-accessing-cues/

Appendix

Further Predicate Phrases

Visual	Auditory	Kinaesthetic
Dim view	Idle talk	Hang in there
Flashed on	Inquire into	Heated argument
Catch a glimpse of	Keynote speaker	Hold on!
Get a scope on	Clear as a bell	Come to grips with
Hazy idea	Call on	Control yourself
Horse of a different colour	Describe in detail	Cool/calm/collected
In light of	Earful	Firm foundations
In person	Give an account of	Get a handle on
Make a scene	Tuned in/tuned out	Know-how
Mental image	Grant an audience	Lay cards on table
Mind's eye	Heard voices	Get the drift of
Naked eye	Hidden message	Pull some strings
See to it	Utterly	Sharp as a tack
Short sighted	Voiced an opinion	Slipped my mind
Showing off	Within hearing	Smooth operator
Sight for sore eyes	Word for word	So-so
Staring off into space	Manner of speaking	Start from scratch
Take a peek	Pay attention to	Stiff upper lip
Tunnel vision	Power of speech	Stuffed shirt
Under your nose	Purrs like a kitten	Too much of a hassle
Up front	State your purpose	Topsy-turvy
Well defined	Tattle-tale	Hand in hand

& Words

Visual	Auditory	Kinaesthetic	Auditory Digital
appear	harmonise	grasp	think
reveal	sound(s)	unfeeling	decide
envision	melodious	slip through	change
illuminate	attune	catch on	perceive
foggy	question	tap into	conceive
focused	be heard	contact	know
flash	clatter	throw out	describe
fade	sing	turn around	question

Chapter 7

The Power of Language – listen between the lines

"All the accomplishments of the human race, both positive and negative, have involved the use of language. We as human beings use our language in two ways. We use it first of all to represent our experience – we call this activity reasoning, thinking, fantasising, and rehearsing. When we use language as a representational system, we are creating a model of our experience. This model that we create by our representational use of language is based upon our perceptions of the world."
Bandler and Grinder, Structure of Magic

Concept

The map is not the territory. The words we use are not actually the event or the item they represent. Although they describe the event we

> *"Good words are worth much and cost little"* George Herbert

have chosen them to represent the words themselves are not the actual event itself. We create our own reality based on our past experience.

Our language becomes a 'map' of the 'territory' of our constructed reality, through the information we have obtained through our five senses. We code, order and give meaning (through deletion, distortion and generalization) to our experience in words, sounds, pictures, feelings, tastes and smells. Five different people might all experience the same event but each will take a different experience away from it depending on their own beliefs and values. NLP is the art of changing our map to create more choices.

Language is one of our most powerful filters and often beyond our conscious awareness. Words communicate much more than we can process consciously. When we accept the presupposition, "The meaning of communication is in the response you get," we are able to take 100% responsibility for all of our communication. Put simply, you cannot not communicate; by taking responsibility and appreciating that whatever you say will affect the receiver's communication, doesn't it makes sense to use language that produces the most effective results?

Lets return to our original definition of NLP "how we use the language of the mind to consistently achieve our specific and desired outcomes." If the language we currently use has created a world that does not serve us, then by changing the structure of the language we use, surely we can create more choices for ourselves and others, it is just a matter of how.

Language is one of the main filters in the communication model, it is how we speak to ourselves and most importantly it is how we speak to others. Therefore I hope you see that language is in itself a huge topic, one that I am going to divide into the following four sub-sections in an attempt to break the chapter down into more manageable chunks and to also help you find techniques in future reference.

Overview of language topics

Subchapter 7.1 Linguistic Presuppositions

Overview: Linguistic Presuppositions are what is assumed in a sentence. The power of linguistic change presupposes that the unconscious mind has to accept the presuppositions inherent in the sentence in order for the unconscious mind to make sense of the sentence.

Subchapter 7.2 Milton Model & Meta Model

Overview: The Milton Model looks at using the language of ambiguity. By being artfully vague in our language we can induce trance states enabling individuals to overcome their problems and discover new resources.
In contrast, the Meta Model was developed to recover information about how the client has created their Model of Reality. By gaining more specificity, new choices become actualised.

Subchapter 7.3 The Hierarchy of Ideas Model

Overview: The Hierarchy of Ideas Model looks at the order of our thinking. By being flexible in our language, we can pace a client's model of the world and influence them to higher or lower levels of abstraction or specificity.

Subchapter 7.4 Logical levels.

Overview: Logical levels are very useful for assisting with or understanding change from an individual, departmental or organisational point of view.

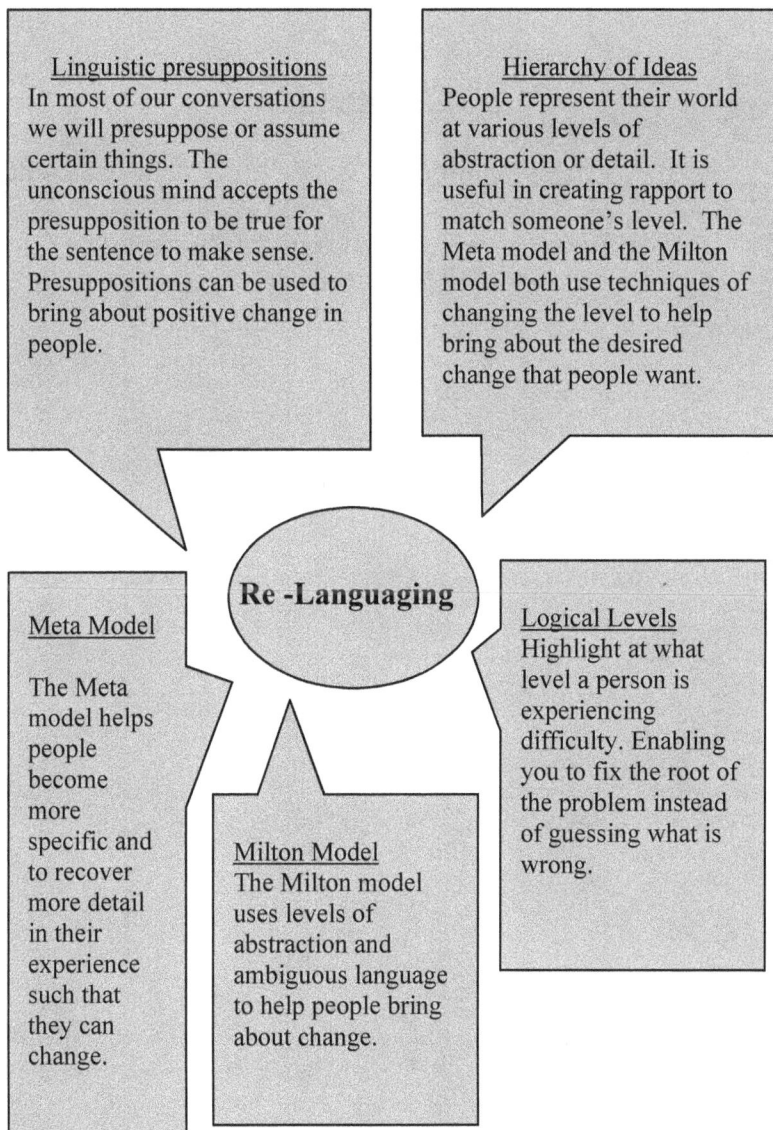

Linguistic presuppositions
In most of our conversations we will presuppose or assume certain things. The unconscious mind accepts the presupposition to be true for the sentence to make sense. Presuppositions can be used to bring about positive change in people.

Hierarchy of Ideas
People represent their world at various levels of abstraction or detail. It is useful in creating rapport to match someone's level. The Meta model and the Milton model both use techniques of changing the level to help bring about the desired change that people want.

Re -Languaging

Meta Model

The Meta model helps people become more specific and to recover more detail in their experience such that they can change.

Milton Model
The Milton model uses levels of abstraction and ambiguous language to help people bring about change.

Logical Levels
Highlight at what level a person is experiencing difficulty. Enabling you to fix the root of the problem instead of guessing what is wrong.

Chapter 7.1

Linguistic Presuppositions – Assumptions made in advance

"The human race is governed by its imagination"
Napoleon

Concept

This technique is based on the presupposition; The map is not the territory. The words we use are not actually the event or the item they represent. They are just the words the person has used in order to explain their meaning. Linguistic presuppositions help you to listen between the lines and separate the truth from your assumption, and are the foundation to this language section.

Benefits

Linguistic presuppositions enable you to recognise what another has assumed to be true by the words that they use.

- Communicate more effectively by becoming aware and understanding the power of the words you use.
- Ideal for selling; to pick up on and resolve the false assumption a client has made about your product/service, instead of guessing why they are saying no.
- Avoid misunderstandings; by noticing the linguistic presupposition in another's sentence to ensure or if necessary create colouration/congruence.
- Find solutions quicker.
- Help change someone's ideas and thinking around a problem to realise a solution themselves.
- To understand the assumptions within objections.

Just like Presuppositions are convenient assumptions, Linguistic Presuppositions are assumptions made in advance; the implied meaning within a sentence. Simply, what we presume to be true from what the other person is saying for their statement/sentence to make sense.

Every sentence that we say has a presupposition (assumption) in it. Think back to the communication model: Language is one of our main filters which we use to delete, distort and generalise the external event. When we make bold statements such as "*I can't do..........*" we limit our options for success as we have deleted the

123

possibility that we could. Just as the person you are speaking to has to assume you feel the task is too hard, you are inadequate to complete it or worse presumes you have been unsuccessful before.

For example, if someone makes the assumption *"That's too hard for me"*, then they will have instantly deleted the possibility that they could do it easily, leaving themselves with far fewer choices. By paying attention to the linguistic presuppositions someone uses will allow you to help them explore how they are limiting themselves, so you can find and implement strategies to produce better results.

Think of the statement 'The window is broken', what do you presume for this statement to be true? We can assume that, it's cracked, it's shattered, it does not open, the hinge has gone, the window needs fixing, the window has been smashed, etc. The truth is simply; there is a window, it is broken. The thing about Linguistic Presuppositions is that it aims to distinguish between the truth (there is a window, its broken) and an assumption/mind read (someone has smashed it, the hinges have gone).

Likewise in project management, a statement such as *"We have tried that method before"* can have a negative impact on the team as they delete the possibility that it could work this time by making the assumption that it will not work again. Ignoring the fact that; that was THEN and this is NOW, with a potentially whole set of different circumstances; the team has more experience, with new recruits with fresh ideas and strengths. Regardless of the political, economic, environmental, social, technological or legal changes since you last tried that method.

As previously touched upon linguistic presuppositions can be used to help someone change their internal representation of an experience, thus creating more

> *"My life has been full of terrible misfortunes, most of which never happened"* Michel De Montaigne

choices so that they can make the changes they want more

efficiently. Think back to Cause and Effect in chapter 2, cause and effect looks at behaviours; are you at "cause" or at "effect" for what takes place in your life? For example you wake up to the sun coming through your window, you're shocked as it should only be 06:00 and it's October! To which you panic, checking the alarm clock which confirms you are late, it is actually quarter past eight and you panic even more as you remember you have a job interview at 09:00 on the other side of town. As you run down stairs you trip and stub your toe, the hot water is not working in the shower and it is now twenty to nine, you can't find your car keys and have to hail a taxi. What do you already know about this day?

Your assumption of it is going to influence your outcome. People who are at cause apologise for being late, get over it and move on; people who are at effect assume it is going to be a bad day and stay in a un-resourceful state, which leads to them stuttering and passing upon questions they should know from the interview panel. Later that day they drown their sorrows with a friend and tell them: x, y and z caused me to not get the job. Their friend would assume all this to be true in order to make sense of what they have said. (x=y) the reality is you were late, the results of the job interview could have gone either way, could be due to you being at effect, not shining to the best of your ability in the interview room, or it could have been due to the next candidate after you was exactly what the interview panel were looking for.

We use linguistic presuppositions all the time, think how many times you have said to a junior member of staff how simple or easy a task is, regardless of what it is, they have the implied knowledge that it is going to be easy as that is the assumed truth within your sentence. This is one of the main ways in which we can use linguistic presuppositions consciously to change somebody's mindset. Compare the impact of the following two sentences on someone's internal representation and their expectation of the experience:

1. *"You have to be fit to be able to swim"*

2. *"You will be surprised by how fit you become once you have learnt how to swim"*

Which sentence would have the greater chance of helping the person to achieve their outcome? Which would give them a useful internal representation for them to start out on their quest to learn how to swim? What are the presuppositions in each of the sentences?

How many times have you heard a nurse say *"I am afraid this is going to hurt"* or even *"this should not hurt that much"*. How do these sentences make you feel? Now compare these sentences' to; *"this may be sore and it will be over quickly."*

Therefore you can use presuppositions to create internal representations in yourself and others that can help bypass the other person's resistance. By being aware of the presuppositions you use in your internal dialogue you can help yourself to change your own internal representations. By being aware of the presuppositions others use you can help them change their internal representations.

History

In NLP this technique came about through modelling Milton Erickson's hypnosis techniques on patients. He would frequently make statements or suggestions such as *"Do you want to tell me what is bothering you now or would you rather wait a while"* which presupposed certain behaviours or responses in his patients. In this example it presupposes that the patient was going to tell him what was bothering them, it was just a matter of when. Linguistic presuppositions also stem back to pragmatics, which is a sub-field of linguistics, studying the ways in which context contributes to meaning. Work done by Lauri Karttunen during 1973 – 1974 can also be related, where after numerous articles around

Presuppositions and Linguistic Context, she concluded that we make use of linguistic presuppositions in communicating indirectly and in inferring what someone is committed to, without them precisely saying it.

Linguistic presuppositions are not a mind read. As the receiver of communication it is important to distinguish what is presupposed in the communication and what you assume based on your interpretation of the communication through your filters (beliefs/values, memories, attitudes etc.) How often have you been in a conversation with another only to find that they had meant something completely different? Or in extreme examples you had assumed the opposite of what they had meant. Deductions created on the basis of how we see the world are called "Mind Reads" (in plain English; assumptions). Linguistic presuppositions are what we presuppose to be true in order for the sentence to make sense (e.g. the broken window example).

Think back to the communication model: our internal representation is created by us filtering the external events (deleting, distorting and generalising information) through our unique set of filters, one of which is Language. By listening to the language used (external event) we decide what is true (our internal representation) which influences our state, behaviour and therefore how we respond.

Therefore if we choose our language wisely we can influence our own internal representations and more importantly that of other people, so that you can remove obstacles giving a person a whole range of options. Likewise, becoming more aware of the words you use and the impending results they have on other people makes you use language more appropriately and less derogatively. Which, when we think back to Cause and Effect, puts it very much at cause as we are 100% responsible for our communication.

How many NLP presuppositions does this lead back to?! One I want you to think about is the system (person) with the most flexibility (choices) of behaviour will have the most influence on the system. By being responsible for the words you use, you increase your own choice of behaviour but also that of the person you are communicating to, a technique which is very useful for problem solving.

How to do it!

The advantage with linguistic presuppositions over just being more aware and responsible for your language is that it is a formalised structure for obtaining a different perspective on a problem due to the linguistic presuppositions being broken down into different types.

Types of Presuppositions
Linguistic presuppositions are the most powerful of the Meta and Milton model language patterns.

1. **Existence** – Is the first and most basic of all the linguistic presuppositions and relates to *a noun, a person, place or thing* in a person's language, based on their memories, decisions or values. Regardless of whether it is stated as a positive or a negative, the effect of the presupposition is still the same.

For example:

Jack realised the new stock was left in the forecourt - notice to make sense of that sentence you have to accept the fact that there is a forecourt, new stock and Jack. Now I just want you to notice this as well, if I said Jack didn't realise there was new stock in the forecourt, or Jack just realised there was new stock in the forecourt, or Jack was angry the new stock had been left in the forecourt, whichever way I say it, in order to make sense of it, you have to accept the presupposition of forecourt, new stock and Jack. The purpose of the Existence presupposition is to displace any resistance in the core matters (forecourt, new stock, Jack) to

128

build the basis of agreement before moving onto the detailed matters(didn't, just, angry).

2. **Modal Operators** – A word we use to talk about either in Possibility or Necessity.

Possibility - Whether or not the client believes something is possible, words that imply if something is possible. Cue words like *can, could, will, would, might, possible*.

*Sue realised that she **could** go shopping.*

From the previous example: *It is **possible** for Jack to bring in the new stock by himself.* The purpose of the Modal Operator-Possibility presupposition is for someone who is towards achieving their goal to assist in motivation and access a person's belief around a task.

Necessity – Words that suggest the client is motivated by necessity, implying that they need to do something. Cue words like *should, must, got to, have to,*

*Sue realised that she **had to** be sailing on that boat.*

*John finally knew that he **must** climb the mountain behind the house.*

Small words with Big Meanings:
But, although, however.
Contradicts what has just been said, if that is not your intention, try to use: And!

Try; implies difficulty and/or a high possibility of failure.

Or; can limit our thinking to 1 or 2 options.

Don't; usually contradicts its intended purpose. *'Don't think of an oak tree now'.*

Yet; an empowering word, symbolises that something can be achieved in the future.

129

From the previous example: *Jack realised he **had to** bring in the new stock by himself.* The purpose of the Modal Operator-Necessity presupposition is for someone who is away from motivated to achieve their goal to assist in motivation and access a person's belief around a task.

3. **Cause - Effect** – is probably the most important of all the linguistic presuppositions and relates to something occurring that causes a specific effect. There is an implied connection. Cue words like *because, in order to, makes, as you . . . then you . . . , if . . . then........., to make."*

From the previous example; *because it was raining Jack had to move the new stock quickly off the forecourt inside the building.* The purpose of the cause—effect presupposition is to imply a sequential chain of events.

4. **Complex Equivalent (X=Y)** –involves constructing beliefs out of generalisations. It is making two experiences equal. Cue words like: *to be, means,* that ascribe meaning to something.

For example: *You purchasing this book means that you are interested in NLP.* The purpose of the Complex Equivalent presupposition is to imply a simultaneous reaction, you doing that, means this.

5. **Awareness** –Verbs that imply perception of some sort. Cue words such as notice, *know, realise, aware of,* and any of the predicate words & phrases covered in representational systems of the senses (chapter 6).

For example: *You may not have realised just how much you have learnt from this book already.* The purpose of the awareness presupposition is to draw your attention to things.

6. **Time** - Verb tenses that move the client through time, *-ing* implies ongoing; *-ed* implies in the past. Cue words like, *stop, now, yet, before begin, after, during, end, future, when, again, still, soon, etc.*

Tense type words like *was, had, been, went* (past tense), *am, have, are, stop, start, continue* (present tense) *will, going, getting* (future) can create powerful assumptions.

For example; *"What **has been** the problem?"* not only respects their model of the world but also re-categorises their problem as if it is in the past, opening up new avenues to deal with it. As it is in the past it is not so strongly held, with emotions clouding judgements or restraining. You could also say *"What have you not been able to do **yet**?"* which implies they will be able to do it in the future. The purpose of time presupposition is to change the time frame of a problem to make it seem much more achievable.

7. **Adverb/Adjective** – modifies or qualifies a Verb/Noun, where this modification is accepted.

Adjective (Noun): *big, small, heavy, light, green, happy, tidy* etc.
Adverb (Verb): *only, simply, easily, successfully, happily, typically, effortlessly, willingly*, words ending in **ly**

From the first example: *Jack didn't realise how **easily** he would move the new stock from the forecourt.*

Adjective *example: Jack didn't realise how **easy** it was to move the **light** new stock boxes from the forecourt.*

The purpose of using an Adverb/Adjective presupposition is to modify a task to show it in a new light.

8. **Inclusive / Exclusive – OR.** Gives the illusion of choice

   Inclusive example: *"Would you like to pay by cash or credit card"*. implies you have the choice, the reality is you're going to buy today. The purpose of using an Inclusive Or presupposition is to take the emphasis off what they are doing will ultimately result in what you want, by giving them choice in the way they do it.

   Exclusive example: *"Would you like to do it now or later"* implies you still have an option; the reality is that you're going to do it! The purpose of using an Exclusive Or-presupposition is instead of saying *"my way or the highway"* and causing upset and/or confrontation, you give the illusion of choice.

9. **Ordinal -** Signifies numeric order or a list, and can use a word like *Firstly, Secondly, Lastly, next, again, then, finally etc.*

   For example: *"**After** noticing the stock on the forecourt, Jack **then** went to bring it inside the building"*.

   The purpose of the Ordinal presupposition is to put the problem into context and order so as to see the steps needed to achieve it and to evaluate how you/another person is progressing.

Linguistic presuppositions applied to learning

Existence: You know, don't you, that learning is easy . .

Possibility: It is possible for you to learn this quickly . . .

Cause-Effect: Because you are learning, you are

Complex Equivalence: Understanding language patterns you'll become excellent communicators

Awareness: As you become more aware of your language you will realise the effectiveness of linguistic presuppositions

Time: Before you read this, did you know you were fascinated by language?

Adverb /Adjective: Learning easily enables big.....

Inclusive / Exclusive Or: Will you realise now or after the next exercise the benefits this technique gives to you?

Ordinal: First I want you to read the explanation and then carry out the exercise.
You to be aware of how much you already know.

Exercises

Exercise 1 – Distinguish "mind reads"

In the following sentences, please distinguish between a presupposition and a mind read. Put a 'P' or an 'MR' next to each one:

1.   *"I'm not sure whether I should leave my job."*

_____   A.   He has a job

_____   B.   He hates his job

_____   C.   He is currently looking for another job

_____   D.   He's a low life lazy slob!

2.   *"I don't see why I can't do it. All my colleagues are doing it!"*

_____   A.   He feels that he is treated unfairly

_____   B.   He wants to be liked by his colleagues

_____   C.   This person's colleagues do something he doesn't do

_____   D.   All his colleagues are better than he is!

3.   *"If I don't learn how to communicate with my boss, I won't get a promotion."*

____   A.   He feels that he is treated unfairly

____   B.   He doesn't know how to communicate with his boss

____   C.   He wants to learn new behaviours

____   D.   His position is connected to his communication skills

4.   "I have always set unrealistic standards."

____   A.   She can't stop setting unrealistic standards

____   B.   She has standards

____   C.   Only she sets her standards

____   D.   She knows when she is being unrealistic

5.   "My new job makes me feel great! I can see now how my old job was making me unhappy"

____   A.   He was bullied in his old job

____   B.   He got a promotion

____   C.   He has much more control of his life now

____   D.   He has a new job

Exercise 2 – Distinguish presuppositions

Per Tad James

In the following sentences, please circle the <u>major</u> presupposition(s):

1. "If the cat meows again, I'll have to put him outside."

2. "It was her friendly smile that made me walk up and say 'Hi'."
3. "If only he had come home on time, the party wouldn't have gotten out of control."
4. "People have always given me more to do than I can handle."
5. "His easy-going personality is good PR for our company."
6. "Stop watching over your shoulder."
7. "Only you can learn this."
8. "Either she goes to the store or I do."
9. "First the winds came then the rain."
10. "Opera makes me want to cry.

Exercise 3 – Create your own motivational statements

1. In whatever context you desire, create a motivational statement as outlined above using linguistic presuppositions,

a) Existence
b) Possibility
c) Cause-Effect
d) Complex Equivalence
e) Awareness
f) Time
g) Adverb/Adjective
h) Inclusive / Exclusive Or
i) Ordinal

Summary

Our linguistic communication conveys meaning which is not expressly stated in the words we use. Presuppositions are the name given to the implied fact that must be assumed before a given sentence can be accepted to be true. Linguistic presuppositions are ways to identify what someone has presupposed to be true, to respond or behave the way they have done.

By becoming aware of linguistic presuppositions you can gain greater understanding of another person's model of the world, rather than assuming or imposing your model of the world on them.

The increased awareness along with your sensory acuity will provide you with far more information and insights than the meaning expressed by the words themselves.

Presuppositions enable you to identify the root cause of misunderstanding, helping you gain insights into the situation to support your staff even more effectively. Linguistic presuppositions are the foundation to language in NLP: it is on this foundation that we become aware of the language we use and therefore more responsible in the way that we talk to others, either being more precise or open for answers/interpretation, so as to get the greatest impact/response from them.

References

- Rosen. S, (1991) *My Voice Will Go with You:* The Teaching Tales of Milton H. Erickson, W. W. Norton
- Sevi, A (2001) *Review of Kasher: Pragmatics, vol. IV: Presupposition.* Terence Langendoen
- Kasher, A. (1998) *Pragmatics.* Routledge (Taylor and Francis)

Appendix – Answers to exercises

"I'm not sure whether I should leave my job."
A.   He has a job = **P**
B.   He hates his job = **MR**
C.   He is currently looking for another job = **MR**
D.   He's a low life lazy slob! = **MR**

2.   "I don't see why I can't do it. All my colleagues are doing it!"
A.   He feels that he is treated unfairly = **P**
B.   He wants to be liked by his colleagues = **MR**
C.   This person's colleagues do something he doesn't do = **P**
D.   All his colleagues are better than he is! = **MR**

3.   "If I don't learn how to communicate with my boss, I won't get a promotion."
A.   He feels that he is treated unfairly = **MR**
B.   He doesn't know how to communicate with his boss = **MR**
C.   He wants to learn new behaviours = **P**
D.   His position is connected to his communication skills = **MR**

4.   "I have always set unrealistic standards."

A. She can't stop setting unrealistic standards = **MR**
B. She has standards = **P**
C. Only she sets her standards = **MR**
D. She knows when she is being unrealistic = **P**

5. "My new job makes me feel great! I can see now how my old job was making me unhappy"

A. He was bullied in his old job = **MR**
B. He got a promotion = **MR**
C. He has much more control of his life now = **MR**
D. He has a new job = **P**

Exercise 2 – Distinguish presuppositions

Answers in brackets after the highlighted words.

1. "If the **cat** (existence) meows **again** (ordinal), I'll **have to** (modal operator of necessity) put him **outside** (existence)."

2. "It was **her** (existence) **friendly** (adverb) **smile** (existence) that **made** (complex equivalent) me walk up and say 'Hi'."

3. "**If only** (cause effect) **he** (existence) **had** (modal operator of necessity) come **home** (existence) on time, the **party** (existence) wouldn't have gotten out of control."

4. "**People** (existence) have always given me more to do than I **can** (modal operator of possibility) handle."

5. "**His** (existence) **easy-going** (adverb) personality is good PR for our **company** (existence)."

6. "**Stop** (time) **watching** (awareness) over your **shoulder** (existence)."

7. "Only you **can** (modal operator of possibility) **learn this** (awareness)."

8. "Either **she** (existence) goes to the **store** (existence) **or** (exclusive or) I do."

139

9.   "**First** (ordinal) the **winds** (existence) came **then** (ordinal) the **rain** (existence)."

10.   "**Opera** (existence) **makes** (complex equivalent) **me** (existence) **want** (modal operator of possibility) to **cry** (awareness).

Exercise 3 – Example answers

    a) Existence- Thank you for coming to this presentation today.

    b) Possibility- We can do it!

    c) Cause-Effect- The problems have caused us to want to have this meeting

    d) Complex Equivalence- Being here means you want to sort things out.

    e) Awareness- Our assessment of

    f) Time- Now that

    g) Adverb/Adjective- Successfully

    h) Inclusive / Exclusive Or- Sooner or later we will resolve the problem.

    i) Ordinal- Firstly we will do 'X' then we will do 'Y'; thirdly we will do 'Z'.

Chapter 7.2

The Milton and Meta models – the art of being vague or specific!

"The limits of my language mean the limits of my world"
Ludwig Wittgenstein

Concept

This technique is based on the NLP presupposition; The system (person) with the most flexibility (choices) of behaviour will have the most influence on the system. The more flexibility you have with your language the more options you have open to you. By using both ambiguous & specific language you can firstly give yourself more options at how to look at an issue and then by using directive specific language question how these options will benefit in reacting to the issue.

Benefits

The **Milton Model** is a model for indirect interpersonal communication, enabling a person to resolve issues more effectively and is useful in sales, therapy, family relations and in gaining rapport in general.

- Access unconscious resources of another person, enabling them to gather more information or to lead them into an altered state through rapport.
- Help someone deduce the answer for themselves.
- To create truly motivational speeches.
- To induce trance.
- Create empowering metaphors.
- Passes potential conscious interference in a subtle and non-confrontational manner.

The Meta Model on the other hand is a model for changing our maps of the world, it provides a number of problem solving strategies.

- Resolve confusion and misunderstanding by getting specific on what the problem truly is.

> *"Language is the source of misunderstandings."*
> Antoine de Saint-Exupery

- Understand what people say is not the experience itself & use language to deduce what actually happened.
- Uncover/acquire additional information.
- Save time when acquiring information by asking the right questions & avoid going off-piste.
- Put a problem into the correct context.

What are the Milton and Meta Models?

The use of language is essential in directing a person's experience and focus of attention. The Milton Model, named after Milton Erickson, lists the key parts of speech and key patterns that are useful in subtly and effectively directing another person's line of thinking. The principles of the Milton Model basically state that using very general language can lead to more rapport, where specific language is more limiting and has a greater chance of excluding concepts from a person's experience.

> *"(Specific) Language helps form the limits of our reality"* Dale Spender

Robert Dilts states that the Milton Model "provides fundamental structures for forming suggestions by passing potential conscious interference in a subtle and non confrontational manner."

In contrast the Meta model provides a framework for reconstructing what someone has deleted, distorted or generalised about the external event.

> *"A different language is a different vision of life."*
> Federico Fellini

143

The principles of the Meta Model are based on the map is not the territory, the words we use are just the words we have chosen to explain the event and the meaning that event had to us. By using language specifically we can obtain additional truer information relating to the event.

The Meta Models seek to challenge linguistic distortion, clarify generalisation and recover deleted information which occurs in a speaker's language. The Milton Model enables people to make their own meaning from a sentence as so much has been left out, whereas the Meta Model allows you to obtain more information so you can acquire and take on the speaker's true meaning of a sentence.

> *"The devil is in the detail"* Old German Proverb

How many times have you made a deal only to find out that when it came to signing the contract it all fell apart? This is because the idea of the deal was accepted but the finer details of what it entailed were not discussed... that dreaded small print.

Furthermore those cheeky politicians use the Milton Model all the time! Think about the following phrases;

"People are ready for change" Who? How?!

"We deliver on education and health" Again, How??!!

"The economy is already in much better shape" HOW???!!!! Dont make me come over there!!!

"We believe in a good standard of living for everyone" OK my definition of a good standard of living is daily pedicures and massages, what I got was three different colour bins and a box, instead of black bags.

Notice the deletions, distortions and generalisations in these statements. To top it all off, think back to the UK's New Labour political party's anthem in the late 1990's *"Things can only get better"* leaving the voter to make up for themselves which things might get better - and better than what?!.

Finally the biggest criminal of them all; Advertisers. Think of every advertising slogan you have ever heard and you will uncover the artfuly vagueness of the Milton Model language patterns.

Examples:

"Every little helps" Tesco

"Because you're worth it" L'Oréal hair products

And who can forget Lynx's infamous *"Spray more, get more"*

As previously discussed the Meta Model is the direct contrast and pretty much the answer to the Milton Model. When you hear or see a statement that is artfully vague your natural response is to clarify it (the who, how, when, and what, if you like). It provides us with a way of gathering information in a concise and timely manner.

Politicians don't restrict themselves by only using the Milton Model, oh no, they also use the Meta Model to undermine their opponents, turning abstract nominalisations back into a verb. I am sure you can think of many examples where one party has attacked another party's campaign, publicly questioning where are they going to get the money from to give everyone a good standard of living. How are they going to increase the standard of education in schools, and then coming in with a sweeping statement like *"By increasing tax payer's money!"*

Furthermore, how many times have you heard the phrase *"That's not what I said"*, *"That's not what I meant"*, or *"You have taken it the wrong way."* What does the word 'intelligence' mean? Well to

145

you, me or another it could mean a range of things such as wise, intelligent, knowledgeable, wisdom, being articulate, capability, comprehension, understanding, reason and before you know it could change into 'intelligence' 'informative' 'like the MI5' and 'spies!' This is where the Milton Model can potentially become difficult and where miscommunication arises. The Meta Model prompts questions such as "how specifically, what specifically do you mean by: intelligence", aiming to avoid misunderstanding and confrontations.

History

The Milton and Meta Models were the first two models of NLP developed by Bandler and Grinder. Through their modelling of Milton H. Erickson, psychiatrist and pioneer of medical hypnosis, they concluded that the success he had with his patients was through his ability to use artfully ambiguous language, from this they developed the Milton Model Patterns.

In contrast, when modelling Firtz Perls, a gestalt therapist, and Virginia Satir, who was a family systems therapist, they noted Perls and Satir used very specific language in the way they achieved success with their patients by being able to very quickly establish the specific root cause of the problem.

Bandler and Grinder's work was influenced by ideas of human modelling and the rationale of cause and effect, which was work carried out by Alfred Korzybski (a philosopher) and his notion that the map is not the territory, which also features in Gregory Bateson's work.

It is important to appreciate that the Meta and Milton Models are not given solutions to resolving problems. If someone wishes to hold onto their problem (why? believe me some people just don't think they are living unless they have some problem to moan about), or in a business context, if a partner/contractor is hell bent on getting the lion's share of the profits, then no amount of artfully vague language or specific questioning is going to resolve it.

If we think back to the NLP Communication Model both the effects of the Milton and Meta Model can be explained. All of our experiences are subjective, we delete,

> "Change your language and you change your thoughts."
> Karl Albrecht

distort and generalise the external event differently according to our unique set of filters. The Milton Model uses this fact to make the listener go inside and give meaning to what has been said, for example- "you know you deserve it", dependant on your frame of mind at the time of hearing this comment, will determine the meaning. The Meta Model also uses the knowledge of this to recover what we have (more importantly what another has) deleted, distorted and generalised, basically determining why we placed the meaning on it.

Think back to the presupposition; The map is not the territory. This presupposition is what the Meta Model is based upon, as the Meta Model looks at the meaning the words somebody uses actually have and establishes what they mean by what they have said.

How to do it

Whether at a conference, meeting or party, every person in the room is likely to be different, with different needs, different maps of the world, different priorities, different filters, values and beliefs: finding one specific message that will reenergise all those different people is rarely going to happen. The Milton Model gives you a way to connect with the whole group regardless of their individual differences or the agenda of the meeting.

Going back to our examples of advertising slogans they all make you feel good and seem positive, but none are very specific. When you want to influence large audiences, whatever the medium, the more vague you are with your language the more effective you are in engaging them and creating the effect you want, as people will take what you say and look to apply it to themselves.

Model language patterns

<table>
<tr><td colspan="3" align="center">Patterns that relate to the Milton & Meta Models</td></tr>
<tr><td>1. Mind Reads</td><td>2. Lost Performatives</td><td>3. Cause and Effect</td></tr>
<tr><td>4. Complex Equivalents</td><td>5. Presuppositions</td><td>6. Universal Quantifiers</td></tr>
<tr><td>7. Model Operators of Possibility and Necessity</td><td>8. Nominalisations</td><td>9. Unspecified Verbs</td></tr>
<tr><td colspan="3">10.a. Lack of Referential index   10.b. Comparative Deletion</td></tr>
</table>

Other Patterns – that only relate to the Milton Model		
10. Tag Question	11. Pace Current Experience	12. Embedded Questions
13. Embedded Commands	14. Double Bind	15. Conversational Postulate
16. Extended Quote	17. Selectional Restriction Violation	18. Ambiguity
19. Analogue Marking	20. Utilisation	

Patterns 1 – 10 are directly transferable into Meta. 11- 21 are just for the use in the Milton Model. The Meta is the answer you give to a Milton Model pattern. e.g. 1. Mind Read; the Milton Model "*I know you are wondering*", the Meta Model "how specifically do you know what I am wondering?" (I.e. simply their answer, the person you are speaking to's response).

The Milton Model patterns explained:

1.　Mind Read

Claiming to know the thoughts or feelings of another person, without making assumptions specifying the process by which you came to know the information.
I know that you are wondering . . . (how)
I can understand that . . .
I knew you were curious . . .
With a forced mind read, you, "Start a sentence and don't quite . . ."
Your client will gladly fill it in for you.

2.　Lost Performative

Value judgements where judger is left out.
Learning is easy . . . (say's who)
And it's a good thing to wonder . . . (is it)
And it's a good thing to . . .
That's right . . .

3.　Cause & Effect

Where one thing causes another, x=y because of x, y happens.
If . . . then . . .
As you . . . then you . . .
If you study, you will learn.
Because you're listening, you are gaining understanding.

4.　Complex Equivalence

Where two things become equivalent to each other, x means y.
The more you study, the more you learn.
Gaining more perspectives means gaining more understanding.

150

5.   Presupposition

The linguistic equivalent of assumptions, what you have to presuppose to be true in order for the sentence to make sense.
You are learning many things . . .
And you are absorbing all the learning's.
Have you noticed how easily you learn language patterns?

6.   Universal Quantifiers

Are universal generalisations with no reference words such as; *all, every, never, always, nobody, everybody, everyone, all 'ism's' ageism, sexism.*
And all the things . . .
Everybody says so
We always do this

7.   Modal Operators

Words which imply possibility or necessity and which form our rules in life, such as *will, can, may, could, must, should, need.*
You can learn . . .
You could
One should ......
It is possible for you to absorb all of the learnings now.

8.   Nominalization

Process words (verbs) which have been frozen in time by making them into nouns that delete a great deal of information.
Provide you with new insights, and new understandings.
Accessing your own inner knowledge will give you unlimited wisdom and understanding.

9. Unspecified Verb (unspecified predicate)

The listener is forced to supply the meaning of the sentence, as it is left open to interpretation.
And you can . . .
I want you to become . . .

10. A Lack of Referential Index

Phrase in which the subject of the sentence is unspecified/left out, which encourages you to accept the meaning.
One can, you know, learn language patterns easily.
Some people know.
Others may begin to feel . . .
You know the feeling.

10. B Comparative Deletion

Where the comparison is made and it is not specified as to what or to whom it was made. *Right and Wrong; Now and Then; Sooner or Later; At One Time or Another; More & More.*
And it's more or less the right thing.
Sometimes it's better to feel now and then . . .

11 Tag Question

Tag Questions displace resistance to the end of a sentence *don't they?*
They set up a place to create agreement, as well as to strengthen agreement in a pacing situation.
Isn't it?
You can can't you
....weren't they?
Can you not?

152

12   Pace Current Experience

Where client's experience is described in a way which is undeniable, describing what they are doing right now - encourages acceptance.
You are sitting here, listening to me, looking at me, (etc.)
When you understand this.
You are sitting here, listening to my voice, writing your notes in your own words or mine.

13   Embedded Commands

Directives that are embedded within the sentence, which direct a person to do something. This is a double message and sends one message to the conscious mind and another message to the unconscious mind.
You will <u>absorb the learnings</u> . . .
I don't know if you'll <u>remember this now</u> or later . . .

14.   Embedded Questions
A sentence with a question included which keeps the conversation flowing freely rather than direct questions.
I wonder whether you know <u>how quickly you want this problem to go away</u>.
If you were to know when . . . <u>will you solve it</u> . . .?

15.   Double Bind

A paradox which on the surface implies the client creates choice for the client but where either choice is acceptable.
You can change as quickly or a slowly as you want to now.
Will you take your tablets before or after you've had a quick drink?

16. Conversational Postulate

A question to which the response is either a *yes* or a *no:* it's what must be present in a sentence so that you will do what I want you to do. It allows you to choose to respond or not.
Do you feel this is something you understand?
Will you feel more comfortable with your arms unfolded?

17. Extended Quote

Distracting the conscious mind by the use of many referential indices.
Yesterday I bumped into Jack, who told me about a course he went on in Cardiff where Jessica lives, her daughter Hannah came to Alex's party . . .

18. Selectional Restriction Violation

A statement that is made about an inanimate object referring to them as if they were alive.
A chair can have feelings . . .
The car knew how to get there.
The walls are listening; they have ears.
You're pen is learning everything that you are.

19. <u>Ambiguity</u>

    a.   Phonological homophones: words that sound the same yet mean different things
        Hear and *Here. To* and *Too* and *Two. No* and *Know.*
        As you sit . . . here . . . the sound of my voice

    b.   Syntactic: where the function (syntax) of a word cannot be immediately determined from the immediate context.
        Hypnotising hypnotists can be tricky.
        They are visiting relatives.
        Running water.

    c.   Scope: where it cannot be determined by linguistic context how much is applied to that sentence by some other portion of the sentence.
        Your deep breathing and trance . . .
        Speaking to you as a child. . ..
        The weight of your hands and feet . . .
        The comfort of the couch and floor . . .

    d.   Punctuation: pauses within sentences
        I want you to notice your . . . hand . . . me the salt.
        Seeing the waves . . . as you go into trance.

20. <u>Analogue Marking</u>

Marking out a portion of the sentence verbally or non-verbally (with gestures).
You can . . . go into trance . . . now . . .
Will you . . . let your eyelids close . . .

21.   Utilisation

Utilise all that happens or is said, using the client's language.

Client: *"I am not sold"*. Response: *"That's right you are not sold, yet, because you haven't asked the one question that will have you totally and completely sold."*

Practitioner: *"Notice how the room fills with light as you become more comfortable, lighter and lighter . . ."*

Putting it all together in order to induce a trance like state, for example in teaching:

I know that you are wondering..... (mind read) and it's a good thing to wonder . . .(lost performative) If you wonder, you will learn (cause & effect).Gaining more understanding means gaining more learnings . . .(complex equivalents) you have learned many things . . .(presuppositions) and all the things that you should learn . . .(model operators of necessity) you can learn .(model operators of possibility).   Provide you with new insights, and new understandings (nominalization), and you can, (unspecified verb) can't you? (Tag questions). You may understand (simple deletion) one can, you know (lack of referential index), at one time or another (comparative deletion).   As you sit there, reading this book, thinking about how you can use these Milton Model patterns you realise it will be through practice...(pace current experience), and you will absorb all these learnings (embedded command), wont you? (Tag question).

The theory is if you are in a trance like state, you can speak directly with the unconscious mind, stopping the conscious mind from getting in the way with objections and emotions. Another example of how to put it all together as a motivational opener to a meeting. *Thank you all for coming here today... (presupposition) The fact that you are here means that you want to get things sorted...*

(complex equivalence) ready for change... (unspecified verb). You may already have started to become aware of the problems that we are experiencing... (mind read), and it is good (lost performative)... isn't it (tag question)? That as a team we will be able to sort them (model operator of possibility), won't we? (tag question).

As you all sit there relaxed (pace current experience) as the seat supports you (lack of referential index) I know you are wondering (mind read) because you are committed to achieving a solution (cause and effect) which is what makes us already successful... (nominalization). Sooner or later you will see (double bind) that our solution is in reach (presupposition) and just think how much better things will be once we have sorted them... (complex equivalence)

One further example of how to use Milton Model patterns to a group, this example is to a group of health care professionals used when introducing new government initiatives and targets.

Meta Model Overview

The Meta Model aims to uncover the deletions, distortions and generalisations said in conversation:

Deletion
Your outcome: gather and/or recover information;

Exactly? Specifically? Precisely? Where? When? What? How? Who?

Distortion
Your outcome: challenge and change the meaning, recover the evidence;

Who says?
How specifically do you know?
How does X mean Y...?

Generalisation
Your outcome: expand the limits of the speaker's model of the world;

All? Every? Never? What would happen if...? What stops you...?

Meta Model - Overview of usage:

Language Pattern another person uses	Response - the question you would ask	Outcome – recovering what that other person has Distorted, Generalised or Deleted
DISTORTIONS		
1. Mind Reading: claiming to know someone's internal state. Ex: "You don't like me."	"How do you know I don't like you?"	Recovers source of the Info.
2. Lost Performative: value judgements where the person doing the judging is left out. Ex. "It's bad to be inconsistent."	"Who says it's bad?" "According to whom?" "How do you know it's bad?"	Gathers evidence. Recovers source of the belief, the Performative, strategy for the belief.
3. Cause—Effect: where cause is wrongly put outside the self. Ex: "You make me sad."	"How does what I'm doing cause you to feel sad?" (Also, counter Ex., or "How Specifically?")	Recovers the choice.
4. Complex Equivalence: where two experiences are interpreted as being synonymous. Ex: "She's always yelling at me, she doesn't like me."	"How does her yelling mean that she doesn't like you?" "Have you ever yelled at someone you liked?"	Recovers complex equivalence. Counter example. Or simply recovers/gives more choice.

159

5. Presuppositions: ex: "If my husband knew how much I suffered, he wouldn't do that." There are 3 presuppositions in this sentence: (1) I suffer, (2) my husband acts in some way, and (3) my husband doesn't know I suffer.	(1) "How do you choose to suffer?" (2) "How is he (re)acting? (3) "How do you know he doesn't know?"	Specify the choice & the verb, & what he does. Recover the internal representation and the Complex Equivalence.

GENERALISATIONS

6. Universal Quantifiers: universal generalisations like all, every, never, everyone, no one, etc. Ex: "she never listens to me."	Find counter examples. "never?" "what would happen if she did?"	Recovers counter examples, effects, outcomes.
7. Modal Operators: a. Modal Operators of Necessity: as in should, shouldn't, must, must not, have to, need to it is necessary. Ex: "I have to take care of her." **b. Modal Operators of Possibility:**(OrImpossibility.) As in can/can't, will/won't, may/maynot/possible/impossible. Ex: "I can't tell my boss the truth."	a. "What would happen if you did?" ("What would happen if you didn't?" Also, "Or?" b. "What prevents you?" ("What would happen if you did?")	Recovers effects and outcome. Recovers causes.

DELETIONS

8. Nominalizations: process words that have been frozen in time, making them nouns. Ex: "There is no communication here."	"Who's not communicating what to whom?" "How would you like to communicate?"	Turns it back into a process, recovers deletion and referential index.
9. Unspecified Verbs: ex: "He rejected me."	"How, specifically?"	Specifies the verb.

10. a. Lack of Referential Index: fails to specify a person or thing. Ex: "They don't listen to me."	a."Who, specifically, doesn't listen to you?"	a.Recovers referential. index.
b. Comparative Deletions: as in good, better, best, worst, more, less, most, least. Ex: "She's a better person." "That's too expensive"	b. "Better than whom?" "Better at what?" "Compared to whom, what?	b.Recovers comparative deletion.
c. Simple Deletions: ex: "I am very uncomfortable."	c."About what/whom?"	c.Recovers deletion.

Example - Questioning

When speaking, people delete, distort and generalise all the time (yes, all the time!). At times it is useful to be able to help clients/colleagues etc be more specific when they are discussing their issues and challenges. Here are some examples:

Comment	Possible Challenges
"They always do that!"	*"Always?"* *"Who specifically does that?"* *"What specifically do they do?"* *"How do you know?"* *"How is that a problem?"*
"That's the way things are done here."	*"What would happen if they were done in a different way?"* *"What stops things from changing?"* *"What stops you/us from changing things/doing it differently?"* *"What specific things are done this way round here?"*
"They don't care."	*"How do you know?"* *"Who specifically doesn't care?"*
"There's no communication here."	*"Who is not communicating?"* *"What is not being communicated?"* *"How would you like people to communicate instead?"*

NB When deciding whether to 'challenge' or seek more information, do so with a positive intention in mind, not just to be clever!

Exercises

Exercise 1 – Discover your personal hierarchy of modal operators! (With thanks to Joseph O'Connor)

1. Think of something you want to do.

2. Now say to yourself, 'I *should* do that'. Notice how you feel about that and the internal pictures, sounds and feelings it generates.

3. Then say to yourself, 'I *must* do that'. Notice your response.

4. Next, say to yourself, 'I *have to* do that'. Again, notice the submodalities associated with those words.

5. Next say to yourself, 'I *ought to* do that'. Again, notice your submodalities.

6. Finally, say, 'I *can* do that'. What does that feel like? Is it important enough to *want* to do?

7. Which sentence did you feel was the strongest?

Exercise 2:

Watch a television interview with a celebrity, politician or sportsperson. You may find it easier to record all or part of the interview for this exercise. Identify four Meta Model Patterns that they use. Write down the sentence that illustrates the pattern and the name of the pattern.

Exercise 3:

For each of the sentences you wrote above, write a Meta Model response that would help you get the person to become more specific had you been the interviewer?

Summary

The Milton and Meta models of language patterns show you the impact of your own language and how to use it to get the results that you and the person you are communicating to wants.

An understanding of the patterns will explain areas of miscommunication and enable you to accurately deduce the root of a problem, without mind reading the other person.

The patterns enable effective rapport, give insights into the effectiveness of your communication and, when used alongside your sensory acuity, help you to understand the response you get.

The Milton Model can be seen as the big picture; abstract language, the big chunk, promoting people to apply their own meaning and reference to what you have said.

The Meta Model can be seen as the specifics, the finer details, the small chunk, drilling down on the exact problem rather than holding a problem at a higher level. A negative example of *"People don't respect me"* allows you to ask *"Who specifically?"* and *"How do you specifically know that?"* This establishes the route of the problem whilst putting it into perspective, respecting their model of the world and maintaining rapport to create a foundation to go on and to resolve it.

References

- Erickson M., H. (1975)*Patterns of the Hypnotic Techniques of Milton H. Erickson Volume I*
- Erickson M., H. *(1977)Patterns of the Hypnotic Techniques of Milton H. Erickson Volume II*
- Erickson M., H. (1975)*The Structure of Magic I: A Book About Language and Therapy*
- Grinder, John & Carmen Bostic St Clair (2001.). *Whispering in the Wind*

Chapter 7.3

The Hierarchy of Ideas – the Order of Thinking

"Whoever sets the agenda controls the outcome of the debate"
Noam Chomsky.

Concept

Like the previous subchapters on language, this technique is based on the NLP presupposition; The system (person) with the most flexibility (choices) of behaviour will have the most influence on the system. The more flexibility you have within your language and ability to move between big picture to small detail then the greater the impact you will have on the system.

Benefits

The hierarchy of ideas technique is a very easy way to learn and utilise the difference between abstract and specific. People who can see the big picture and get into the appropriate detail are more successful than those who can't. You can significantly enhance your cognitive abilities and communication skills by developing your abilities to utilise chunking.

Hierarchy of ideas is a way of;
- Grasping the overall big picture or delve into the detail, depending on what is called for.
- Promoting lateral thinking.
- Achieving agreement and commonality between groups of people.
- Gaining agreement quickly by establishing the higher intention to then enable you to go into the details of how to achieve it. (Useful in negotiation)
- Putting yourself firmly in control of your meetings ensureing your agenda is covered, by being able to easily reach agreement on the overall agenda.
- To establish rapport quicker; being able to match the level of content that the other person is working at. If someone is big picture and you give them too much information, then you will simply overwhelm them with the details. Just as giving a detail/small chunk person the big picture will leave them feeling lost without knowing what it is they are meant to do.
- Give information in manageable chunks – respective to the party you are talking to.

What is the Hierarchy of Ideas?

The Hierarchy of Ideas is a linguistic tool that allows the speaker to traverse the realms of abstract to specificity easily and effortlessly. The Hierarchy of Ideas model is a simple way to work out what level of abstraction or specificity that we have in our language compared to what other people have in theirs. This enables us to match that level, allowing communication to flow better.

Have you noticed how language can be, at one extreme, vague and general and, at the other, very specific? Big words have a hypnotic effect as they cause us to search around in our minds to

> **Chunking** - Moving a "chunk", or a group of bits of information, in the direction of a deductive or inductive conclusion through the use of language.

find some meaning: our meaning, how we represent that word, which can be difficult. We can gain specificity in inter-personal communication by chunking down to uncover increasingly fine levels of detail by asking the questions *'What are examples of this?'* or *'What specifically?'*. When we've been *'down in the detail'* and we want to move up to take look at the *'Big Picture'* or, if you like, take a *'bird's eye view'* of things we chunk up.

By understanding the limitations of language you can get a great deal more from it, by learning the difference between the general and the vague, to the detailed and specific, there are a number of gradations expressing things less generally or specifically. Through changing our language, we can affect the client's state and their behaviour. The hierarchy of ideas also utilises the concept of chunks of information and our ability to take such a chunk and *'chunk up'* to a higher level of abstraction, *'chunk down'* to a lower level of abstraction and even *'chunk sideways'* (laterally) between two chunks at the same level of abstraction.

As we get more and more abstract, we deal with larger and larger chunks of data. As we get more specific, we deal with smaller and smaller chunks of data. Imagine being on top of the Eiffel Tower, from the top you have a lovely overview of Paris, seeing for miles and miles in all directions. However you cannot see what is going on in the streets, houses and shops below until you come down the tower and walk from its base. The most abstract and all-embracing concepts are at the top, with the most concrete at the bottom. When we "chunk up," we move up the hierarchy of ideas. When we "chunk down," we get more and more specific.

> **Inductive** (Chunking Up) - drawing a general conclusion (abstract) from specific facts. To chunk up ask the questions, "What's the purpose of . . .?" or "What is this an example of . . .?" or "What's the intention of...?" This also leads to agreement.

There are many examples of when we can utilise chunking up or down, one example of how we use this hierarchy of ideas technique is in a meeting or during a discussion to get back on track with the agenda by chunking up and then chunking down a different way back to the topic that was being questioned and resulted in the meeting going off-piste. We tend to differ less on the bigger-chunk items as most people in a meeting could agree on such sweeping statements as "*We want the company to succeed.*" So when there is disagreement, chunking up to a place where people agree can help remove personal agendas and emotion to defuse the tension and give everyone the same context. You can then carefully chunk down, preserving agreement, to ensure the agenda is met and to develop the details that you require.

> **Deductive** (Chunking Down) - reasoning from the general to the specific. To chunk down, ask the question, "What specifically . . .?" or "What are examples of this?" This leads to distinctions.

So far we've looked at chunking down to fine detail and chunking up to the big picture. Now I would like you to consider the benefit of being able to chunk laterally (sideways).

168

How do we chunk sideways? Simple - first chunk up one level, then chunk down someplace else. For example if we take the word *Music* and chunk up one level we could chunk up to *Entertainment,* then if we ask ourselves *"What are other examples of entertainment?"* we could chunk across and down to TV, theatre, dance, cinema, opera, ballet or any number of *Entertainment* forms.

By using this process of chunking up then back down we've effectively chunked sideways - in this particular context we chunked up from Music entertainment and then sideways and down to TV, theatre, dance, cinema, opera, or ballet. The chunk(s) we end with are on the same level as the chunk we started with.

> **Laterally:** you will benefit even more from being able to chunk laterally or sideways. How do we chunk sideways? First chunk up one level, then chunk down some place else. The question to ask is *'What are other examples of....*

Communication tends to flow better and be more useful when all of the people involved are using similar sized chunks from the same hierarchical level. This is also one of the reasons why the person controlling the level of abstraction also controls the communication; lateral chunking is particularly good in negotiation for this reason.

When you become skilled at chunking up, down and sideways one of the things you will notice is an exponential increase in your communication skills. Another thing that you'll notice is your increasing ability to cognitively grasp concepts quicker than you were previously able to.

> **Nominalization** - a noun describing a state of being which exists in name only. Not a tangible item (e.g. Fulfilment, Peace, Oneness, Existence, Divinity). Can be a verb or another process word that has been formed into a noun (e.g. Decision, Realisation, Thought). Chunking up tends to result in nominalizations.

The Hierarchy of Ideas is a good concept for a manager to learn and understand, as most communication difficulties arise from the mismatching of chunk size. Managers who can move up and down levels of abstraction will be able to use this skill easily and effectively in dealing with people.

Programmers are used to moving easily up and down levels of abstraction. For example a directory is made up of files, with each file containing many records, each record has many fields and each field has many bytes. Expressions give rise to statements, grouped into functions, libraries, and then applications. The ability to operate over so many levels of abstraction is arguably one of the traits that make us human.

As a manager, you probably need to process bigger chunks than your employees and smaller chunks than your manager. Ideally, your employees will learn that you don't want to hear all the details of their jobs, and you will learn the same from your line manager. For example if you were to go the CEO of your company and give him all the details of your new idea they will more than likely become impatient with you and tell you to get to the point or worse to go away and write it down as they do not have the time. If you were to go straight into the big picture i.e. the benefit of your idea, you will immediately grab their attention to which you can then go into the details of how. It is useful to be able to "chunk up" and "chunk down" to enable you improve your communication and get your point across.

> When talking to someone using bigger chunks, you can ask the question, "*What, specifically?*" to get more details. When talking to someone using smaller chunks, you can ask, "*What is the intention of this?*" or "*What is this an instance of?*" to encourage larger chunks.

As a manager there are two very useful ways one can "chunk up" an employee, for example the employee's job can be seen in the context of the team and the entire company. By the employee understanding their importance in the workings of the entire company, something that may be undesirable or unpleasant to the employee may appear more tolerable. The second way of chunking up a job is to see it in the context of the employee's career, by asking the employee where they want to be in five or ten years time, will often show the employee that this job is a logical step on the path that they really need to travel to reach their career goals. By seeing the job in this way, both you as their manager/leader and the employee can change your attitudes toward it, showing the job to hold more attraction than previously thought.

History

Lateral Thinking was a term used by Edward DeBono to describe how he was able to get his clients to expand their thinking. He would ask his client to chunk up one level and then ask the client what else this would relate to, allowing the client to chunk up to find connections and relationships and then chunk down to relate these new learnings to their current situation.

There is more power in abstract ideas because they control the concrete ideas. Since all change takes place at the unconscious level and this requires trance, chunk up!

George Miller furthered this theory and introduced the concept of the 'magic number' 7+/-2 in 1956 which was rated as one of the most highly cited papers in psychology. Essentially, people can normally only deal with between 5 and 9 'chunks' of information before becoming overloaded. One of the keys to successful learning is to be able to 'chunk' information appropriately.

Hierarchy of Ideas is not a way to manipulate people. It is simply a way to find a common ground that you can both agree on, making you able to put aside your own personal agendas and emotions that could restrict you from reaching an agreement.

Think back to Sensory Auity: by using your sensory acuity you can tell whether the information you are using is leaving a person feeling confused, anxious or overwhelmed. Here you need to pay attention to your language, have you given that person too much information where they have become overwhelmed and turned off before they have grasped the reason why you are giving them the information? Or is your language so vague that you have only given them the big picture, in a way that makes the task seem so vast with no starting point?

Also in Rapport: being able to match the content chunks that the other person is working at will enable you to get into rapport much more easily and quicker as you are singing from the same hymn sheet. If they prefer an overview of the information and you overwhelm them with the fine details the chances are they will shut off from what you are saying. Likewise if you give a subordinate a task without giving them a detailed explanation of what the task entails, you may well leave them feeling lost without knowing what you want them to do!

The NLP Communication Model introduces the concept of information being divided up into chunks through our unique set of filters were we delete, distort and/or generalise the external information. When you are chunking up, you are chunking up towards words that will relate to someone's values and beliefs, which is one of our main filters. By looking to find a common ground, using words that appeal to their values and beliefs, allows the words you are saying to go through instead of being instantly deleted or distorted. Thus attracting their attention and focusing on the agenda in hand.

N.B Think back to the Presupposition of NLP; Respect for another person's model of the world. This is one of the ways to do it, instead of arguing on the conclusion they have drawn, you can simply keep rapport by chunking up to the bigger picture, or laterally to help them gain another perspective.

How to do it!

Think back to the Milton and Meta Models. The Milton Model uses artfully vague language to which the listener apples their own meaning and can induce a trance like state. In contrast the Meta Model is used to get into the specifics of a situation, into the finer detail.

Basic model of Hierarchy of Ideas

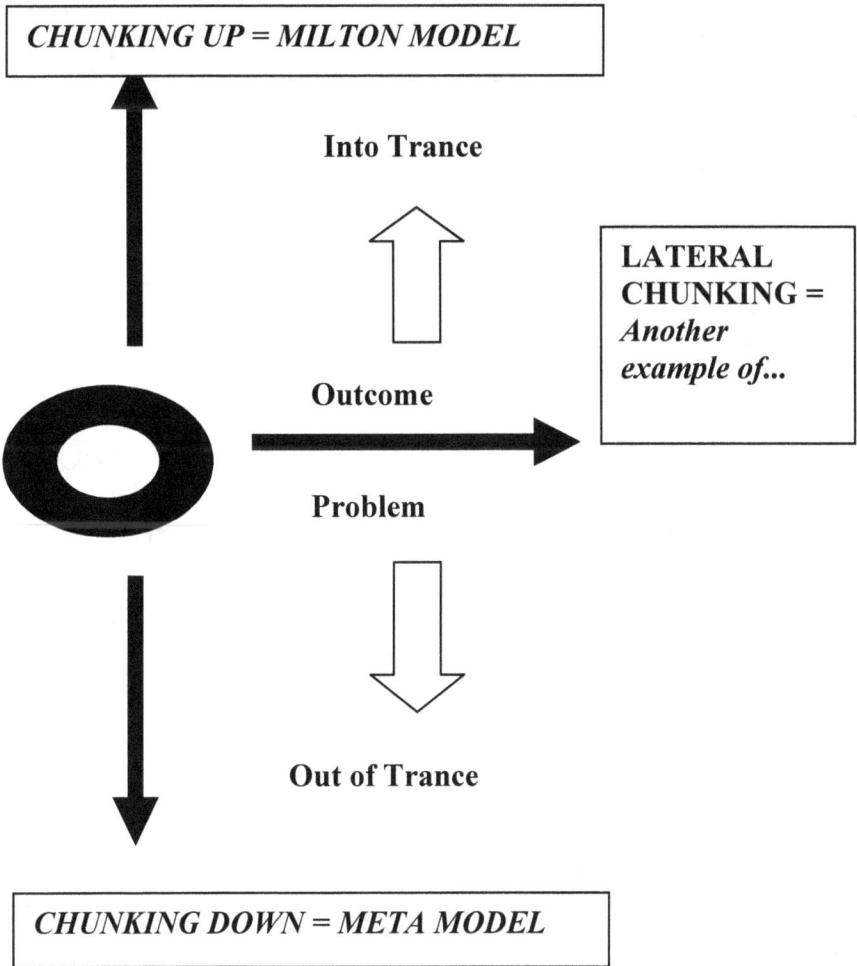

```
┌─────────────────────────────────────────┐
│  CHUNKING UP = MILTON MODEL              │
└─────────────────────────────────────────┘
              ▲
              │        Into Trance
              │           ⇧
                                        ┌──────────────┐
                                        │  LATERAL     │
                        Outcome         │  CHUNKING =  │
   ⬤  ────────────────────────────▶    │  Another     │
                                        │  example of...│
                        Problem         └──────────────┘
              │            ⇩
              │
              ▼        Out of Trance
┌─────────────────────────────────────────┐
│  CHUNKING DOWN = META MODEL              │
└─────────────────────────────────────────┘
```

<u>Detailed Example: Model of the Hierarchy of Ideas</u>

Big Picture/Big Chunk/Overall Small Picture/Detail/Small Chunk

Getting to a BIGGER picture is called 'Chunking Up'.
Examples of questions that enable us to 'Chunk Up' are:
- For what purpose?
- What will that get you/do for you?
- What is your intention..?
- What is the intention of …?
- What is this an example of?

Flora

Edible Plant

Vegetable

Laterally: Being able to chunk laterally or sideways gives you other examples.

First chunk up one level, then chunk down some place else.

For example, what is a onion an example of?
Chunk up = a vegetable
Chunk Laterally, what is another example of a vegetable?

Getting to more detail is called 'Chunking Down'.
Examples of questions that enable us to 'Chunk Down' are:
- What are examples of this?
- What/who/how/ when specifically?
- Compared to who/what/when?
- How specifically do you know?
NB. Avoid using 'WHY?'

| Mushy | Split | Pod |

Small Picture/ Detail/Small Chunk

Example of using Hierarchy of Ideas model for chunking and negotiations

Step 1: Getting into agreement

Given the variability of peoples need, it is not surprising that disagreements often arise. In many instances the disagreements will be in the details of what people want to happen. People are often quite oblivious to the fact that they can gain agreement at a higher level.

It is possible to first chunk up to the principle of the discussion, to get the other person's agreement on that principle. Following this you can then chunk down and start defining details of the discussion. From time to time throughout the conversation you will need to check in with the other party's viewpoint, which can be done by simply asking something like:

'Are these specific details in alignment with the agreed principle?'

If each party chunks up from the specifics to a higher level using the questions previously mentioned in this chapter, examining the basic principles, fundamental needs and desires, they will most likely discover that there is indeed some common aim or purpose that they all can agree with 'in principle.'
For example:

- To make sure that all parties are treated fairly

Once the parties acknowledge that there is a shared aim that they can agree with the principle of, then it is possible to begin negotiations – with each party chunking down to plan the next steps. Often the role of the negotiator is to remind all parties that there is a fundamental point of agreement. There is a great deal to achieve from regularly returning to the principles of agreement to validate that the negotiation is still on course.

```
┌─────────────────────────────────────────────────────┐
│              Shared Principles or Values             │
└─────────────────────────────────────────────────────┘
```

Chunking
Up/Down
as
appropriate

Specific Details for Person or People in Group X	Specific Details for Person or People in Group Y	Specific Details for Person or People in Group X	Specific Details for Person or People in Group Y

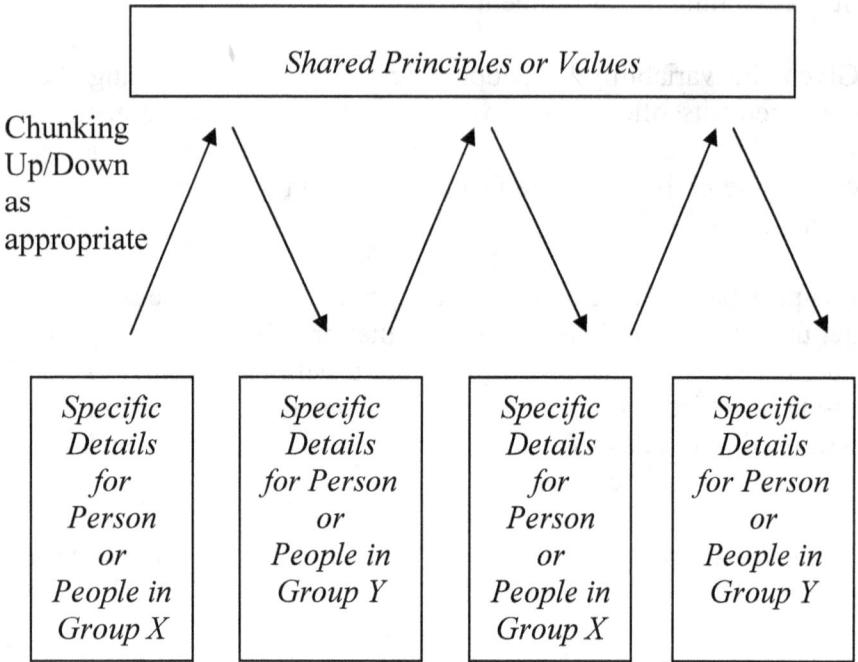

As outlined above the purpose of chunking as well as for negotiation and agreement, is to be able to think outside of the box, to notice the other options available to you in order to achieve the same higher intention.

Exercises

Exercise 1: Practice chunking!

1. This exercise involves three people – Person A is the 'client', Person B is the NLPer carrying out the exercise and Person C is Person B's assistant.
2. Person A and Person B face each other, seated. Person C stands behind Person A, facing Person B.
3. Person A begins talking about any topic they wish.
4. Person C uses their thumb to signal whether they want the Person B to ask a question that chunks up (thumb pointed up), chunks down (thumb pointed down) or chunk laterally (thumb pointed sideways). (To practice the technique properly; Person C needs to make Person B go to both extremes of chunking up and down).
5. Person B asks an appropriate question to chunk accordingly.
6. To add a further level of challenge to the exercise, after 4 minutes Person A can say which direction they are being chunked.
7. After about 7 minutes in all, swap over, and then swap over again so that the exercise is done 3 times and everyone gets the chance to be in each role.

Exercise 2 - Practice chunking up by yourself

Practice chunking up. Take an object you can see and chunk up three levels by asking at each level "What is this an example of?"

What is this an example of?

↑ _____

What is this an example of?

↑ _____

What is this an example of?

↑ _____

Object

| Start | _____

Exercise 3 - Practice chunking down by yourself

Practice chunking down. Take the same object chunk down three levels by asking at each level "What is an example of this?"

Object

| Start | _____

↓ What is an example of this?

_____

↓ What is an example of this?

_____

↓ What is an example of this?

_____

Exercise 4: Practice chunking laterally by yourself

Practice chunking laterally. Take the same object chunk up one level by asking;

"What is this an example of?" then chunk laterally by asking "what is another example of this" repeat 3 times

| Start | Object |

↓ _____

What is an example of this?

↓ _____

What is another example of this?

↓ _____

Summary

We use words as tools for putting forth our ideas, explaining concepts or expressing feelings and emotions. These words can either be extremely specific in nature, very vague or anywhere in between. The Hierarchy of Ideas enables you to navigate up or down to achieve understanding and reach agreement.

The Hierarchy of Ideas is a simple technique that enables you to build rapport and respect the other person's model of the world by chunking your language appropriately. We gain specificity by chunking down to uncover increasing fine level s of details and chunk up to look at the big picture, the overview/purpose of the task in hand, the key benefits being to relate to negotiation and agreement. Lateral thinking, asking what is another example of this is basically looking at how else the task can be achieved, enabling people to think outside the box and gain other perspectives. As you practice this technique, using your sensory acuity and rapport skills you will gain multiple perspectives on a situation and assist others in seeing those perspectives, and how they relate to achieving the higher goal.

References

- www.microdot.net/nlp/hypnotic-language/hierarchy-of-ideas.htm
- www.nlpworld.co.uk/nlp-practitioner-hierarchy-of-ideas-language-for-changehttp://www.microdot.net/nlp/hypnotic-language/hierarchy-of-ideas.htm
- Rosen. S, (1991) *My Voice Will Go with You:* The Teaching Tales of Milton H. Erickson, W. W. Norton
- Ellerton R. (2005) *Live Your Dreams Let Reality Catch Up:* NLP and Common Sense for Coaches, Managers and You, Trafford Publishings, Oxford, UK
- Sevi, A (2001) *Review of Kasher: Pragmatics, vol. IV: Presupposition.* Terence Langendoen
- Kasher, A. (1998) *Pragmatics.* Routledge (Taylor and Francis)
- Molden, D. (2007) *Managing with the Power of NLP*: Neurolinguistic Programming, a Model for Better Management 2 ed, Prentice Hall, Great Britain, Bell &

Chapter 7.4

Logical levels – the ability to understand, predict and influence behaviour

"You don't have to see the whole staircase, just take the first step."
Martin Luther King

Concept

All the subchapter techniques in this language section have been based on the NLP presupposition; The system (person) with the most flexibility (choices) of behaviour will have the most influence on the system and this Logical Level technique is no exception! Basically the more options you have in the techniques available to you the greater the chance of change and success in resolving the situation.

Benefits

Logical Levels are a way to;

- Logical Levels is a very useful technique for assisting with or understanding change, from an individual, social or organization point of view.
- Recognise the level a person is expressing concern with a problem.
- Truly listen and understand what a person is saying, so they feel empowered and valued.
- Ensure your staff get what they need from you to perform a task.
- Get to the root cause of the problem, not guessing what it is.
- Motivate someone to do a task they previously thought was not important by showing them the overall purpose behind doing it.
- Identify inconsistencies in the organisation culture.
- Make sure the whole team, in whatever context, is all pulling together

What are Logical Levels?

The NLP logical levels (also known as the logical levels of change, the logical levels of thinking and the neurological levels) are very useful for assisting with or understanding change from an individual, departmental or organization point of view. The Logical Level model assumes that human processes can be described along a ladder of categories

> *"Language and word choice form a manager's primary tool. Used wisely, sound guidance can grow from the seeds of aligned words. Used poorly and all you get are weeds"* Michael Lissack & Johan Roos.

that represent the cause of the problem. This ladder suggests a natural hierarchy, the levels influence each other in both directions, where a change on a higher level will have a greater impact on the lower levels whereas a change on the lower levels will not necessarily affect the higher levels. For example redecorating the office will not affect the productivity of the staff who work within it, but it will affect their mood. Whereas a manager who values their employees invests in staff development which indicates how important they are to the success of the organisation, improves staff morale, increases capabilities and improves staff productivity, making the company a better place to work.

How often have you heard the phrases below?

"**I** can't do that here"
"I **CAN'T** do that here"
"I can't **DO** that here"
"I can't do **THAT** here"
"I can't do that **HERE**"

Notice the difference? The verbal emphasis illustrates where the root of the problem lies, Logical Levels set out how to solve it:

"**I** can't do that here" is the person's identity.

"I **CAN'T** do that here" is the person's belief/values.

"I can't **DO** that here" is the person's capabilities.

"I can't do **THAT** here" is the person's behaviours.

"I can't do that **HERE**" is the person's environment.

Listening to and understanding the weighting behind the words used will often determine at what level (whether environment, capability, identity, etc.) change will be most effective. Without this understanding, an intervention may occur at a level below where the issue resides. In which case, no change will occur, or an unforeseen change will occur, which generally tends to further exacerbate the challenge and opportunity for change. In order to bring about successful change it is necessary to work at the level above the one you wish to influence.

For instance, we can teach someone a new behaviour, they may even make the effort to demonstrate this behaviour for some time, but there will always be a point where they will check that behaviour against their identity, beliefs\values and capabilities (checking up through their higher levels) to whether or not that behaviour is congruent. When our beliefs and/or identity are incongruent with an action at a lower (logical) level, they will prevent or sabotage implementing change.

When an employee says 'I **CAN'T** do presentations' then all the training courses in the world will not teach them how to do presentations if they simply do not believe they can do it. Linking back to the paragraph above, an unforeseen change in this example could be as dramatic as demoralisation of staff, with the employee walking out of the presentation training course having anxiously confirmed their belief that they **CAN'T** do presentations. If they say 'I can't do presentations **HERE**' then changing their environment will enable them to do so.

So what are these logical levels?!

For those not familiar with the model, here is a quick overview. 'Environment' is at the base, as without an environment or context for the problem 'Behaviours' either cannot take place, or are meaningless. 'Capability' is the logical level 'up' from behaviours because without behaviour we cannot develop capability. Furthermore we could not have "Beliefs and Values" without the capability of thinking, and finally our beliefs and values enable us to develop a sense of self; our 'Identity'. 'Mission' is our purpose, our aims and intention; are personal mission. Who are we serving, what's the bigger picture that goes beyond just 'being', why do we do what we do?

The Logical Level model can help you align your environment, behaviours, competencies, beliefs/values, identity and purpose, to make you aware of any in-congruency. Why? An example would be to ensure your behaviours represent your overall identity so that every part of you is working towards achieving your personal mission.

A simple example would be a person might think it important to be on time for a meeting but in practice will often be late. So the belief (timeliness is important) is contradicted by their behaviour (lateness). Think of any key note speaker, their personal mission is for their voice to be heard, their views to be understood and appreciated. They live and breathe their purpose with every ounce of their fibre, from the environment they are in, the way they behave all the way up to their identity in working to achieve it. As they are not pretending to be in an environment that they do not belong in, or because the beliefs and values they are speaking about are their own and are not simply dictating what they have been told to say, their passion and charisma shines through so much that their speech motivates and interests all who listen to it.

> *"Coherence results from people feeling that the actions required of them are consistent with their own sense of purpose and identity and that of the organisation of which they are a part. This feeling can occur when the values and guiding principles embodied by the corporate process and expressed identity align with how the person defines and embodies their sense of self"* Michael Lissack & Johan Roos.

Likewise a self initiated task compared to a task that has been set by someone else. You go about the former with such excitement and rigour as you want to do it, it is important to you, you see its purpose, it is something you believe in, you are already capable of it and because of this you enjoy and see how it will help your personal development. Whereas the set task will not have the same motivation or drive until we have sat back and thought about it, and even then it still may not have!

Furthermore evaluating your logical levels has the great benefit of deducing where your in-congruency lies; for example if you are unhappy at work, evaluating your logical levels will deduce why you are unhappy. Is it the workplace, the behaviour of your boss, or do your beliefs & values contradict with the tasks you are paid to perform?

To conclude, logical levels provide insights into the most effective way to create change. The higher the logical level of form at which intervention is made, the more comprehensive the field of change. Now in these ever changing times; companies increasingly look to use management consultants to offer re-engineering, re-structuring, or new approaches to transform their organisation. Yet most of these "innovative" approaches seek to only change our environment and behaviour, or at most increase our capabilities.

Changes at these levels will not only be limited, they will be temporary. Unless we change the belief(s) that create our capabilities and behaviours, we tend to revert back to our former methods because some belief, generally unconscious, directs us how to plan and where and when to do it. As long as we believe that sales are always slow in the third quarter of each year, nothing will change the number of sales in the third quarter until we change that belief.

History

Every organisation in the world operates on values whether it knows it or not. This statement is true because every organisation in the world has preferences and priorities. Those that operate with their values in a deliberate and organised manner create for themselves a distinct advantage over competitors in their market, by shaping and defining their own culture, levels of performance and success.

American anthropologist Gregory Bateson identified that any culture can be observed as operating within a distinct set of levels.

His theory was later adapted and extended by Robert Dilts in 1975 whose work suggests that an organisation is the result of the interaction of what he refers to as its Logical Levels.

This work can be seen as an adaptation of Maslow's Hierarchy of Needs, where in 1943 he produced a paper on "A theory of human motivation" which he subsequently extended to include his observations of humans' innate curiosity.

In his paper he studied what he called exemplary people such as Albert Einstein, Jane Addams, Eleanor Roosevelt, and Frederick Douglas rather than mentally ill or neurotic people, which was the practice at the time. His controversial reasons for this were, in his own words *"The study of crippled, stunted, immature, and unhealthy specimens can yield only a cripple psychology and a cripple philosophy"*.

Maslow's hierarchy of needs, like logical levels is often depicted as a pyramid consisting of five levels: the lowest level being associated with physiological needs, while the uppermost level is associated with self-actualization needs, particularly those related to identity and purpose. Deficiency needs must be met first. Once these are met, seeking to satisfy growth needs drives personal growth. The higher needs in this hierarchy only come into focus when the lower needs in the pyramid are met. Once an individual has moved upwards to the next level, needs in the lower level will no longer be prioritized. If a lower set of needs is no longer being met, the individual will temporarily re-prioritize those needs by focusing attention on the unfulfilled needs, but will not permanently regress to the lower level. For instance, a businessman at the esteem level who is recovering from cancer will spend a great deal of time concentrating on his health (physiological needs), but will continue to value his work performance (esteem needs) and will likely return to work during periods of remission.

Maslow Hierarchy of Needs Model:

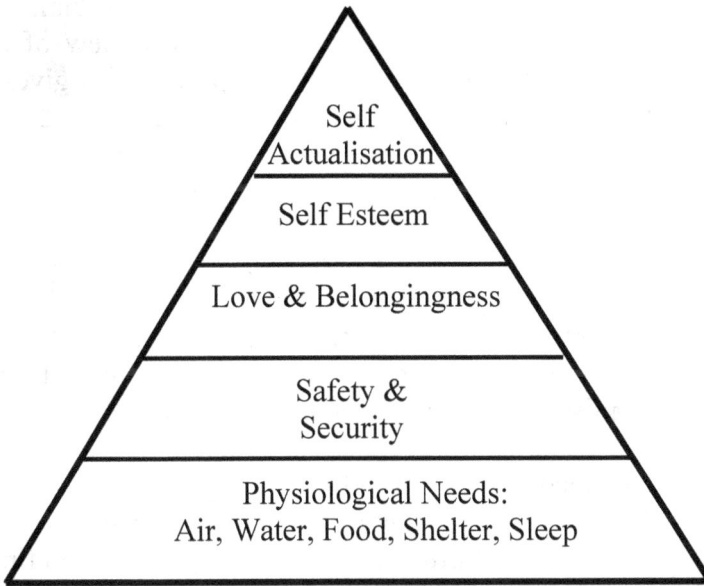

An interpretation of Maslow's hierarchy of needs, represented as a pyramid with the more basic needs at the bottom

Now I know there is no quick fix, and you can all think of examples where in first instance logical levels would not stand true in aligning an organisation. Saying that, successful people in business are those who walk their talk. Logical levels will not work for very unaligned organisations who have company missions or organisational values written on the wall never to be spoken of again. I think we can all think of a company where the CEO makes the decisions, yet the work force at the bottom don't feel valued enough (or paid enough!) to carry them out effectively. Or simply, in change management the reasons why things don't work is because they don't capture the hearts and minds of the people needed to carry them out.

Logical Levels enables the client (individual, department or organisation) to analyse a situation through the levels up to "Mission" to access where the client is at now and establish the root of the problem. Once the client has a clear view of their Mission it puts the situation back into perspective and gives the client direction, so that as they come back down the levels in the model they can see the incongruences that were previously causing them the problem. They look at who they are as an individual, department or organisation, within any given context

> "We first make our habits, then our habits make us" John Dryden

(manager, HR, blue-chip), then evaluate what their beliefs are in regards to their mission, looking at why it is important for them to fulfil their mission, which enables them to address their capabilities; to examine whether there are any other skills or attributes they need in order to fulfil their mission. They can then access their behaviour, distinguishing what behaviours might need to be addressed to fulfil their mission so that they can finally look at their environment, deciding whether it is appropriate to where they need to be. Where else could they develop?

If we think back to the NLP communication model, beliefs and values are one of our filters through which we process information. If we believe we cannot do something, we delete and distort learnings that would enable us to do it. This belief is represented in our behaviour (lack of enthusiasm, motivation, commitment etc.) and therefore our results. For example if you simply believe you can't do a task but yet you manage to do it, you delete or distort this information putting it down to "beginners luck" or a fluke.

Expanding on the presupposition; All procedures should increase wholeness, fewer parts mean less conflicts and more congruence. In an organisational context, Logical Levels allows us to see which areas are not congruent to the organisational culture, or what behaviours are not congruent with the company's identity.

190

The most critical skill for any business is the ability to translate vision into action. This is dependent on two factors: leadership and alignment. Assuming that you have a clear vision and are able to communicate that clearly and vividly, you must then align people and processes with that vision. If we consider a hierarchical model of an organisation, we can find misalignment between the levels of an organisation which is under performing compared to the potential of its people.

In an organisation, misalignment causes loss of energy through frustration, waste and a thousand other side effects which you and your colleagues can feel. Eventually that misalignment will destroy the business - not because of the cost of waste, but because the frustration sucks the energy and passion out of the employees. Work becomes a chore. Customers become an irritation. Problems become show stoppers. The business grinds to a halt.

By creating alignment through the business, we ensure that the energy and passion of your vision is translated into action. That work means anything from play to a noble cause. Customers mean an opportunity to shine. Problems become hurdles to jump over. Your customers continue to buy from you because they feel that passion, that enthusiasm, that energy. They see and feel it in the products, in the marketing, in the customer service and in the dedication of your people.

The outcomes of most motivational speaking and behavioural course training (unless it specifically addresses changing beliefs) at best, reinforces a belief in underperformance. Through aligning logical levels we can more efficiently implement individual and organizational transformations, ensuring that the mission is being worked towards.

How to do it!

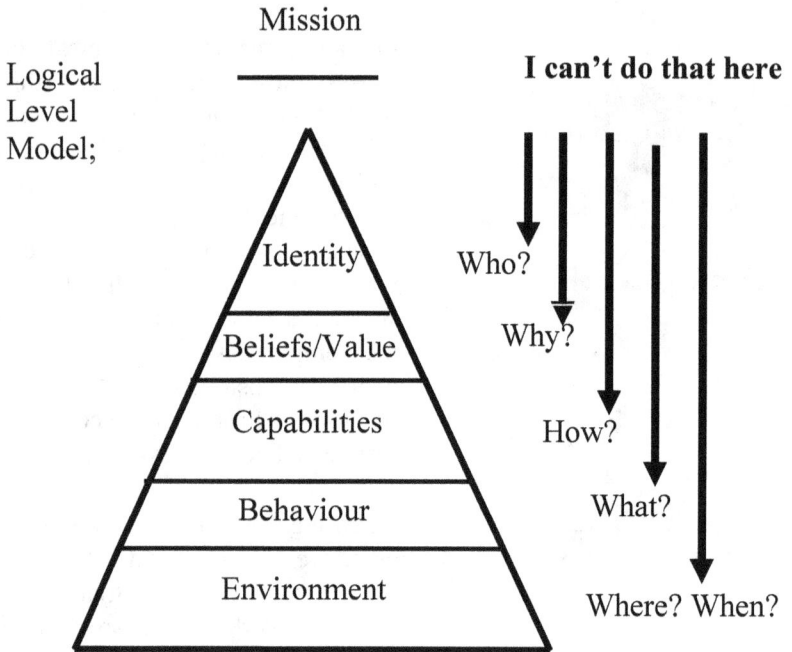

These logical levels can be viewed from an individual, departmental or organisational point of view:

Mission	The bigger picture. What is our purpose; aims and intentions
Identity	What is unique about you? Who are you? What makes you different from everyone else? Identity is your sense of self
Beliefs / Values	Beliefs are generalisations we make about ourselves. They are deep seated views that influence our behaviours. Values are about how we think things ought to be or how people ought to behave. They are made up of beliefs and ideas arising from the person's culture and own life experience.
Capabilities	These are the skills, qualities and strategies within a given context.
Behaviour	Behaviour is about what you do, and say. Basically the external expressions of self.
Environment	This level concerns the external conditions to which you react. Where you work, the people around you, your friends, the company customers etc.

Using these Logical Level distinctions allows you to access certain states.

Spatially mark out six spots on the floor, and assign the logical levels as illustrated in the leadership exercise below:

Example 1 - Leadership

End

Start

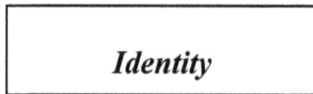

Start		End
Where are you as a leader?	**Environment**	Where else are you a Leader? Where will you be leading in the future?
What behaviours do you have as a leader?	**Behaviour**	What behaviours do you want as a leader in the future?
What Capabilities do you have as a leader? How do you lead?	**Capability**	What capabilities do you now have or want to learn for the future? [X]
What do you believe, what is important to you as a leader?	**Beliefs/Values**	What do you believe **now?** What is important to you **now** about being a leader?
Who are you, as a leader?	**Identity**	Who are you **now** as a leader?
Who else are you serving? What is your mission or purpose as a leader?	Mission	Now that you have seen your purpose, take a moment to reflect on yourself as a leader.

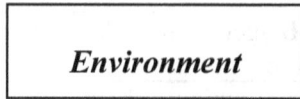

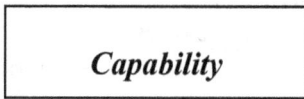

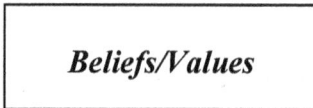

Exercises

The exercise below involves two people – Person A is the 'client', Person B is the NLPer carrying out the exercise.

Exercise 1

1. Person B spatially marks out six spots on the floor and assigns the logical levels as illustrated in the leadership exercise, you can either work on leadership or substitute the word leadership and input any other area you wish to work on.

2. Person A walks through the levels step by step, starting at environment and moving all the way to "beyond identity" with person B asking the appropriate questions at each stage going down the left hand side of the page, eliciting not advising, person B writes down exactly what person A says .

3. Person A moves to the next level when they have said all that they want to say around that level.

4. When they get to 'Mission' and answered all appropriate questions Person B gets them to turn around and starts asking them the questions going from the bottom to the top on the right hand side of the page (asking the questions in a anti clockwise format).

5. Person A then makes a return journey from beyond identity to environment, bringing all that they have now got at mission level, letting it infuse and inform where they are at each lower level. Person B asks Person A the respective questions in each lower level.

6. Once person A has come back to the beginning (environment again) get them to stand on mark X and reflect upon what they need to do.

7. Person A and person B change roles and repeat stages 1-6 again.

N.B instead of Person A being a client, you can define them as the department or organisation you are working with. Likewise instead of examining where Person A is as a "leader" you can examine another field you wish to work on.

Exercise 2 - Defining you.

Realise and define your logical levels:

Environment	Where do you work? What are the external influences in your life and on you? Where do you not work that you would like to work?
Behaviour	What do you do? What behaviour do you have that you prefer not to have? How do your behaviours reflect you?
Capabilities	What are your key capabilities? What skills do you not have yet that would enable you to be who you are or who you want to be?
Values	What is important to you about what you do? What factors influence your decisions?
Beliefs	What do you believe is true about you and those around you that enables you to do what you do? What beliefs do you hold about yourself? What beliefs would you like to hold that are not currently present?
Identity	Who are you? Who are you not that you would like to be?
Mission	What is your purpose in business/life?

Summary

Logical Levels is simple an informative tool that enables you to get insights into situations or problems that have arisen. It is very effective as a management and leadership tool to highlight areas of strength or development.

Using your sensory acuity and listening to the language other people use enables you to notice the logical level in which the problem lies, so that you support and facilitate their development appropriately without guessing what the problem is.

Learning a new skill at first instance (capability level), for example a language, might prompt me to learn the importance of their cultures (values level). Yet if at this value and beliefs level we don't believe we will be able to learn it or we are not good enough (my identity) then I will fail to learn it. If, on the other side, the belief level is changed first, for example, from: I do not have the capacity to learn foreign languages to: It's easy for me to learn languages, the effects for the lower levels are tremendous! It certainly changes my behaviour - suddenly I can talk to people to whom I could not have talked before (capability) I understand and respect (behaviour) their culture (value). There might even be a dramatic change in my environment - I might move to another country.

Logical levels enable you to support and facilitate the learning and development of your team, showing them your understanding and appreciation of where their problem lies. This will ensure you maintain rapport, support your staff , respecting their model of the world.

References

- www.valuesatwork.org/A5LevelsOfAlignment.pdf
- http://en.wikipedia.org/wiki/Maslow%27s_hierarchy_of_needs
- Bateson, G. (1972) *Steps to an Ecology of Mind.* University Of Chicago Press, Chicago, Illinois.
- Satir, V., & Baldwin, M. (1983). *Satir Step by step*: A guide to creating change in families. Palo Alto: Science and
- Behavior Books.
- Maslow, A. (1943) *A Theory of Human Motivation*, Psychological Review, York University, Toronto, Ontario
- Maslow, Abraham H. (1998) *Maslow on Management* John Wiley & Sons
- Chapter 11
- Nietzsche, Friedrich *Twilight of the idols* (1990 Penguin Classics ed.)
- Wake, Lisa. (2008) *Neurolingustic Psychotherapy*, Routledge.

Chapter 8

Submodalities – the brain's language

"Surely, the brain must hold the key to human nature: understanding it will allow us to make sense of so much that puzzles us about ourselves"
Adam Zeman

Concept

This technique is based on the presupposition: We are in charge of our mind and therefore our results. If we are not getting the results we want then it is up to us to change the way we are going about it so that we do get the results we want. If we do not achieve something then it is only ever our fault and our responsibility to change, in order to achieve it.

Benefits

- To change a task you dislike into one you enjoy.
- To make someone seem less intimidating.
- To change values & beliefs.
- To overcome confusion.
- To motivate another.
- To become more internally referenced and a better decision maker.

What are Submodalities?

As previously covered in representational systems, we have five basic senses: visual, auditory, kinaesthetic, olfactory and gustatory, In NLP these are called modalities.

Within each of these modalities we have sub-modalities that are finer distinctions by which we give meaning to our experiences. For example, in visual terms, common distinctions include: brightness, colour contrast, size, distance, sharpness, focus, location, and so on; in auditory: volume, loud or soft, pitch, tonal range, distance, clarity, timbre, etc. Kinaesthetic: internal/external, intensity, still or moving, heavy or light (feeling), hot or cold, high pressure/low pressure etc.

> *"A man cannot directly choose his circumstances, but he can choose his thoughts, and so indirectly, yet surely, shape his circumstances."*
> James Allen

How would you remember what someone was wearing or how they looked the last time you saw them? How can you compare what someone looked liked 6 weeks ago to 6 months ago? You code the two different memories in different submodalities. We create meaning by using different submodalities that code our experience, if we didn't how would we be able to differentiate between 6 weeks, 6 months or 6 years ago?

The technique of changing submodalities is an extremely useful and powerful technique that can change the meaning of an experience; to be less negative, more positive and more empowering. By changing how people represent their own internal representations of themselves, whether past or future orientated, we can help them become more resourceful. For example, by changing an internal picture of a goal, for example, to be more colourful, brighter, clearer, bigger and closer you will make it more appealing, empowering and more able to motivate yourself/the client to achieve it.

Examples of Visual, Auditory, Kinaesthetic submodalities;

Visual Submodalities	Auditory Submodalities	Kinesthetic Submodalities
Size of Picture	Volume	Location
Big/Med/Small	High or Low(Pitch)	Size
Near or Far	Tempo: Fast or Slow	Shape
Location	Direction of sounds	Colour
Black & White or	Internal or External	Intensity High or
Colour	Direction of Sounds	Low
Bright or Dim	Sharp or Soft	Texture-Rough or
Associated or	Timbre-Clear or	Smooth
Dissociated	Raspy	Still or Moving
Number of Pictures	Cadence or Rhythm	Hot or Cold
Focused or	Pauses	Fast or Slow
Defocused	Duration of Sounds	Heavy or Light
Focus-Changing or	Uniqueness of sound	Duration-Short or
Steady	Location of Sounds	Long

How are they useful? Well let's take the following phrase:

"The weight of the world is on my shoulders"

How many times have you heard that being said?

Without eliciting the submodalities, the phrase suggests that the problem is huge (size of picture) and directly (near or far) above their head (location): how would they feel if this weight was on the floor? further away? or the size of pea? Altering the location, distance and size changes the impact this "problem" will have.

How about that "voice inside (internal) your head?" The one that criticises, chastises and makes you feel un-resourceful.

"That voice inside your head is not the voice of God. It just sounds like it thinks it is" Cheri Huber

What would be the impact if you changed that voice to sound like Mickey Mouse (pitch) or if you turned the volume down (volume) or if you made it into a seductive voice (tempo: slow)

Finally a Kinaesthetic example would be a phrase like;

"I feel under so much pressure"

This suggests that the feeling of pressure is high, heavy, and above them from the phrase. We could assume this feeling is an "angry" colour such as a shade of red, so what would happen if we turned the colour to be blue? (colour), or if we associated this "pressure" with a comical shape (shape), or as heavy as a feather (heavy or light). If this pressure was no longer above them (location) but was beneath them, or to the left, to the right or in front of them, so that they can acknowledge and act upon it.

Which leads us into ecology, pressure is needed in some situations, for example GCSE exams or a project deadline. Pressure makes you aware of the importance of the situation, and so taking away the pressure is not always ecological. Submodalities can be used to take away the stress, numbness or the overwhelming feeling pressure may bring, to allow you to realise the pressures significance, remove these restricting feelings and to get on with the task in hand.

I want you to think of a time in the last year when you felt really relaxed. Maybe when you were lying on the beach on your last holiday or when you were sitting in your favourite armchair watching a film... just a time where you remember feeling relaxed and with not a care in the world.

Now close your eyes and picture that scene in your mind. What do you see? Is it black and white or colour? Is it a moving film or a still picture? Is it bright or dim? Are you looking through your own eyes or do you see yourself in the picture? Note down the details and how you perceive the scene.

The answers to those questions are your submodalities for that experience, in other words, how you see the scene now is how you represent that experience to yourself. Seeing the experience is the modality, the way you see it is the submodality; the experience for you.

Now go through the same process with a stressful experience. A time when you remember feeling stressed, anxious or nervous and answer the same questions about the scene; what do you see? Is it a still photo? Is it like a movie screen of a film? Is it in black and white or colour? Is it bright or dim? Are you looking at yourself in the scene or looking through your own eye's? Again note down the details, and compare these answers to the answers of your "relaxed" experience above. You will find that there are major differences between the two, which will be different for each and every one of us and represent how we code, order and give meaning to an event.

By changing these representations, you will change the meaning of that event to yourself. Like a film director, if you change your unhappy scene to be more like your happy scene, you will change your experience. It is important to remember that submodalities are not the solution to the problem; they simply empower us by taking the emotional charge out of a situation, enabling us to be in a more resourceful state to work out the solution.

By understanding how you and how other people store their information, will enable you to make changes to how you/another person perceives a problem. If it is "*Weighing them down*" then no matter how much positive light spirited banter you use, they will still feel weighed down. By respecting this you will respect their model of the world, build rapport and enable you to receive permission to suggest ways in which they could resolve their problem. For example by making it light, or separating it from them, putting it on the floor, making it really small or changing it into a balloon. Once changed, the negative emotions attached to the problem are also changed, enabling the person to focus on the solution and get on with the task in hand.

History

On a daily basis you will be saying and hearing submodalities without even knowing it;

- *"The weight of the world is on my shoulders"*
- *"I've got this big problem hanging over me"*
- *"You're a pain in the neck"*
- *"He gets under my skin"*
- *"You're getting up my nose"*
- *"To close for comfort"*
- *"It's pulling me down"*
- *"It's a strain on me"*

I am sure you can think of a lot more that you hear or perhaps you even say. Unlike a lot of the other techniques you will learn in NLP that have been "discovered" or modelled, having existed previously as part of some long lost culture or one of the modern discoveries made by such pre-NLP schools as Chomsky's transformational grammar, Ericksonian Hypnosis or Fritz Pearls' methodology of Gestalt Therapy, nothing similar to submodalities has ever existed in the past. There has been reference to them in the way that people are able to code, order and give meaning to experience and describe their feelings through pictures of memories but never in the form of the submodalities that we know today.

Submodalities was developed by Richard Bandler one of the co-founders of NLP through his study into Pragmagraphics, which is an area of NLP established by Todd Epstein and Richard Bandler in 1980. This has been further developed by Epstein with Robert Dilts over the following decade. Submodalities relate back to the definition of wanton curiosity, as it was Richard Bandler's curiosity of holography to the human brain that brought about the work of submodalities.

Richard Bandler and Todd Epstein holography, is the study of work done by the Stanford neurophysiologist Karl Pribram that was carried out in the 1960's , where he hypothesised that memories are encoded not in neurons, or small groupings of neurons, but in patterns of nerve impulses that crisscross the entire brain in the same way that patterns of laser light interference crisscross the entire area of a piece of film containing a holographic image. In other words, Pribram believes the brain is itself a hologram. He backed up this theory with the thoughts that explain how the human brain can store so many memories in so little space. It has been estimated that the human brain has the capacity to memorize something on the order of 10 billion bits of information during the average human lifetime, which is understandable if the brain functions according to holographic principles.

If a friend asks you to tell him what comes to mind when he says the word "zebra", you do not have to clumsily sort back through some gigantic and cerebral alphabetic file to arrive at an answer.

Instead, associations like "striped", "horselike", and "animal native to Africa" all pop into your head instantly. Indeed, one of the most amazing things about the human thinking process is that every piece of information seems instantly cross- correlated with every other piece of information--another feature intrinsic to the hologram. Because every portion of a hologram is infinitely interconnected with every other portion, it is perhaps nature's supreme example of a cross-correlated system. Much like a hologram Epstein hypothesized a particular submodality picture (the clarity of an internal image for example) could function like the reference beam used to make a hologram. Altering this submodality, like adjusting the angle or wavelength of the reference beam, would change the resulting interference pattern bringing out different dimensions and facets of the experiences of which it was linked, perhaps shifting it to something else altogether.

Going back to the "What are submodalities" section above, I have tried to give vague examples and descriptions whilst explaining the practical usage of submodalities, because submodalities are different for every person. If I may highlight my "I feel under so much pressure" example, when I am under pressure I visualise a purple pulsing anvil weight as big as the ceiling of the room I am in hanging over me, whereas you could image pressure as a big spiky red cloud floating around your head. Submodalities are different for every person, they are how that person,s perceives/visualises/hears and feels their problem.

Eliciting submodalities helps us avoid guessing, making generalisations and mind reading. Whereas changing submodalities is not the solution to the problem, they empower us by taking the emotional charge out of a situation, enabling us to be in a more resourceful state to work out the solution.

Think back to the presupposition; People have all the resources they need to make the changes they want. People themselves are not un-resourceful, they are simply experiencing unresourceful states, which when changed allows them to access all the resources within them to accomplish whatever they choose. Think back to the communication model of NLP and subjective experience, the internal representation is what we store as our memory of the external event. Submodalities are how we code this internal representation which affects our state, physiology and behaviour. By changing the submodalities of an experience you can impact upon how that experience affects you today; changing the internal representation to be more positive will affect your state and physiology which is reflected in your behaviour and therefore your results, enabling you to be more motivated and work from a more resourceful state.

How it works

In NLP there are two main types of Submodalities that bring about this change of internal representation and therefore changes in a person's state, physiology and behaviour, these are;

Critical Submodalities and Driver Submodalities

Critical Submodalities make the difference in the meaning of an experience, some of the submodalities are more critical than others. For the majority of people, location, size and whether the picture is associated (looking through your own eyes) or dissociated (looking at yourself in the picture) are the most critical. If the picture had a negative emotion attached to it and was located in front of you, just by moving it down to the bottom left (for example, depending on the person!) will take the emotional charge from it.

A Driver Submodality is a submodality so important that it affects all the other submodalities when you change it. If location was the driver submodality, then you would find that the colour, size, brightness and distance (for example, again dependant on the person) will have changed as soon as you move it down to the bottom left.

The two main ways in which you can use submodalities in order to be in charge of your results are;

1) Alter the submodalities of an internal representation
2) Mapping across

Firstly, Alter the submodalities of an internal representation.

Ask the client to identify a picture of 'something' they want to change for example: a food they like

> *"I am always doing things I can't do – that's how I get to do them"*
> Pablo Picasso

and wish they didn't, an activity that they don't like and they wished they did or of an event/situation that makes them feel especially unresourceful.
Elicit each of the submodalities, using the following submodality checklist, making changes to each submodality one by one, asking whether the change makes it Better, Worse or No Difference.

If worse or no difference, then change it back, keep the changes that make it better and if you notice that a certain change makes it a lot better than change that submodality further. For example if "making it small" creates a change for the better then tell the client to make it even smaller and smaller until it feels right to them. You would continue doing this until the client has reached their desired outcome; for example removing a negative memory of their boss shouting at them from; Boss being huge, standing over them, overpowering, to a resourceful memory of boss being small, tiny, at their feet, and the voice being squeaky.

Altering Submodalities Script; the Process:

1) Rapport/Resourceful State/Outcome/Scores on the Doors

2) Ask the client *"Can you think of a food (or something) that you like and wished you didn't?"*

3) Here is where the ecology comes in; Ask the client:
   "Are there are any negative consequences of making this change".
   "What would happen if you no longer liked it?"
   "What would happen if you continued to like it?"
   "What wouldn't happen if you continue to like it?"

208

"What wouldn't happen if you no longer liked it?"
Remember to check for incongruence (using your sensory acuity).

4) Ask the Client to again: *"Think of a food (or something) that you like and wish you didn't (or) situation that you respond to un-resourcefully and which you didn't and Get a picture*

5) Elicit the submodalities using the submodality checklist (on the subsequent page). Go through the checklist asking each point one after another; e.g. is *it black and white or colour, near or far, the location and so on.*

6) Once you have elicited all the submodalities thank the client and then ask them to bring back the picture and make changes to each submodality one by one, asking whether the change makes it Better, Worse or No Difference. For example if the picture was in black and white tell the client to *make it colour....does that make it better, worse or no difference.*

7) Keep the changes that make it better, change it for back the changes that make it worse or no difference.

8) Lock in the changes. *Ask the client to lock in all the changes that made it better.*

9) Test: *Ask the client how they feel in reference to the original situation, so if food-How do they feel now.*

10) Future pace. Ask the client *to go out into the future to the next time they would have done X and ask them how do they feel now? What do they do differently* (this is done as a convincer both to the client and to you to know that the client has had a change).

11) N.B Identify the driver, the submodality that made the difference. Ask the client which one made the difference for the client as knowing this is very empowering for the client as they will be able to apply this method to other things for themselves. (As the NLP presupposition says; we are in charge of our mind then we are in charge of our results).

Submodalities Checklist

VISUAL	1.	2.	3.
Near or Far			
Bright or Dim			
Location			
Size of Picture			
Associated or Dissociated			
Focused or Defocused			
Focus-Changing or Steady			
Framed or Panoramic			
Movie or Still			
Moving fast or slow			
Amount of Contrast			
3D or Flat			
Angle Viewed From			
# of Pictures			

Can you make a picture?

AUDITORY	******	******	*******
Location			
Direction			
Internal or External			
Loud or Soft			
Fast or Slow			
High or Low(Pitch)			
Timbre-Clear or Raspy			
Pauses			
Cadence or Rhythm			
Duration			
Uniqueness of sound			

Are there any Sounds that are Important?

210

KINAESTHETIC	******	******	*******
Location			
Size			
Shape			
Colour			
Intensity			
Steady			
Still or Moving			
Fast or Slow			
Duration-Short or Long			
Humidity-Dry or Wet			
Vibration			
Hot or Cold			
Pressure-High or Low			
Texture-Rough or Smooth			
Heavy or Light			
Internal or External			

Are there any Feelings that are important?

The second way in which you can use submodalities is by a process called; Mapping Across.

Mapping across is a two step process of contrastive analysis and mapping across. Where you would elicit the submodalities of two internal representations; one undesired, one desired and then change the submodalities of the undesired internal representation to be the same as the submodalities of the desired internal representation by;

1. Contrastive Analysis

Contrastive analysis is the elicitation of the two states separately and comparing and contrasting the submodalities of two different states or two different internal representations against each other. The key is finding that critical submodality, which if you remember; is the submodality that defines the desired state to the undesired state.

2. Mapping Across

Mapping across is discovering the driver submodalities that make the other submodalities change and then changing the submodalities of the undesired state into that of the desired state.

Essentially in mapping across we change where appropriate, a food you like and wished you didn't into a food which you don't like or like a lot less. This is done by changing the submodalities of the liked food picture into the submodalities of the disliked food picture. When the mapping across is completed, whenever you think of he food that you used to like and wished you didn't you would find that you had an unappealing picture in mind.

Below is a list of examples of when you could use this Submodality Mapping Across technique:

- To change a task you dislike into one you enjoy.
- To change an activity that you dislike into an activity you like.
- To make someone seem less intimidating.
- To change a negative belief into a positive one.
- To overcome confusion.
- To change a food you like to a food you dislike.

<u>Submodalities Mapping Across Script - the process</u>

1. Rapport/Resourceful State/Outcome/Scores on the Doors

2. Ask the client *"Can you think of a food (or something) that you like and wish you didn't?"*

3. Here is where the ecology comes in, ask the client:

"Are there are any negative consequences of making this change?"
"What would happen if you no longer liked it?"
"What would happen if you continued to like it?"
"What wouldn't happen if you continue to like it?"
"What wouldn't happen if you no longer liked it?"

Remember to check for incongruence (using your sensory acuity)

4. *"Think of a food (or something) that you like less (or) only eat very occasionally (or) a dislike that is of a similar consistency"*. Remember the closer the dislike is to the like the better.

5. Elicit the submodalities of the likes and wishes they didn't or want to like less.

213

6. Elicit the submodalities of the food that the client either likes less or doesn't like.

7. Do the contrastive analysis and look for the driver, i.e. the differences from one to the other remembering the critical submodalities and the drivers.

8. Do the mapping across, **telling** the client to **make** the submodalities of the liked into the disliked or if this is anything other than food making a dislike into a like.

9. Ask the client to lock in the changes. You could say like a key in a lock.

10. Test using the scores on the doors.

11. Future pace. (do this 3 times)

Tips for making these submodality techniques really successful:

1. Do the process below quickly, as the unconscious mind processes quickly.
2. Make sure that your attention is always on the client, and not just the checklist. Remember to use your sensory acuity.
3. Ask do you have a picture rather than can you make a picture: if you say can you then the answer will be yes but not necessarily the true picture.
4. Use shorthand rather than the words.
5. Get the scores on the doors for you to test against and as a convincer to the client.
6. Check ecology.

Below is an example of when I changed a person's Internal Representation of grapefruit juice (which they liked) into lime juice (which they didn't) as they had been started on new medication and was finding it very difficult to stop drinking it.

VISUAL	Grapefruit	Lime	Result
Black and White or Colour	BW	BW	
Near or Far	N	F	* F
Bright or Dim	B	D	* D
Location	Front upper	Side mid	* Side mid
Size of Picture	B	M	* M
Associated or Dissociated	A	A	
Focused or Defocused	F	F	
Focus-Changing or Steady	C	S	* S
Framed or Panoramic	F	P	* P
Movie or Still	M	M	
Moving fast or slow	S	S	
Amount of Contrast	Lots	A Little	* A Little
3D or Flat	3D	3D	
Angle Viewed	Straight On	Straight On	
# of Picture	1	1	

Can you make a picture?

AUDITORY	******	******	*******
Location	Left	Right	* Right
Direction	Forward	Circular	Circular
Internal or External	E	E	
Loud or Soft	L	S	* S
Fast or Slow	F	F	
High or Low(Pitch)	H	H	
Timbre	C	R	
Pauses	No	No	
Cadence or Rhythm	No	No	
Uniqueness of sound	No	No	

Are there any Sounds that are Important?

215

KINAESTHETIC	******	******	*******
Location	Chest	Throat	* Throat
Size	B	Very B	* Very B
Shape	Round	Square	* Square
Colour	Blue	Green	* Green
Intensity	H	H	
Steady	Yes	No	* No
Still or Moving	S	M	* M
Fast or Slow	-	F	* F
Duration-Short or Long	S	S	
Humidity-Dry or Wet	D	D	
Vibration	Y	Y	
Hot or Cold	H	Warm	* Warm
Pressure-High or Low	Yes-High	N	* N
Texture-Rough or Smooth	R	S	* S
Heavy or Light	H	H	
Internal or External	I	I	

Are there any Feelings that are Important ?

216

<u>Principles of Mapping Across</u>

1. Identify the critical submodalities, as these are the submodalities that make the difference in the meaning of an experience.

2. Take charge. Tell the client to make it colour, make it bright, move it to the left. If you say can you or could you the client will either say yes or no or do it saying yes and then move it back, as you have not given them direct instructions.

3. Ensure the client wants the change. If you get anything less than a congruent yes when asking if the client wants to solve their problem or do the procedure then get really curious into why they want to keep their problem. Get the scores on the doors as to where they are now and where they want to get to. They need to want to do it a 100%. If you get a client who only wants to change 80% then get curious.

4. Same context. Ensure what you are changing is in the same context; writing notes into swimming will most likely not work.

5. Ecology. If it doesn't sit right with you then I would urge you not to do it. With ecology you need to check that there are no negative consequences for the client, the client's friends, family neighbours and society, in fact the planet in general. Also check yourself, if there is any incongruence with you, as this will mirror back to the client and make the technique potentially unsuccessful. Remember congruence, if you don't get a congruent answer then don't do it and investigate why.

6. **One** note here is that with food: do not do a dislike to a like. There is usually a very good reason why you don't like a food for example you are allergic. There is also **a lot** of psychology attached to food and I am sure the Dieticians and the Doctors reading this will have seen patients who have negative memories around certain foods. For example being force fed, abused or bullied.

217

Exercises

All the below exercises involve two people – Person A is the 'client', Person B is the NLPer carrying out the exercise.

Exercise 1
1. Persons B elicits Person A's submodalities of something they like (but wished they didn't) using the eliciting submodalities script.
2. Swap over so that Person A has the opportunity to elicit submodalities.

Exercise 2

1. Now these submodalities have been elicited, Person B thanks Person A and then starts to ask them to bring back the picture and make changes to each submodality one by one, asking whether the change makes it Better, Worse or No Difference. For example if the picture was in black and white tell the client to *make it colour....does that make it better, worse or no difference.*

2. Person B tells Person A to keep the changes that make it better, telling Person A to change back the changes that make it worse or no difference.

3. Person B tells *Person A to lock in all the changes that made it better.*

4. Test: *Person B asks Person A how they feel in reference to the original situation, so if food-How do they feel about that food now?*

5. Future pace: Person B asks Person A *to go "into the future" to the next time they would have eaten that food and ask them how do they feel now? What would they do differently* (this is done as a convincer both to the client and to you to know that the client has had a change).

6. After there has been a successful change, swap places so that Person A has the opportunity to elicit submodalities.

Exercise 3

1. Person B follows the mapping across submodalities script, using the submodalities that have already been elicited in exercises 1 & 2.
2. Person B then asks Person A to think of a food (or something) that you like less (or) only eat very occasionally (or) a dislike that is of a similar consistency". (Remember the closer the food they dislike to the food they like the better).

3. Person B then elicits the submodalities of the food Person A likes less (or) only eats very occasionally (or) dislikes.

4. Person B carries out the contrastive analysis and looks for the driver submodality, i.e. the differences from one to the other remembering the critical submodalities and the driver.

5. Person B carries out the mapping across, **telling** Person A to **make** the submodalities of the liked into the disliked or if this is anything other than food making a dislike into a like.

6. Person B asks Person A to lock in the changes.

7. Test: *Person B asks Person A how they feel in reference to the original situation, so if food-How do they feel about that food now?*

8. Future pace: Person B asks Person A *to go "into the future" to the next time they would have eaten that food and asks them how do they feel now? What would they do differently* (this is done as a convincer both to the client and to you to know that the client has had a change).

9. After there has been a successful change, swap places so that Person A has the opportunity to elicit submodalities.

Summary

Submodalities are how we code, order and give meaning to our experiences (through our five basic senses of visual, auditory, kinaesthetic, olfactory and gustatory) if we have coded it one way then just as easily (by changing the submodalities) we can code it another; changing its order and meaning during the process.

Submodalities are fantastic in goal setting as they bring the goal alive, they make it bigger, brighter and closer to you (if that is what works for you) making it even more compelling and achievable.

Using submodalities not only puts you in charge of your brain, but also enables you to help others be in charge of theirs. Even if not formally used linguistically acknowledging that a person has a big problem hanging over them, accepting it and agreeing with them will respect their model of the world. To tell them that it isn't that bad when they are physically seeing it over their head will cause friction and make the other person feel like you are ignoring them...causing a breakdown in rapport.

Use their words and your sensory acuity and say, "*I appreciate what you mean, I have felt like that, it is like you feel squashed/under the pressure/ weighed down*" (the words they have used) when they agree match them further, saying that "*I have felt literally flattened in the past*" (a play on their words). Going on to say "*Pressure is often a good thing as it makes you aware of what needs to be done*" (checking ecology) when they agree say something like "*It would be nicer if it was below you though*" "*you know, just there*" (pointing in front of you down towards the floor) when they agree with a sigh of relief (sensory acuity) you could say "*let's keep it there then hey.*"

Submodalities is a simple technique that can completely transform a person's problem as long as you act ecologically and respect their model of the world.

References

For more information and deeper understanding into submodalities I recommend you read:

- Andreas, S., Andreas, C. (1987) *Change Your Mind and Keep The Change.* Utah, Real People Press
- Bandler, R. (1985) *Using Your Brain for A Change.* Real People Press
- http://twm.co.nz/hologram.html
- http://www.nlpu.com/Articles/artic25.htm
- Bandler, R., Macdonald, W. (1989) *An Insiders Guide to Submodalities.* Utah, Real People Press

Chapter 9

Anchoring – the confidence switch

"It's lack of faith that makes people afraid of meeting challenges, and I believe in myself"
Muhammad Ali

Concept

This technique is based on the NLP presupposition; People are doing the best they can with the resources they have available. It is just a case of getting hold of the resources when you want them. Anchoring works by creating an association between an emotion and an external trigger. The response can be 'conditioned' or 'automatic'.

Benefits

I invariably cover the skill of anchoring in most classes I teach. Groups usually grasp the principle quickly and after we have run at least three anchors and taken the group through the complete sequence mentioned below, participants find they have been helped into a significant state change. In the longer term, this technique offers people greater confidence and a calm realisation that they can succeed in a challenge (as more often than not they have done something like it before).

> If I was to ask you to go back to a time when you felt really, really happy, a specific time, then go back to that time now......go right back to that time....and step into your body......see what you saw, hear what you heard and really feel those feelings of happiness wash over you. How do you feel now?

- To influence your state
- Silencing that inner critic
- Obtaining confidence in your abilities
- To intensify positive & resourceful experiences
- To diminish unpleasant, unresourceful or stressful experiences
- To put yourself firmly in control of your actions
- To be able to feel at your best when you want to; for example for an interview, presentation, date or meeting.

What is an Anchor?

An anchor is a stimulus that creates a response in you or another person. Therefore the process of anchoring is using a memory (Visual, Auditory, Kinaesthetic, Olfactory or Gustatory) of a positive resource to produce a positive state of mind and change your behaviour. A psychotherapist might anchor positive states like calmness and relaxation in the treatment of phobias or confidence in the treatment of anxiety, such as in public speaking.

> *"Confidence contributes more to conversation than wit"* Francois De La Rochefoucauld.

All memories work on the same principle; Think of your strongest memories; your first day at school, your first kiss or Christmases with your family, the strength and depth of the memory is determined by the intensity of the experience. By using anchoring we can make positive, resourceful memories; bigger, brighter, louder & vibrant to diminish the adverse affects of time and to allow this memory to put us into a truly resourceful state.

Bear in mind that we have both negative and positive anchors. Being called for a meeting, job interview or yearly appraisal might and can bring up negative connotations and memories encouraging you to move away from the task instead of actively embracing it.

One of the things about anchoring is that when people are about to do something that is particularly unpleasant or something they are not looking forward to, they get in 'A' RIGHT state. With anchoring you get into 'THE RIGHT' state, deliberately triggering the positive memory to put you in a more resourceful frame of mind.

Likewise, due to their very nature; we often emphasise negative experiences. NO! Find and learn the lesson of that experience and then make it smaller, duller, quieter, mono-colour so that the emotions applied to it do not negatively affect your performance, because after all there is no failure, only feedback. By learning the positive intent in a negative experience and ignoring the emotions we have attached to it, enables you to use it for the better.

There are examples of anchors all around us, taking the one example of TV advertising. Television commercials mercilessly use a range of Visual, Auditory and Kinaesthetic anchors for their own agendas, marketers try to create an association between the desired product and your wants; Visual examples are obvious such as Lynx's body sprays "Lynx effect", Lynx hungry women that just so happen to be stunningly beautiful. Auditory examples such as the Pentium processor jingle for quality, or the more recent example of Cadbury using Phil Collins "In the air tonight" song to rekindle your love affair with chocolate and for kinaesthetic examples, well there are just too many to list! Herbal Essences 'orgasmic' shampoo, basically every beauty product ever invented, Full stop!

Finally more extreme advertisements such as the THINK! Road safety campaigns use a range of anchors to elicit powerful states within each of us. Do you remember the "80% of people live when hit at 30mph compared to 80% die when hit at 40mph with the little girl? That advert will always stay with me, springing to mind every time I get in the car.

Anchors can be Visual, Auditory, Kinaesthetic, Olfactory or Gustatory, or a combination of these. Anchors are everywhere, all around us, we are responding to them constantly without being aware of what they are.

Here are some examples;

Visual

- The blue flashing lights of a police car or ambulance.
- A photograph of a loved one or a special day.
- Your child sleeping.

Auditory
- Your favourite love song or up-time song.
- Your alarm clock.
- The school bell or church bells.

Kinaesthetic
- A hug or a kiss from a loved one.
- Your favourite jumper.
- An open fire.

Olfactory
- The smell of the aftershave /perfume of a loved one.
- The smell of freshly baked bread.
- The smell of freshly ground coffee.

Gustatory
- Your Favourite meal.
- Ice Cream.
- Chocolate, say no more!

I am sure you can think of some examples in your own life where a certain thing causes you to feel a certain way. Once you have learnt anchoring you will be able to have that for yourself and also help people feel the way they want to.

History

Anchoring is nothing new. In 1902, Dr. Edwin B. Twitmyer submitted a paper to the American Medical Association called "Stimulus Response"; where he tested the knee-jerk reflex of college students by sounding a bell 0.5 seconds before hitting their patellar tendon. Twitmyer found that after several trials, the bell was sufficient enough to elicit the reflex in some of the students. But the American Medical Association were not very interested.

That is until 1927 when Ivan P. Pavlov (who had read Dr. Twitmyer's paper!) submitted a paper to the Russian Medical Society called "Conditioned Reflexes", where he paired a conditioned stimulus (food) that normally elicited a conditioned response (salivation) with an unconscious stimulus (bell ringing).

226

Famously, Dr. Pavlov took a group of dogs and, before each time he fed the dogs, he rang a bell. He repeated this process over and over again. Eventually, the dogs were so conditioned to the sound of the bell that all Pavlov had to do was ring the bell and the dogs would begin to salivate in anticipation of their meal. Over time, the dogs became conditioned to the sound of the bell. The bell became an auditory stimulus, or auditory anchor, for the dogs, which is known as classical conditioning, and anchoring in NLP. Classical conditioning/anchoring requires the pairing of a known stimulus with a new conditioned stimulus to create a conditioned response.

The Science- The Brain and Neurotransmitters

Altogether, the brain consists of some **10 billion neurons**. Each neuron reaches out to one or more other neurons using minute fibres known as axons and dendrites every time we under-take any sort of mental activity.

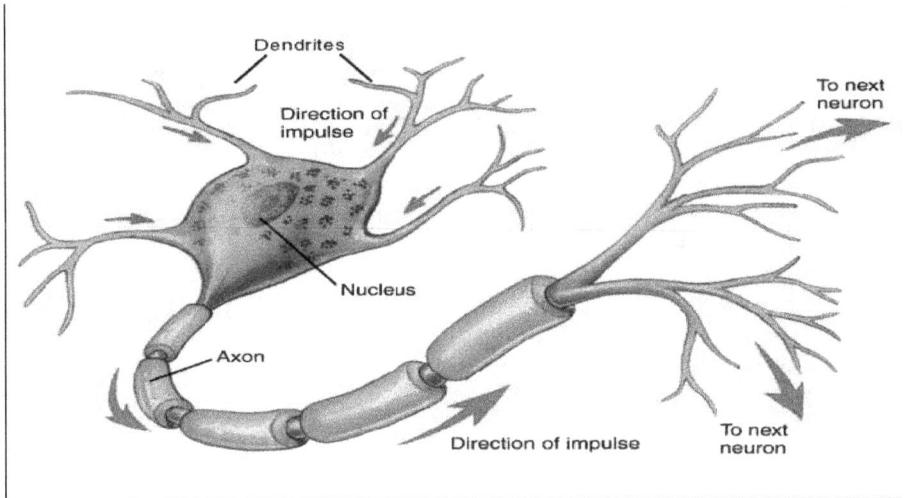

There are recognisable groups of neurons in the brain, but in principle a neuron can communicate with any other brain cell to form a thought or a memory, or to precipitate a course of action. Every time we use our brain to make a memory, certain neurons transmit electrical impulses at lightning speed along their axons.

The impulses are picked up by the dendrites of other cells, forming a type of electrical circuitry in the brain.

Each neuron may have hundreds of dendrites. Between each dendrite and each fibre at the end of the receiving cell's axon is a tiny gap, known as a synapse. In 1911 Santiago Ramon y Cajal, the father of neuro-anatomy, discovered that the number of synapses was the real measure of genius. Importantly, though neurons stop reproducing after infancy, axons, dendrites and synapses keep growing as long as we keep learning.

Damasio (1994) took anchoring and identified that excitation of the neurons causes an electrical current to be sent from the nerve cell, down the axon and into the synapse. A response within the synapse is triggered releasing neurotransmitters that directly affect the nerve receptors. This affects the next neuron, again releasing neurotransmitters, causing a neurological chain from that neural memory.

In 1982 psychoneuroimmunology was developed by Ader and Cohen through demonstrating that the immune system could be conditioned and was directly under the influence of the brain. This was a ground breaking discovery that was inspired by Pavlov's work, where they experimented with mice that had lupus. When giving the mice the cyclophosphamide injection they would give them a saccharine solution to drink, which elicited a specific response in their immune system. Later when the mice were only given the saccharine solution to drink, their immune system reacted as if it had been given the cyclophosphamide.

Pavlov's work has been further developed by Pert (1997) who states that within our bodies we have a 'state dependant recall' which means that a person is more likely to recall positive emotional experiences when in a positive state, just as a negative experience is easily accessible in a negative state. An example of this would be when we are upset or depressed; we always manage to amalgamate every negative thing possible, memory, actions, events, even songs become sad.

Pert (1997) also developed Ader and Cohen's work, whereby she postulated that there were 'molecules of emotion'. Pert states that the endocrine system is flooded with neuropeptides when positive emotions are experienced as the result of neurotransmitter activation. These neuropeptides are throughout the body especially around the spinal column and gut, which is why feelings are experienced both in the body and the brain. An example of this is serotonin which acts as a natural painkiller and dopamine inhibits some of our movements.

In 1986, Deepak Chopra wrote in his book, Quantum Healing, where he explains that "the neurotransmitter touches every single cell in the human body". "The immune system constantly eavesdrops on your internal dialogue, because of the ability of the neurotransmitter to affect every single cell in the body". Memories are therefore stored throughout the body, in the nerve cells that control the muscles.

Anchoring is fundamentally the process of stimulus-response which you already use everyday; your reaction to hearing your favourite song, the taste and smell of your favourite food (or the thought of eating brussels sprouts!) and words like: "holiday", athletes even call it "getting into the zone".

The process of classical conditioning forms the basis of much of learned human behaviour. The understanding of classical conditioning has also been successfully used by the big advertising firms on Madison Avenue. An effective commercial will influence the viewer to create some positive emotions to a product. Initially, the product does not provoke any feeling. The goal is to "train" and condition the viewer's nervous system to make an association between the product and some positive emotion, like feeling powerful, feeling smart, or feeling like an Olympian. In order to understand how classical conditioning works, it is important to be familiar with the basic principles of the process.

Classical conditioning process

The Unconditioned Stimulus

Is one that unconditionally, naturally, and automatically triggers a response. For example, when you smell one of your favourite foods, you may immediately feel very hungry. In this example, the smell of the food is the unconditioned stimulus.

The Unconditioned Response

Is the unlearned response that occurs naturally in response to the unconditioned stimulus. In our example, the feeling of hunger in response to the smell of food is the unconditioned response.

The Conditioned Stimulus

Is a previously neutral stimulus that, after becoming associated with the unconditioned stimulus, eventually comes to trigger a conditioned response. In our earlier example, suppose that when you smelled your favourite food, you also heard the sound of a whistle. While the whistle is unrelated to the smell of the food, if the sound of the whistle was paired multiple times with the smell, the sound would eventually trigger the conditioned response. In this case, the sound of the whistle is the conditioned stimulus.

The Conditioned Response

Is the learned response to the previously neutral stimulus. In our example, the conditioned response would be feeling hungry when you heard the sound of the whistle.

Another example of stimulus response is a song, for example, when you hear Christmas carols, you may begin to feel those feelings of Christmas; or you may have a favourite song that reminds you of a certain person, and when you hear that song, you begin to feel certain feelings. A song, like the sound of a bell, can become a powerful anchor and create certain emotions.

By consciously understanding this concept, we can create these anchors that will assist us to be more resourceful at will, being more successful in sports or in the classroom for example. The next time you are feeling great because you scored the winning point or aced that exam, all you need to do is apply an anchor (whether visual, auditory or kinaesthetic).

While anchoring is a powerful state management tool, it is important to appreciate that anchoring cannot influence external factors; for example linking back to our 100 meter sprint example in "Goals and Outcomes." Anchoring yourself into a positive state of mind will not guarantee you win the race and beat all your fellow contenders, but it will put you in the positive resourceful state to beat your personal best, potentially beating your fellow contestants.

Likewise anchoring in itself is not a phobia cure; it can make you feel confident around spiders but will not take away the fear that was created from the initial event that made you scared (phobic) of spiders.

Principles

If you think back to the NLP communication model, where we discussed how events are filtered through a person's values, beliefs, meta programs, etc and after we have deleted, distorted and generalised the information we end up with our internal representation. Our internal representation leads through our physiology to our internal state, which leads to our behaviour and then to our results. By changing our state we can change our behaviour and therefore our results.

Therefore anchoring is simply about state management and state elicitation, how to use anchors to feel the way you want to feel. Think back to the presuppositions of NLP and how we are in charge of our minds and therefore our results. So if we can be in charge of our state, which we can through anchoring, then we can be in charge of our mind and therefore our results. Which if you think back to Cause and Effect, puts us very much at Cause, which is where I would rather be, wouldn't you?

The technique is further enforced by the NLP presupposition that people have all the resources that they need to make the changes they want, it is just a case of getting hold of the resources when you want them. Anchoring works by creating an association between an emotion and an external trigger, being set up deliberately to give you choice and emotional freedom, so that you can function at your best in any situation, especially situations which in the past made you feel negative or un-resourceful.

How to do it:

State Elicitation Script – to be carried out with two people, one the client & the other the person carrying out the technique; NLPer.

- Can you remember a time when you were totally......(emotion; e.g. confident)......?
- Can you remember a specific time?
- As you go back to that time now ... (pause), go right back to that time, float down into your body and see what you saw, hear what you heard, and really feel the feelings of being totally......(emotion; e.g. confident)......?

Remember the NLPer needs to be in the same state as that being elicited in the client, which through the concepts of rapport you can achieve easily.

<u>The 5 Keys to Anchoring</u>

1) **Intensity** of the experience.-An anchor should be applied when the client is fully associated into the intense state. It is really important to ensure that your client picks a really intense experience and fully associates back into the event.

2) **Timing** of the anchor. (see the application of the anchor diagram below)-As someone thinks about an event, all emotions, be it happiness, calmness, confidence, intensity levels will exponentially rise and then fall again. This will typically last between 5-15 seconds. What you are looking to do is capture the intensity of the emotion at its highest point to make it a very successful anchor.

3) **Uniqueness** of the stimulus-The more unique the stimulus the stronger the anchor will be, touching a knuckle, an ear lobe or perhaps feeling a wedding ring. If you use a body part that comes into contact frequently, for example the palm of your hand, you may find that the anchor is fired every time you pick something up, shake hands or even wash your hands, diminishing its effects and making it useless.

4) **Replicability** of the stimulus-It is really important that you can easily perform your anchor. For example your knee or ankle, yes it's unique but not very practical to perform during a presentation. Squeezing your fingers or ear lobe is easy to replicate without anybody noticing.

5) **Number** of times-Repetition of the stimulus, the number of times the anchor is repeated, i.e. steps 2-6 on the script, the 7 steps to anchoring. The more you stack it the more effective it will be.

I.T.U.R.N is a useful mnemonic to help you remember these 5 keys.

Application of an Anchor

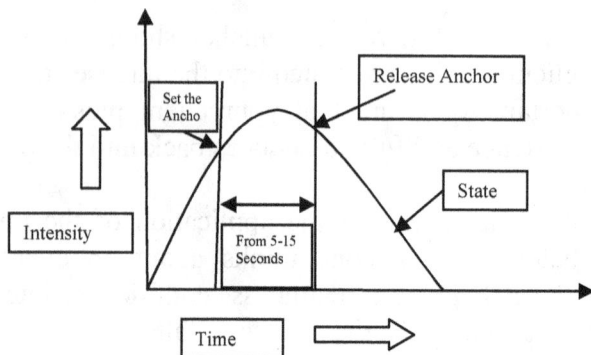

Method 1: The Seven Steps to Resource Anchoring

1) **Pre-frame**; get into rapport and establish the outcome. Explain the process that you and the client are going to go through in brief, so that they know what to expect and what is expected of them. Ask the client what the scores on the doors are (on a scale of 0-10 out of 10 how ....Emotion.... do they feel where 0 is not at all and 10 is totally...... Then ask the client where on a scale of 0-10 they would like to get to).

2) **Recall** a past vivid experience of the state that you are going to elicit (this is very important, the experience has to be the most vivid and intense experience you can imagine) It is important that you as the practitioner are in the same state as that, which you are eliciting. If you sound tired or bored or emotionless when saying remember a past vivid experience when they felt really, really confident, then it is not going to have the same effect as it would if you said remember a past vivid experience when they felt really, really confident.

> "*I never hit a shot, not even in practice, without having a very sharp in-focus picture of it in my head*" Jack Nicklaus

3) **Associate**; make sure the client is fully associated into the state. Ask them "to go back to that event, see what they saw, feel what they felt, and hear what they heard". This is where your sensory acuity comes in, watching the client ensuring they are fully associated. For you would expect to see the client sit/stand tall, head held high. Taking deep thoughtful, assertive breaths. Looking chuffed with themselves, or happy or assertive.

4) **Anchor**; See the graph on Page 234. The anchor needs to be applied when it is at its most intense point, which usually lasts for 5-10 seconds.

5) **Change** state. Ask the client about anything, the weather, where they bought their top, shoes or watch. Something that will make them change completely from the feeling they are currently experiencing in this case; confidence.

6) **Repeat** steps 2 - 5 at least 3-5 times as necessary.

7) **Test** and future pace. What should happen is that when the client fires the anchor you will become aware of them experiencing that state by using your sensory acuity. If not; go back to point 2 and repeat ensuring that the client gets fully associated back into the past vivid event where they experienced that state.

Method 2 Circle of Excellence – for those who are kinaesthetic and like to physically put on a confidence ring.

The "Circle of Excellence" is a tool using an imaginary circle on the floor as a spatial anchor to install new or additional resources relative to a situation where different behaviour or thinking is desired.

Moreover the Circle of Excellence uses a kinaesthetic anchor to activate a "Moment of Excellence", i.e. a moment in which you are at the top, were you feel like superman, and were you are untouchable. Imagine a circle on the floor in front of you: in this circle is a picture of you being in a specific state. This picture of you behaves the way you want to behave when you are in that state. When you walk into this circle, you will be in that specific state.

This method is ideal for planning and troubleshooting, as you can mentally rehearse potential things that could happen, noticing how you deal with it. In the actual event if the things you have rehearsed happen then not only are you aware of them rather than shocked, but you also know ways in which to deal with them. This ensures you stay calm, relaxed and confident rather than flummoxed by them.

The Script

1. Identify the situation or event which is coming up which the client is nervous or anxious about.

2. Associate the client into the event and find out what resources the client would need in order to not feel un-resourceful. Aim for 3 resources, no more than 4, writing down the client's exact words (not short hand, as this can encourage mind reading, if the client says "to feel more confident", write "to feel more confident", not simply "confidence").

3. Build a powerful resource anchor or all of the resources which the client has listed in step 2. Draw an imaginary circle on the floor large enough to step into, when you anchor each state get the client to step into the circle. Follow the resource anchor script and the state elicitation script.

4. Once all of the resources have been sufficiently stacked in the circle; step back into the circle and fire the anchor, this time imagining the future situation/event which you were nervous/anxious about. Imagine the situation/event on a

movie screen in front of you where you can see yourself in the movie (dissociated), with all the resources that you have anchored. Watch the movie, seeing how resourceful you are. When the movie has finished step back out of the circle.

5. Ask the client how that was, what did they see, hear, feel and learn about the event. Are there any other resources that the client would need to know that they are resourceful? If yes anchor these as in position 2, if no go to step 6.

6. Step back into the circle and fire the anchor, start watching the movie again only this time you are looking through your own eyes (associated). See what you would see through your own eyes in the situation/event, hear the sounds and language used, and get in touch with your posture, breathing and emotions when inside the desirable resourceful state. Notice how well the situation is going and how well you are being perceived by others. Take whatever learnings you need to take to know that there is no need to be nervous or anxious about the situation. When the movie has finished step back out of the circle taking all those learnings with you.

7. Test and future pace. When finished get the client to imagine the circle shrinking to the size of a ring or a bracelet, so that whenever they need it they can just drop to the floor and step into it.

Exercises

The exercises below involve two people – Person A is the 'client', Person B is the NLPer carrying out the exercise.
Exercise 1- Visual Calibration

1. Person B gets the scores on the doors now about how Person A feels about an event/situation.
2. Person B carries out the resource anchor state elicitation script outlined in the "seven steps of resource anchoring" above on Person A.
3. Final scores on the doors about how Person A feels about that event/situation now, to serve as a convincer.
4. Swap places so person A gets the opportunity to practice the technique.

Exercise 2

Follow the circle of excellence script.
1. Person B gets the scores on the doors now about how Person A feels about an event/situation.
2. Person B carries out the circle of excellence script state elicitation script outlined in the "the circle of excellence – the script" above on Person A.
3. Person B tests and future paces, getting the final scores on the doors about how Person A feels about that future event/situation now, to serve as a convincer.
4. When finished Person B gets Person A to imagine the circle shrinking to the size of a ring or a bracelet, so that whenever they need it they can just drop it to the floor and step into it.
5. Swap places so person A gets the opportunity to practice the technique.

Summary

Anchoring is the study and application of a simple concept 'memory' and how, through neuro-associative connections, an environmental, physical or mental trigger can stimulate a separate emotional or physical response.

In NLP we use anchoring to elicit resourceful states that are already within us, empowering ourselves and developing our resources.

The circle of excellence enables you to preview a future event from a dissociated position. This dissociated position allows you to notice things you would not have previously. You can then take these findings into an associated position realising that you do have the resources available to you.

In the circle of excellence you will have experienced association (looking through your own eyes) and dissociation (seeing yourself in the event/picture). When we are associated we are in touch with the emotions, just as with dissociation we are detached from the emotions, enabling you to gain a different perspective of the situation as it is no longer clouded by emotions. This enables you to be more objective and see other options of behaviuor that previously you were not aware of.

References

- Bandler, R., Grinder, J. (1979) *Frogs into Princes*. Moab, Utah. Real People Press.
- Henwood, S., Lister, J. (2007) *NLP and Coaching for Healthcare Professionals*. Chichester, John Wiley & Sons, Ltd.
- Boyes, C. (2006) *Need to Know NLP;* Achieve Success with Positive Thinking. London. Harper Collins Publishers.
- Pavlov, I.P. (1927) Conditioned Reflexes. London: Routledge.
- Damasio, A. (1994) Emotion, Reason and the human Brain. New York: Penguin
- Ader, R. Cohen, N. (1982) Behaviourally Conditioned Immunosuppression and Murine Systemic, *Lupus Erthematosus, Science.* 215:1534-1536
- Pert, C. (1997) Molecules of Emotion. Why You Feel the Way You Feel. London: Pocket Books
- Chopra, D. (1989) Quantum Healing. Exploring the Frontiers of Mind/Body Medicine. New York: Bantam Books

Chapter 10

Perceptual Positions – wisdom comes from multiple perspectives.

"Wisdom is your perspective on life, your sense of balance, your understanding of how the various parts and principles apply and relate to each other. It embraces judgment, discernment, and comprehension. It is a gestalt or oneness, and integrated wholeness."
Stephen R. Covey

Concept

This technique is based on the NLP presupposition; Respect the other person's model of the world, by stepping into another's "shoes" you gain insight into their model of the world and a better understanding of their point of view.

> *"No matter how thin you slice it, there are always two sides."*
> Baruch Spinoza

Benefits

Perceptual Positions is a dissociative technique that is used to take the emotional charge out of a situation, enabling you to obtain multiple perspectives and therefore a greater understanding of a situation.

- Gaining new insights into the other person's point of view.
- To see the "Big Picture"
- Enables people to feel resourceful in situations that previously made them feel un-resourceful.
- To give you more flexibility by opening out your thinking.
- To see the effects your own behaviour and communication has on others.
- To resolve relationship/behavioural conflicts.
- To efficiently negotiate (whether upwards or downwards) to the end solution.
- For strategic planning to be able to see things from the point of view of the managers, doctors, patients, relatives and other Trusts.
- Clients will give you insights into how to plan company goals that (1) make sense, (2) are needed and (3) everyone will actively embrace.
- To help people become more creative.
- To dream up solutions, realise how to implement and criticise whether or not they will be successful.

What is it?

Perceptual Positions is the skill of adopting more points of view than your own in an experientially rich and organized way, which allows us to have multiple perspectives in a situation so that we can feel more resourceful, have a greater influence and be more flexible. It represents a profound contribution to the study and practical applications of the human mind.

Essentially, perceptual positions is a dissociative technique that is used to take the emotional charge out of a situation, allowing you to gain greater understanding of the other person's perspective of that certain situation.

> "Do not judge your neighbour until you have walked a mile in his moccasins; do not evaluate until you have, through multiple descriptions, gained news of difference."
> (Turtles All The Way Down, pp200) John Grinder and Judith De Lozier

The principle behind Perceptual Positions is the very simple idea of standing in another person's shoes. In other words, you can't really understand someone until you have experienced what it is like to be in their situation. Which in the NLP Perceptual Positions technique is "second positioning" as you look at it as if (when have we heard these word before?) you were the other person.

The ability to see things from the point of view of another is a key skill in understanding people and is important to the communication process in relationships, negotiations and interviewing, as well as to healthy boundaries and the concept of self.

Consider walking a mile in another man's shoes. That's fundamentally a kinaesthetic and behavioural representation. If you were actually to do it, you'd have many other perceptions as well. What you could and couldn't see, as you walked along in those shoes, would be pretty important. What you heard in the environment around you, in your own head, perhaps words or a song, what people said to you, would also be important to that

243

experience. As will the state of your body while walking, your posture, and internal physical sensations. Add to this what you believe about what you are perceiving, will that affect what you perceive? What other perceptual filters might you have working? How do you interpret what you do perceive? Are you cautious in interpretations, or do you produce conclusions rapidly?

Using NLP Perceptual Positions you can create a very rich sense of another person's experience using only your own memory, imagination and physiology.

History

Perceptual Positions was created by John Grinder; one of the co-founders of NLP and Judith De Lozier, a lady who played a big part in the development of NLP in the 1980's. They published a book called Turtles all the Way Down; Prerequisites to Personal Genius in 1986.

John Grinder and Judith De Lozier studied highly successful people the likes of Milton Erickson (a linguist and hypnotherapist), Virgina Satir (a family therapist) and Fitz Pels (a gestalt therapist), who dealt professionally with conflict resolution and family therapy.

They modelled what it was that made them so successful in their therapy and noticed that they were all using the same, or very similar, thinking strategy without consciously realising it. In family therapy for example they would get each family member to sit in different chairs as the mother, the father and the child, enabling each family member to see the situation from the perspective of the other family members.

They also modelled a man called Gregory Bateson who was an anthropologist, whose interest lay in linguistics, cybernetics, system theories and social sciences. He used a double description and perpetrated that double or triple descriptions are better than one. His belief was that you can develop new choices of responses when you can move between different perceptual positions. If you think back to the presuppositions of NLP, the law of requisite variety the person with the most choices and flexibility has the biggest impact on the system. Their modelling produced what was known initially as the three sphere technique, which was renamed to the Perceptual Positions that we know today.

Robert Dilts (a developer, author, trainer and consultant in NLP) took this theory further forward still, using multiple perceptual positions in his Disney Creativity Strategy. In this work, based on his modelling of Walt Disney, he teaches people to examine a goal from the perception of the Dreamer, the Realist (the one who brings it into reality) and the Critic.

But remember one thing: that perceptual positions is not is a MIND READ, and you may be thinking that you can never really know what the other person is thinking, which on the one hand is true but by putting yourself in their shoes you can at least get a better picture of it, or at least get insights into what they are thinking and how your behaviour is impacting them.

By taking responsibility for our results and changing our internal thoughts of someone enables us to see them in a different light, giving us more flexibility and choice in our actions and communication. If your approach to another person changes, then they will change their approach back. If we are projecting bad vibes out, all we will see is those bad vibes being sent back.

This is further enforced by the communication model which looks at what we delete, distort and generalise through our filters of the external event (the other person). One of our major filters is our values and beliefs. Well, if we hold a negative belief about someone we delete all their positive attributes as it does not conform to our beliefs. By changing our beliefs and our behaviour towards the other person we will see new things that we have not seen before. As we see these we see and respond to the other person differently, especially if we are 50% to blame.

Furthermore look at the NLP presupposition at the start of the chapter; Respect another person's model of the world. By using perceptual positions and "second positioning" someone you can create a very rich sense of that person's experience using only your own memory, imagination and physiology. By respecting their model of the world and gaining insights into it, you will find it is a lot easier and quicker to build rapport.

Combine this with the NLP presupposition; People are doing the best they can with the resources they have available (remembering that a person's behaviour is adaptable to the situation, their present behaviour is simply the best choice available to them at that time with the resources they have available and has a positive intent for them). By "second positioning" someone you can see what their positive intention was and appreciate that the person's behaviour is not who they are, so you can support and assist them to change their behaviour to resolve the situation or to find a solution.

How to do it!

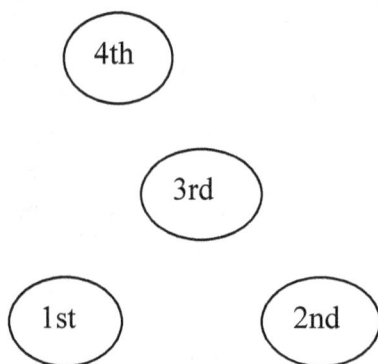

- Position 1 is you as you, fully associated into the problem or situation.
- Position 2 is the other person or persons in the problem or situation.
- Position 3 is a neutral position, someone who is completely independent. The wise old owl if you like.
- Position 4 is a doubly dissociated position, which is used to advise the neutral position in position 3 if the client is struggling to step back from the situation.

Now most people, particularly if they are stuck in a situation or a conflict, are in position 1. They might not have even considered that there might be another point of view. One of the things we do in perceptual positions is to move them to another position to get that other perspective.

Detailed explanation of the different positions;

First position is your own perceptual position as you, yourself, experience it looking at the world through your own eyes-from your point of view and not taking into account anyone else's point of view. In NLP, we would call this a fully associated position. That is, you are fully in it and living it as if it is happening right now.

The second position is the perceptual position of an 'other'. It's the walking, seeing, hearing, feeling, thinking, believing, etc., in another man's shoes. This position can be in direct communication with First Position. This time you are looking through another person's eyes; appreciating the other person's point of view. That is, if you adopted Second Position, and spoke to yourself in First Position, you would address yourself as 'you'.

From third position, you are like an interested, but not directly involved, a neutral observer, someone who is completely independent of the other two. It's a useful position for gathering information and noticing relationship dynamics going on between them. Being dissociated from both and seeing the situation from an outsider's point of view, as an independent observer, this is an objective point of view. In third position, if you were to refer to yourself in first or second position, you'd use third person pronouns such as "he", "she" or "they".

Fourth position is also known as the Meta Mirror, is a doubly dissociated position, which is used if the client is struggling to step back from the situation. From this position you are advising the neutral observer what to say to the 'you' in position one and two. You would notice what the neutral observer is noticing, Using language such as "down there is a wise old owl looking down on X and Y" "What advice would you give the wise old owl to give to X and Y". Basically this position is to get the client further away from the situation so that they can see from the third position.

<u>Example</u>

Ok so let's look at the process. Before we start let's put some names to this rather than practitioner and client and other person. Let's say that the client is Anne, and the other person who she has a problem with, is Bob

1. Firstly you need to mark out three positions either with chairs or just points on the floor.

2. Explain the process to Anne so she knows what to expect.

3. Then what you would do is to ask Anne the nature of the problem and ask her for marks out of 10 for the current level of the problem, which you would explain the mark to be >7 as if it is less than this the client won't have as powerful a result.

4. Then you would ask Anne where she would like to be instead. What would be an appropriate mark out of 10 for the current situation?

5. So let's say Anne wants to move from 8/10 to 3/10 I would check that she is motivated and wants to get from 8 to 3/10 (because if they are not motivated it is probably not worth doing the exercise with them). This exercise will work well if there is a big gap between the present state and desired state, as if there is only a small cap then the results won't be so powerful.

6. When you know that the client is both motivated and that there is a good gap, do an ecology check. So what is ecology anybody know?

Yes, you're right, essentially ecology in NLP deals with the relationships between a client and their natural, social and created environments and how a proposed goal or change might impact on their relationships and environment. It is a frame within which the desired outcome is checked against the consequences on the client's life and mind as systemic processes. It treats the client's relationship with self as a system and their relationship with others as subsystems that interact, so when someone considers a change it is important therefore to take into account the consequences on the system as a whole. To do this you would ask them if there are any negative consequences in resolving the problem and then the 4 ecology questions of:

1. What would happen if you solve this problem?
2. What won't happen if you solve this problem?
3. What would happen if you didn't solve this problem?
4. And finally the big one- What won't happen if you don't solve this problem? Which will identify if there are any secondary gains of the client keeping their problem, which if there are the technique will not be as successful, as at an unconscious level the client won't want to.

Once you know from an ecological perspective that it is appropriate for the client to solve their problem then start the process.

7. Ask Anne to go to position 1 whether standing or sitting

8. Then ask Anne 'What are you thinking, feeling and hearing as you look over there at Bob-keep Anne in this position until she has associated back into the "situation". Once she has associated back into the emotions take her out of position 1, do not leave her in position 1 for longer than necessary.

9. Once you have a few points ask Anne to either stand/or step towards the middle and break state. A break state is when you say anything in order to make the client think of

something else, for example if the fire alarm were to go now you wouldn't be in the same frame of mind as you are now sat listening to me, you would probably be in a state of alarm, worry or even panic. Just by asking the client to stand up or move away from the position they are in could be enough of a break state, or ask them *"how do you take your coffee or do you prefer tea?"* any question that will give you a short answer.

10. Then move them into position 2. In position 2 ask Anne to in effect become Bob. Stand like Bob, think like Bob, what would Bob say. Now the language in this part is very important, always address the client as the other person so in this case it would be: so Bob as you look over there towards Anne what are you thinking, feeling and or hearing. Ensure that you speak to Anne as if she is Bob

11. So Bob as you look over to Anne what are you thinking, what are you thinking? and what are you feeling?

12. And Anne as Bob will say Blah, Blah, and Blah.

13. I certainly think that as the practitioner whilst they are in position 2 to keep on asking what else, what else, anything else Bob, to uncover and elicit further information from Bob's point of view.

14. After the client has finished, when they have been exhausted of all insights (of which you should find several, or at least one very big insight) move the client into the middle, out from position 2 and do another break state.

15. Then take the client into position 3, the completely neutral position. I use the wise old owl in a tree, which for me works really well as it uses the metaphor of the 'one that knows all' and it dissociates the client in distance from the other two positions. Again the language you use is very important. You would say something like: So here you are the wise old owl and over there you can see two people Anne and Bob who have been having some problems. From up here you can see the whole relationship between them

and you can see both sides of the story. Now that you have the different perspectives from those two people down there is there any advice that you want to give them? Wait for the response and ask 'anything else?' Keep on asking 'anything else until the client says no. Then you can ask is there anything that Anne wants to say to Bob, then again 'anything else'. Then ask if there is anything Bob wants to say to Anne and again say 'anything else'. Before you take the client back to position 1 ask is there anything else you need to notice about their situation.

16. Give Anne the chance to reflect then move to position 1 without breaking states getting Anne to take the learnings with her. Then ask Anne 'How's that different now?, take note of the presumption that it is different, that something has changed. Then ask Anne what are the 1, 2, 3 things she is going to do differently in order to take things forward. Then ask Anne what the scores out of 10 are now. If they are 3/10 then great, you're done; if they are 5/10 you could ask Anne if she knows what she needs to do in order to get the problem down to a 3/10. Often you will hear things like yes; I need the 1st and 2nd thing to have happened then I can plan how to further resolve the conflict. If necessary you could take Anne round again starting from the position she would be in if she had done what it was that got them down from an 8/10 – 5/10.

17. Then future pace Anne by asking her what she will be seeing, hearing and feeling in 1 week after she has initiated her plans that she said in position 1. Then take Anne to 3 months into the future: what will she be seeing, hearing and feeling with regards to her relationship with Bob now that the conflict had been resolved? Then do the same for 6 months.

Summary of process

Follow the script. Remember to elicit. Do not advise.

1. Build rapport
2. Check ecology
3. Take the client into position 1
4. Break state
5. Go to position 2 - speak to the client as the other person
6. Break state
7. Go to position 3 - remember elicit, do not advise
8. Return back to position 1
9. Test
10. Future pace

Key Points

1. Have a checker, score out of 10 the situation as it is now (8/10) how would you want it to be (2/10).

2. Always break state in position 1 and 2, otherwise the client will go into the next position with the mind set and emotions of the previous position. It is hard to want to look at the other person's point of view when you are angry or upset with them.

3. Always use the appropriate language to the position that you are in, as this will keep the client in the position and focus them. For example $1^{st}/2^{nd}$ position = I, 3rd = they.

4. When you are doing the exercise make sure you are stood next to the client so that you can use your sensory acuity, be in rapport and support the client. You will be able to use your own body language to direct the focus of the client. By nodding your head or pointing in the direction of the position you are talking about.

5. Always start and finish in position 1, draw the client's attention to how things have changed. 'How's that different now'.

6. Resist the temptation to suggest or advise or coach. Ask open questions. (The client can't argue with their own advice).

7. Just another couple of key points that I want to mention. I have used an example where the client has moved from position 1, to 2, then to 3 equally. This may not always be appropriate, especially if this is a particularly traumatic or emotional situation with the client. After you have explained the process to your client, if you feel there is any resistance to going into position 2 take a note of it. Especially if you find that the client is having real difficulty to even look over to position 2 when they are in position 1, or that after you have broken state, about to go to position 2, if you sense any resistance or fear or uncertainty from the client then don't go to position 2, go straight to position 3 instead. This usually happens if there are a lot of negative emotions attached to the situation. It is more ecological to move the client to position 3 where they are dissociated from the situation. The client will still have really big insights and take the learnings away that they need in order to move forward.

8. If the situation has improved from, say, 8 out of 10 to 5 out of 10, and the client would ideally like it to be 2 out of 10, firstly congratulate the client and ask the client 'How would it get to a 4?' (i.e. reduce incrementally).

9. Look, Listen and Feel- sensory acuity.

10. Now some people doing this exercise will say that you will never really know what the other person is thinking. Which on the one hand is true, but on the other hand if one person in the system changes then the whole system changes. If Anne changes her approach to Bob then he will change his approach back. I have done this technique countless times and in multiple different ways and I have never known it not to work. Even when the situation has not been completely

resolved the client has always got enough insights in order to move the situation forward.

Now I am guessing that some of you are wondering how you can apply this in practice, as there may be certain people that you don't feel would get up and walk around, or that wouldn't want to do this technique. Well this is one of the beauties of perceptual positions. You can do it sitting at a desk by just moving your body, so that you are facing different directions, ensuring that you break state between position 1& 2 and 2 & 3 (ideal if you are in an appraisal or with a senior member of staff who you don't feel would walk around the room); or Perceptual Positions can be done all linguistically in the form of a conversation without you having to tell the other person what you are actually going to do.

An example of when I have used this technique linguistically is when I had a member of staff (Pam) come thumbing into the office.

"I am sick of Mrs. Blogs; it's as if she doesn't trust you." Pam declared "Mr. Blogs is just fine until she comes in." [There was my position 1!]

I smiled and broke up the conversation by asking if she had her break yet – to which she replied she had. [That was my break state.]

I said to Pam; "If you were Mrs Blogs and had just heard Pam say that (I am sick of Mrs Blogs; it's as if she doesn't trust you......Mr Blogs is just fine until she comes in.) what would you be thinking and feeling?" [To move Pam into position 2]

She said "I am NOT! Mrs Blogs." I said "I know you're not (laughing) but imagine you were, what would you be thinking and feeling?"

She said "Well I am just scared for my husband and myself, we have never been apart in 46 years and I feel like I am not needed."

"Anything else" I asked?

"Well I only get to see him for 4 hours a day and miss him terribly; I don't understand all the mumbo jumbo they say which makes me feel even more useless." Pam replied.

"Anything else" I asked.

"I am terrified that I might lose him." To this Pam got upset.

I stood up and said "did you say you had had a break?" [To break state again].

"Yes 1hr ago." Pam replied. From standing I went to sit in the chair at the other side of Pam, grabbing some files as I went past her.

Then I said "I was in the same situation as you are now with Mr Jones' wife a couple of months ago and I said the same things about Mrs Jones. She was scared to lose her husband too I think they had been married 50 years next anniversary." "What advice would you have given me and Mrs Jones to resolve our problem?" [To move Pam into position 3]

She said "Well really it was down to you Donna; you are the professional and at the end of the day you know what was happening with Mr Jones, where as his wife was clueless and terrified."

"So what would you tell me to do?" I replied.

Pam went on to say "Well you need to go through everything with her really, or at least get the Doctor too, then you can explain properly."

"Oh. Anything else?" I said

"Mainly you just needed to show more empathy and maybe take time when she comes in to acknowledge her." Pam concluded.

I then stood back up, to stand facing her, and asked if she could see any similarities between my situation with Mrs Jones and hers with Mrs Blogs. [To move Pam back into position 1]

Pam said "Yes, yes, very clever pass me the notes" and walked out.

255

I gave it 5 minutes then walked passed Mr Blog's bed where Pam and Mrs Blogs both were and they were getting on really well, chatting back and forth instead of the usual higher pitched three word sentences they usually said at each other. With Mrs Blogs smiling and appearing relaxed.

As mentioned earlier, a famous example of this is the Disney Creativity Strategy developed by Robert Dilts in 1998, where instead of looking at resolving conflicts he looked at the processes required in new product development.

Instead of you, the person you are having conflict with and then a 3rd unbiased person, Disney changed and relabelled the positions to; Dreamer, Realist, Critic and a meta position to review the 3 other positions.

In Dreamer anything goes, the team were allowed to fantasise new ideas without any inhibitions. Negativity just is not allowed! No can't, won't, no, unrealistic, but instead a child- like imagination of the final vision, of what if and how.

Then the team went into another room as a Realist, thinking more realistically about the ideas they came up with in "Dreamer" to devise a specific plan of what was needed to put those ideas effectively into action.

Finally the team went into a third room where they constructively criticised the plan, offering positive and constructive criticism as well as finding problems to their ideas.

They moved back and forth, finding problems, dreaming up solutions, planning those solutions, criticising those solutions etc until the idea was finished from concept to completion.

Perceptual Positions Script

1. Rapport/Resourceful states/Outcome

2. Practitioner assists the client in identifying a problem she is experiencing with an individual, or situation she would like more insight into. Check Ecology.

3. Set three chairs or mark out three spaces as shown:

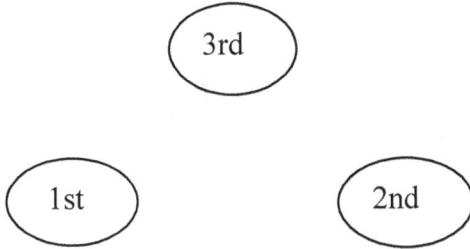

4. The Client sits/stands in 1st position as 'themselves' and describes problem as briefly as possible. Practitioner asks 'what are you thinking, what are you feeling?'

5. The client breaks state and then moves into 2nd position as the 'other person' in the problem relationship/situation. Practitioner refers to the client by the name of the other person, and ensures that the client's language reflects them being the other person in 2nd position. Practitioner asks the other person 'So as you look at the client (1st) what are you thinking, what are you feeling about this?' and keeps asking 'What else' until there is no more useful information from the client (as the other person). Practitioner calibrates physiology, tonality, etc.

6. The client then goes to 3rd position after breaking state, as the observer of the relationship between 'those two people down there/other there' and describes the situation. Practitioner asks open questions to help this 'neutral observer' to gain insights, learnings and suggested action-points. Practitioner calibrates physiology, tonality, etc.

7. Adjust the position of 3rd as required. Possibly dissociate further by standing on a chair, or moving even further away or move into a 4th position, doubly dissociated from the situation.

8. The Client is guided back to first position taking the learnings of all 3 positions. 'So how's that different now?' Check ecology.

9. Repeat Steps 4, 5, 6 and 7 as required. Check ecology.

10. Test and future pace.

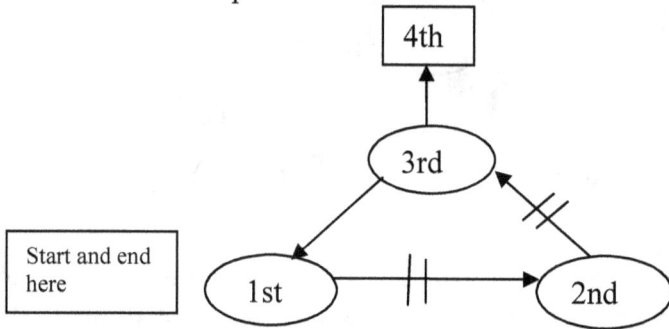

Exercises

The exercises below involve two people – Person A is the 'client', Person B is the NLPer carrying out the exercise.
1. Person B sets out the 3 positions, either chairs for positions 1 and 2 and a mark on the floor for position 3 or mark out 3 positions.
2. Person B follows the perceptual positions script. Remembering to elicit NOT advise.

It will take 15 minutes each way.

Summary

Perceptual Positions is a technique that allows us to have multiple perspectives in any situation, so that you can have greater influence and be even more flexible.

Use your sensory acuity and the power of rapport, watching your client's breathing skin tone, posture etc.

One of the key points I want you to remember is that it is really important to your client that you understand their problem without mind reading it. When your member of staff or client tells you their problem they assume that you understand their problem. One of the ways you can understand their problem is by asking "*How is that a problem?*" Keep on asking until you get some kind of complex equivalent X equals Y or a comparative deletion which will enable you to fully understand their problem and then reframe it.

Being able to see things from another person's perspective enables you to understand what is important to them; knowing that, it helps you to empathise with them and communicate even more effectively as you will be respecting and relating to their values.

References

- De Lozier, J., Grinder, J. (1987) *Turtles All The Way Down*, Prerequisites to Personal Genius. California, Scotts Valley.
- Bostic St Clair & Grinder, Whispering in the Wind 2002 p.247
- Dilts, R. (2000) *Encyclopaedia of NLP*. Http://NLPuniversitypress.com

Chapter 11

Reframing – it's all just a matter of perspective

"There's no such thing as bad weather ...only the wrong clothes"
Billy Connolly

Concept

This technique is based on the NLP presupposition; People have all the resources they need to make the changes they want. People are not un-resourceful, they just experience un-resourceful states.

Benefits

Reframing is one of the most fundamental techniques of NLP that is used to separate intention from behaviour by turning negatives into positives, which is done by changing the meaning of a certain situation into a more useful and positive one.

- It's the basis behind all negotiations.
- Helps you understand and overcome standard responses to objections.
- Helps you and your staff become even more effective in their communication.
- To enable you and your staff see the solution to a problem that previously could not be seen.
- To disassociate emotional ties to a problem enabling it to be overcome.
- To be able to conduct effective meetings that get results.

What is Reframing?

NLP uses frames to provide a context, focus or guidance for our thoughts and actions. They provide focus on our activities and a context in which we can assess our progress, to explore other possibilities and ensure common understanding. The meaning of all experience is dependent upon the frame we put around the experience or the context of the experience.

For example; whispering. Whispering in itself is harmless yet for that patient lying in bed it means that there is something seriously wrong with me, or if two colleagues are whispering and suddenly stop when you walk towards them it means something sinister like they are talking about me, but a group of people behind you whispering in a library is not even given a second thought due to its circumstance and where it is taking place. So as you can see a whisper in and of itself is harmless unless meaning and context is attached to it.

All meaning is context dependant, for example, a scream will have one meaning if it comes from a happy child having just opened the present they always wanted and a different one if the scream is from someone who has just fallen over and hurt their ankle.

There are several different types of frames that in and of themselves will improve your communication and your ability to handle objection which we need to look at before we go into reframing.

a. Backtrack

The backtracking frame is a simple tool, that enables you to check understanding and agreement during and when concluding a meeting. It is accomplished by summarising the information obtained so far, just using the keywords and tonality of those who brought the information forward. Think back to the communication model, we all have our own unique set of filters, explaining how each individual may come to significantly different conclusions. The frame enables you to ensure everyone has the same understanding of what was discussed and decided and helps to maintain a course towards the desired outcome.

b. Relevancy

This is a very effective frame that has to be used appropriately with a good level of rapport. It is basically how is this relevant to the situation or topic? This could be seen as rude and how it should be used is in relation to an agenda. For example in a meeting, if a meeting is going off track as they routinely do, with the rapport that you will have built, agree with what has been said, stating that it is a valid point that we could look at in a lot more detail in the next meeting if that is ok with you as I am not sure how relevant it is to our agreed outcome and I will put it in the meeting ensuring that it is the first thing we deal with at our next meeting as we are running short on time. This will refocus the group and move them on. Every unchecked irrelevancy, takes 20 minutes to get the meeting back on tract.

c.   As If
This is based on acting "as if" a desired state or outcome has already been achieved, or "as if" someone else is giving you information.

When problem solving, you can explore possible solutions by acting "as if" the problem was solved, then looking back at how you solved it.

> Live your dreams now and allow reality to catch up!

If there is a key person who would know the answer, then you may say, Lets act as if Robert was here; "What would he say/suggest"?

The "as if" frame is hugely beneficial in project planning. Acting as if the project has been successfully completed and asking what steps were necessary to successfully complete this project. This approach may also be beneficial if it is necessary to negotiate, during the project planning: 'What would happen if we did this?', 'what would you want if we did this?

d.   Open
"Are there any further questions?" This may be used to clarify situations and gain agreement to move on to the next topic in a meeting, or when doing training or teaching.

e.   Contrast
This is very useful in selling and in putting the problem into reality. Comparing where they are currently to where they will be. For example compare how you feel now to how you will look and feel after completing the training, or in sales; yes you can buy the product marginally cheaper elsewhere, but do they have the same level of customer service?

f. Ecology

This is a very important frame because if a person pursues their outcome without regard for whether or not it is appropriate to their beliefs & values then it will more than likely not have the desired long term effects that the person originally desired, or simply will never be achieved through clashing values. (Think back to the family man/woman who values spending a lot of time with their family when looking at job adverts and career options).

Before you set an outcome at work, think what is the effect on your colleagues and are there any negative consequences of the outcome being met? Same at home, what effects would this change have on your family, friends neighbours, and most importantly on yourself.

g. Agreement

The principle behind the agreement frame is two words '**And**' and '**But**' used to put your opinion across or disagree, yet giving the other person the impression that you completely agree with them. If you are given a particularly un-resourceful or negative statement, instead of getting into an argument with them it is a lot more professional to use this frame.

For example "I agree the government targets have not been achieved **but** I am doing everything I can to correct that; I have had a problem with being short staffed **but** I am dealing with that to ensure the targets are met". Compared to "I agree the government targets have not been achieved '**and**' I am doing everything I can to correct that; I have had a problem with being short staffed **and** I am dealing with that to ensure the targets are met". If I had said **but** straight away the other person has chance to interrupt as you were about to give an excuse, which I have using **and** without negating the fact I agree. By pacing the colleague's experience they will feel listened to, which is very useful in building rapport.

By using the word **and** (think back to influencing language) allows me to get my whole answer across, which takes in the other person's view point before they have chance to interrupt me.

h.   Outcome

An outcome frame provides a focus for what you want to achieve, the ensuing effects and the resources required to achieve it.

Clearly defined outcomes provide you with a context for making decisions and assessing your behaviours. Without appropriately defined outcomes, you can limit your accomplishments, take on too much and become overwhelmed or simply not accomplish your dreams.

i.   Problem Frame

A problem frame is focused on what is wrong or needs to be fixed rather than what is sought after. When setting a problem frame you would ask "What's wrong", "What's not working". These answered would be how the meeting or coaching or discussion would start. A problem frame is the opposite of an outcome frame.

j.   Evidence

This frame looks at what your evidence criteria is for reaching and fulfilling your outcome; how you will know when you have got there (achieved your outcome)? What will you see, hear, feel and/or be experiencing? It is a gauge to see how well you are progressing towards your desired outcome, and to assess whether or not your outcome needs to be changed or modified in any way.

k.   Purpose Frame

Essentially this frame is to question for what purpose somebody wants something, what would it do for them? This is another useful link to the outcome frame; what do you want? What will you get from it? You can then further contrast this using the contrast frame against what they have already or questioning the expense or time required.

Now that you have an idea of the concepts of framing we will look at what reframing is, the history of reframing, the principles of how it works and how to do it.

Reframing is the process whereby an element of communication is presented to transform an individual's perception of the meanings or "<u>frames</u>" attributed to words, phrases and events. By changing the way the event is perceived responses and behaviours will also change. Reframing with language allows you to see the world in a different way and this changes the meaning. Reframing is the basis of jokes, myths, legends, fairy tales and most creative ways of thinking and there are numerous examples in children's literature.

Another meaning or another sense is assigned by reframing a situation or context, thus seeing a situation in another frame. A frame can refer to a belief, what limits our view of the world. If we let this limiting belief go, new conceptions and interpretation possibilities can develop.

Changing the frame of reference is called reframing in NLP. The purpose of reframing is to help a person experience their actions, the impact of their beliefs, etc. from a different perspective (frame) and potentially be more resourceful or have more choice in how they react.

Psychologically to 'Reframe' something means to transform its meaning by putting it into a different framework or context than it has previously been perceived. Frames greatly influence the way that specific experiences and events are interpreted and responded to, because of how they serve to punctuate those experiences and direct attention.

In NLP reframing involves pulling a new mental frame around the content of an experience or situation, expanding our perception of the situation so that it may be more wisely and resourcefully handled.

Your experience of life is primarily affected by the perspective you view it from. Depending on the meaning you give to situations or events will make

> *"I have not failed 700 times, I have not failed once. I have succeeded in proving that those 700 ways will not work. When I have eliminated all the ways that will not work, I will find the way that will work"* Thomas Edison

you feel and behave differently. By positively reframing the experience you give yourself more choices, more choices gives us greater flexibility leading to greater influence in any situation.

Essentially reframing is separating intention from behaviour and its consequence. Reframing is used to take a situation that you have given a negative meaning to and show you how to see that situation differently, so that you can give the situation a more positive meaning. This is done by changing the meaning of a certain situation into a more useful and positive one.

Reframing is going on all around us!

> *"You carry your own weather around with you"* Steven Covey

Here are some examples of reframes you experience everyday; Excerpted from "Live Your Dreams Let Reality Catch Up: NLP and Common Sense for Coaches, Managers and You", roger Ellerton, 2006, pages 116 & 117. Used with permission.

- Politicians are masters at reframing. It seems no matter what happens, they can put a positive spin on it for themselves or a negative spin for their opponents.

- You may be frustrated at your wife for inviting the elderly gentleman next door for supper. Until she points out that if you were in his shoes, then you may find this simple act to be the highlight of your week.

- Consider that old wooden table in the basement that you use as a temporary workbench for sawing wood, nailing things together, etc. Instantly, it is seen differently if some tells you that it is a valuable antique.

- Jokes are reframes - you are guided to think in one frame and then the frame (meaning or context) changes. 'How many psychologists does it take to change a light bulb?' Answer: "Only one, and the light bulb must want to change"!

- Fairy tales often use reframes to help children see different perspectives or consequences - crying wolf.

- An excuse is a reframe that attributes a different meaning or context to your behaviours.
- Or in the healthcare context, all the patients in a hospital will on more than one occasion have been asked by the doctor to get undressed, if this were any other person or out of the hospital setting they would either tell them where to go or call the police. Same as with Nurses, if the Doctor asks you to get undressed when you are at work you would probably feel quite uncomfortable, tell him where to go or get him sued for sexual harassment. Yet if you were at work and suddenly fell ill, this instruction wouldn't faze you.

> *"We're not retreating we're just advancing in another direction"*
> General George S. Patton

- Another example is whispering, which in and of itself is harmless yet for that patient in bed it means that there is something seriously wrong with me. If two colleagues are whispering and suddenly stop when you get close to them it means something sinister like they are talking about me, not that they have finished their conversation. Think of two little toddlers, if they are whispering it's cute or they are up to something. So as you can see a whisper in and of itself is harmless, unless meaning and context is attached to it.

Some more notable examples of reframes are

- During the 1984 campaign, there was considerable concern about Ronald Reagan's age. Speaking during the presidential debate with Walter Mondale, Reagan said I will not make age an issue of this campaign. '*I am not going to exploit, for political purposes, my opponent's youth and inexperience*'. Reagan's age was not an issue for the remainder of the campaign!

- There is a story about Thomas Watson Sr. the first President of IBM. A young worker had made a mistake that lost IBM $1 M in business. She was called in to the President's office and as she walked in said, '*Well, I guess you have called me here to fire me'. 'Fire you?* Mr. Watson replied, *"I just spent $1 M on your education!'*

Changing the frame of an experience can have a major influence on how you perceive, interpret and react to that experience. Being told that you have one hour to complete a task will most likely result in a different emotional state, approach and quality of work than if you are told that you have one week to accomplish the same task.

This illustrates how a change in frame (in this case a timeframe) can have a significant impact on the choices you make. Changing the frame of reference is called reframing in NLP. The purpose of reframing is to help a person experience their actions, the impact of their beliefs, etc. from a different perspective (frame) and potentially be more resourceful or have more choice in how they react.

Any problem no matter how big is part of a solution that we just haven't found yet (that in its self is a reframe); reframing is one way in which we can gain access to the solution, our ability to reframe depends on our ability to think outside the box. The meaning of reframing is to separate intention from behaviour and the consequence itself.

History

Reframing is nothing new, it has been around forever. Think of all the myths and fairy tales that we tell our children! Each are reframes. The ugly duckling that turned out to be a beautiful swan, Rudolf the reindeer with his funny looking nose turned out to be the one who led Santa's sleigh.

Every joke is a reframe; where we take one statement, transform it and give it a different meaning.

As a NLP technique reframing was modelled by Richard Bandler and John Grinder as they observed the work of Milton Erickson ,Fritz Perls and Judith Delozier. Through their modelling they noticed how all 3 were able to take an un-resourceful statement made by their client and notice what else it could mean (content/meaning reframe) or to notice where else that behaviour could be useful (context reframe).

There is a famous story of a father who brought his head-strong daughter to see Milton Erickson. He said to Erickson, '*My daughter doesn't listen to me or her mother. She is always expressing her own opinion"* After the father finished describing his daughter's problem, Erickson replied, 'Now isn't it good that she will be able to stand on her own two feet when she is ready to leave home?' The father sat in stunned silence. That was the extent of the therapy -- the father now saw his daughter's behaviour as a useful resource later in her life.

Reframing is not a way of sticking your head in the sand or a way to pretend that things are ok when they are not, it is simply a way to notice what else a behaviour could mean, the answer to which could potentially provide the insights to solve the problem.

Principles

If you think back to the NLP Communication model and how we delete, distort and generalise the external event and end up with our own internal representation of the external event. Well when we are reframing this is what we are dealing with-the internal representation, this is what we reframe by asking ourselves what else could this behaviour mean, or where else could this behaviour be useful? Which puts us very much at cause wouldn't you say!

Think back to the presuppositions of NLP. There is no such thing as failure only feedback, this is simply a reframe on failing

Think back to the presuppositions of NLP. There is no such thing as un-resourceful people only un-resourceful states - what does this mean?

If you think back to the presuppositions of NLP. The map is not the territory, what does it mean? It means that all meaning is dependent on the context, so it's dependant on the frame we put around it.

In fact, I hope you start to realize that every presupposition is a reframe!

Reframing Belief

Any problem no matter how big or small is part of a solution that we just haven't found yet, which is one of my personal beliefs that I have in my own life, especially when I am working with clients. People do not have problems they just haven't found the solution yet. That in itself is a reframe.

Reframing is one way in which we can gain access to the solution, our ability to reframe depends on our ability to think outside the box. The meaning of reframing is to separate intention from behaviour and the consequence itself.

Content/Meaning Reframes

The content or meaning of a situation is determined by what you choose to focus on. An electrical power failure when you're making Sunday lunch can be one of the most infuriating things imaginable. It could also be an excuse to not have to slave over a hot stove and have an enjoyable meal out, without having to wash up afterwards.

A content reframe is useful for statements such as:

'I get annoyed when my mum stands behind me while I am working.'

Notice how the person has taken the situation and given it a specific meaning -- which may or may not be true - and in so doing limits their resourcefulness and possible courses of action.

To reframe this situation, remember the NLP presupposition 'Every behaviour has a positive intention' and ask questions such as:

- What other meaning could the mum's behaviour have? Or for what purpose does she do it? A possible reframe might be:

'Is it possible that she is proud of you and enjoys watching you achieve? Or 'Maybe she wants to help and does not know how to offer her assistance in any other way?'

- What is the positive value in this behaviour? The positive value could be related to the mum's behaviour (as above) or it could be related to the speaker's behaviour. A possible reframe might be:

'Isn't it great that you have that relationship with your mum, and that you have her around you?

A meaning reframe which is also known as the content reframe is where we ask what else can this behaviour mean other than the negative meaning the client has placed on it.

272

A meaning reframe works best when there is a complex equivalent or cause and effect, X is Y or X means Y or X causes Y or X makes, basically when X happens I respond with Y.

The way to do a meaning reframe is simply to ask yourself, what is it that the client hasn't noticed in order for them to still have their problem, then tell them.

Context Reframe

A context reframe is where the meaning changes into a more useful one when we consider that same behaviour in a different context. According to Leslie Cameron-Bandler in her book; *They lived happily ever after (1978),* contextual reframing is to change a person's negative internal responses to a particular behaviour by realizing the usefulness of the behaviour in some contexts.

Context reframes work by taking the present negative situation/problem and seeing in what other context this behaviour would be useful.

Exaggeration such as: 'I'm too ……. He's too…..bossy.'

In this type of situation, your client has assumed that this type of behaviour has no value. You job is to discover when it is of value by asking yourself the question:

When or where would this behaviour be useful or viewed as a resource?

A possible reframe might be:

'Isn't that a great to know that he/she knows what they want and what they want it to look like?'

Once you have your client more resourceful, you can then assist them to discover behaviours that may be more appropriate in other situations.

An Example would be

- **Rain in the Sahara Desert is useful - Rain on a wedding day is not.**

  The rain itself is neither good nor bad

- **"My brother is too cocky" - "Isn't it good that he will be able to stand up for himself in the future"?**

  His cockiness is not good now but will benefit him in the future.

Another Example would be

- The ward being full of outlying patients is frustrating. A context reframe would be **"Isn't it nice to know that your staff have the skills and ability to look after such a range of medical and surgical patients?"**. What we have done is to change the problem of having outlying patients to the positive fact that the staff have the skills to look after them.

Compared with the meaning reframe of;

- **"If there weren't the outlying patients the ward would not be busy enough for you to keep all of your staff".**

With context reframes you can change the time, the environment, the frame size, the duration, the context it is in whether work, family or home, comparing the different solutions.

<u>Keys to Successful Reframing</u>

When presenting a reframe to another person:

- Make sure you have rapport and their permission to offer it.

- You may believe your reframe is the best ever and yet it may not work for the other person - simply because they have a different model of the world than you do. Remember the NLP presupposition - There is no failure, only feedback - and explore other possible reframes.

- If you present the reframe in the form of a question or a metaphor (story), it is more likely to be considered by your client than if you present it as a statement of fact.

- The main key with any kind of reframe is that it needs to be plausible and delivered congruently.

- I find too many NLP novices saying they 'reframed' someone, when in fact you can't reframe anyone other than yourself. The best you can do is to ask someone to consider your reframe and then he can choose whether or not it reframes his experience.

One thing to remember is that some people get so wrapped up in their problem that they can't see the solution; they can't see the wood for the trees. By reframing them you show them that there are solutions, you separate the behaviour they are experiencing from the intention of it, enabling them to see the solution. This, in other words, is the positive intention.

Examples of Reframing

Example: My colleague is quiet which means she is annoyed with me.

Possible Reframes;

1. Your colleague might just have things on her mind.
2. Has there ever been a time that your colleague has been quiet and she is ok with you?
3. Your friendship must be really good for you to be able to pick up on that. Has there ever been a time that your colleague has been quiet and she is ok with you
4. Are you being quiet with your colleague too? If yes does that mean that you are annoyed with her?
5. I didn't realise that being quiet automatically meant you are annoyed with someone.
6. At least she is not rowing with you.
7. You're lucky: my colleagues usually row with me when they are annoyed with me.

Exercises

Exercise 1 - Reframe the following statements:

1. I am too weak to get out of bed!

    ....
    ....
    ....

2. That patient is always staring at me!

    ....
    ....
    ....

3. The sister is always checking up on me!

    ....
    ....
    ....

4. She never appreciates all the work I do!

    ....
    ....
    ....

5. If they cared about the welfare of the patients they would provide more staff!

    ....
    ....
    ....

Exercise 2

Form a group of up to 4 and throw each other low level problems or issues that you have, or you can use any everyday objections that you receive at work, for the rest of the group to reframe. Take it in turns going around the group at giving a problem. You may find that one person gives you a reframe that is good and doesn't quite shift the problem for you. If this is the case another member of the group does a reframe. If this happens don't worry or think anything negative, remember we all delete, distort and generalise things differently, just because that didn't work for Bob doesn't mean it won't work for Anne.

Summary

Remember the key to reframing is to separate intention from behaviour. It doesn't have to be true just plausible and delivered congruently. If the first one does not land (noticed through using your sensory acuity and rapport skills) then just use another.

One of the key points I want you to remember is that it is really important to your client that you understand their problem without mind reading it. When your member of staff or client tells you their problem they assume that you understand the complexities of it. One of the ways you can understand their problem is by asking *"How is that a problem?"* Keep on asking until you get some kind of complex equivalent X equals Y or a comparative deletion which will enable you to fully understand their problem and then reframe it.

Reframing is a hugely powerful technique that with practice can assist you in managing and handling all objections. It is the ability to notice what the other person hasn't noticed about a situation, by asking them *"Where else would that behaviour be useful?"* or *"What else could that behaviour mean?"* Reframing is looking outside the box, a technique just like perceptual positions that gives you a different perspective of the problem.

References

- Bandler, R., Grindler, J. (1981) *Reframing.* Moab, Utah. Real People Press.
- Bandler, R. (1983) *Reframing: NLP And The Transformation Of Meaning*; Moab, Utah. Real People Press
- Ellerton, R. (2006) *Live Your Dreams... Let Reality Catch Up: NLP and Common Sense for Coaches, Managers and You.* Oxford, UK Trafford Publishings,

Chapter 12

Your Values – what's important to you?

"Conscience is that ability within me that attaches itself to the highest standard I know, then continually reminds me of what that standard demands. If I am in the habit of always holding it in front of me, conscience will always indicate what I should do"
Oswald Chambers

Concept

This technique is based on the NLP presupposition; The mind and the body affect each other. If something is not

> *"A value is a hot button that drives behaviour."* Anon

congruent with your values, your values can inhibit you from carrying out that task, as it is not important to you.

Benefits

- For selling: find out the desired criteria/values of the client/customer/prospect so you can explain your service in terms that most matter to them.
- In management; find out and utilise what values motivate your staff team.
- Your career: define what values are important to you, so you can choose a career that is most aligned to them.
- For Recruitment: HR advertising: write the job advert including the values that are important in order for the successful candidate to fulfil the role, diminishing the risk of employing someone who passed with flying colours at the interview stage, yet ultimately is not suitable for the role or the company not suited to them.
- Relationships: knowing your values to establish what is important to you in a relationship and to improve existing relationships.
- If someone is getting what is important to them out of their career/relationship the more likely they are to enjoy it, be successful and ultimately give as much as they are getting out of it back.

What are Values?

The Oxford English dictionary defines values as *"Principles or standards of behaviour"*. Moreover, they are the primary source of motivation in people's lives, where when met or matched, people feel a sense of satisfaction, harmony or rapport, but when values are not met, people often feel dissatisfied, incongruent or violated. Values are a powerful perceptual filter that we use to assess situations to basically gauge what we do and don't desire.

If you were asked to specify what values are important to the organisation you work for, would you be able to verbalise it? How about in your own team or department, what is your team or department striving towards? If you don't know the answer to those questions, maybe you don't know where you are going – and if you don't know where you are going, how will you know when you get there? More importantly how will you know what part you have to play?

Most people are not aware of their specific values and are not aware that their values affect everything that they do. Values are the things that are important to us. They are essentially a deep, unconscious belief system about what's important and what's good or bad to us. It is our values that will determine what we pay attention to. It is important to understand your value system so that you can identify what motivates you and what will help you to move forward.

During the course of this book we have touched on beliefs, especially when we have described them as a filter in the communication model, beliefs are convictions we hold to be true. They are statements about our internal representations or generalisations on how we believe the world is, emotionally held thoughts about ourselves, others (person, company or thing) and situations. They are not based on fact, but on our perception of events at the time they were formed. They can either be empowering (for example, I have the ability to influence my department or my team) or dis-empowering (for example, I just come into work to do a job and earn some money, or nobody listens to me so what is the point?).

Fundamentally it is important to realise beliefs are attached or related to a certain value.

Beliefs determine whether or not we believe we can do something. This in turn will determine the interpretation of everything we see, hear and feel, which in turn will determine our behaviour and finally our actual outcomes. Our beliefs are generally formed by the time we are seven years old. We take on board opinions from influential people and then treat them as if they were facts.

Our beliefs often act as a self fulfilling prophecy. By limiting our beliefs, we limit our performance – not only ours individually, but as an organisation. If we believe that the service we offer is as good as it can get, then it will not improve. If we believe we can do things even better, we free up potential to make the changes required to make things even better for clients (and staff alike).

Think back to the presupposition; People have all the resources they need to achieve the changes they want. By being aware of our values and what is important to us provides the motivation to make those changes. Believing this would free staff to develop and grow through questioning and mentoring, rather than the manager simply always telling them what to do.

There are two types of values elicitation, the formal and informal. The formal way we shall go into more detail throughout this chapter as this is the full process of the NLP technique and requires the person you are using the technique on to: a) give their permission to you doing it, b) want to understand and maybe change their values, c) provide truer and more detailed information and d) is a more in depth process. The informal process on the other hand does not require the other person's permission as you are simply trying to better understand what's important to them; it is a quick and easy technique to use as it is simply dropping an open question into a conversation.

For example; simply asking an artfully vague question such as *"I'm curious, what is important to you about your career?"* will result in a list of the person's values. This is in no means as in depth as a formal elicitation but it will provide you insights into the person's character and career aspirations.

How about from a sales perspective; *"What do you look for in a (product) or (service) i.e. a business consultancy firm?"* Or when going for a job interview, asking such questions as *"What do you look for from a customer/employee?"* will enable the employer to honestly tell you what they want. If the answer "matches" or is right for you, you can give them references to how you fit that model.

If personal development is important to you, I am sure you can find examples of when you have become bored within a job/hobby/activity. This is usually because the opportunities to develop have been exhausted and are no longer there.

Likewise respect, if respect is something that is important to you within a relationship and your partner/boss/friend is always dismissing your opinion, this relationship will not be one that you hold dear/close to you as there will always be negative emotions and behaviours attached to it.

Corporate governance has progressed since the last century with people having a lot more rights than they used to. It is not simply the case that "you get paid to go to work, so work!" a phrase that has been introduced in the 21st century relates to your "Work/life balance". If having a good Work/life balance is something that is important to you; then a potential promotion, meaning you are working twenty more hours a week may cause conflict within you.

History

Although controversial, the history of values stems from the work of Friedrich Nietzsche, a philosopher, who literally questioned everything that was going on around him in his lifetime (1844-1900). Starting from his works *The will to power* which was an attempt at a revaluation of all values, which appears to stem from his contempt for Christianity and the entirety of the moral system that flowed from it. This work seems to have been abandoned as he used draft passages to comprise other books, such as the *Twilight of the idols* and *The antichrist* (both written in 1888) as he slipped further into sickness, where a mental breakdown led to his death in 1900.

Work on values continued through psychotherapy and, in particular; understanding personality. Work done by Morris Massey in 1979 looks at the different developmental phases that an individual experiences in growth of personality in relation to their values. His work on imprinting refers back to Instinctive Behaviour (1935) done by Konrad Lorenz, which was further developed by John Bowlby who formulated the attachment theory in 1969.

Robert Dilts continued this psychoanalytic perspective, taking into account Sigmund Freud's theory on Transference, which seems to point to imprint- like phenomena. He proposed that since imprinting has a neurological component, it is possible to access these biochemical states to literally re-imprint new states, thereby creating new neurological choice and behaviour. Further development of values can be seen throughout Dilts' work in reference to Logical Levels.

Massey's work has also influenced the development of values according to generations. He suggests that if a value system of each generational group is examined, it is possible to gain greater insight into their beliefs and behaviours.

In 1943 Maslow identified processes whereby an individual's aim in life is self actualisation. Graves took this work further in 1965 and identified that values develop in response to the environmental conditions that a person is subject to. He postulated that there were 9 levels of value development, each one needing to be worked through and resolved before the individual could evolve to the next level.

This led to the work of Spiral Dynamics in 1996 by Doctors Don Beck and Chris Cowan. Massey, Graves et al and Maslow all provide a perspective on how values are developed and become part of the main identity of an individual.

I would like to stress that understanding Values is not a way to manipulate and control another person's thoughts or decision processes, it is simply a way of understanding their hierarchy of values to enable you to get a better understanding of what makes them tick and what they hold dear.

Now I realise that there is a potential to question the honesty of someone else's responses or the effectiveness of values, and I appreciate where some people may find it hard to transpose them into a business or sales environment, as this is what I felt when I first learnt about understanding values. When you have elicited your own values within a given context you will realise just how important and beneficial they are due to the amount of insights they give you about yourself.

This is more of the formal value elicitation process and how you can gain insights into what is important to yourself and other people within a one to one coaching or career/personal development session, as the person that is there will want to be honest and tell you their values for their own benefit and own insights. Where-as asking this in a job interview/business prospect setting, where you only briefly ask what is important rather than the full elicitation, will make them simply give the answer they think you want. Fundamentally, use your common sense!

How? Think back to sensory acuity, listening to another person's language and watching their body language highlights when someone is talking about their values. Your values are like "hot buttons" - when someone is talking about what is important to them they become passionate and will often over emphasise to put their point across.

Likewise using the perceptual positions technique you learnt in chapter 10, knowing somebody's values allows you to second position them and gain insights into their model of the world and how they could view you (what you are saying, what you represent i.e. a service, business or company image).

More importantly remember the communication model we covered all the way back in chapter 1?! Values are one of your main filters, they determine what you delete, distort and generalise. A statement I think you will appreciate; if something, or if a topic of conversation is not important to you, you're not going to pay much attention; likewise if a task is not important to you, you're not going to be very motivated in completing it.

Some of you reading that may think, well that's obvious! Well the fact is, it is. The key is to look to truly understanding and appreciate another person's values, which enables us to describe the topic/task to appeal to them. For example setting a task as mundane as carrying out a risk assessment is not exactly going to get a junior colleague "fired up" to complete it, however if you take the time to find out what their values are, in this instance let's say personal development is important to them, then explaining that being able to carry out risk assessments is a fundamental requirement for anyone with senior responsibility.

A simple example would be walking down the street with a friend or partner of the opposite sex, have you found it weird how one will notice something which you were completely oblivious to? You would have found from the logical level exercise (in language subchapter 7.4) how your values imprint in your capabilities, behaviour and environment around you and also how they are an example of your identity.

The presupposition; Pay attention to behaviour, reinforces this theory as it explains why people react the way they do. What you have labelled as your husband/colleague/client "overreacting" to a situation is simply the correct reaction for them, as you/the situation has directly conflicted one of their values. Actions speak louder than words, behaviour is the truest and best quality information people can give to you.

Values - Organisation of Hierarchy

All values are interlinked and they form a natural hierarchy. They are what are important to us, and from each value we form beliefs which will verify that value and govern our behaviour.

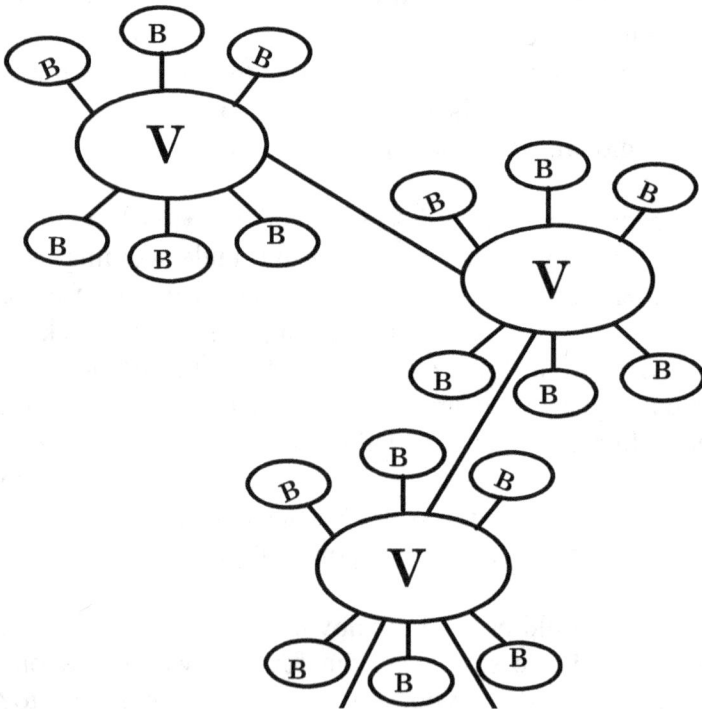

<u>Sources of Values</u>

Values are built from our life experiences: what we learned at home, in school, at work, and anywhere we have spent time. Politics, religion and culture can also affect our values. Those closest to us often influence our values, whether they try to do so or not. Parents and immediate family members are often the first influence on our values and as we grow older; friends, peers, teachers, etc. also start to influence them, your main sources are indicted below;

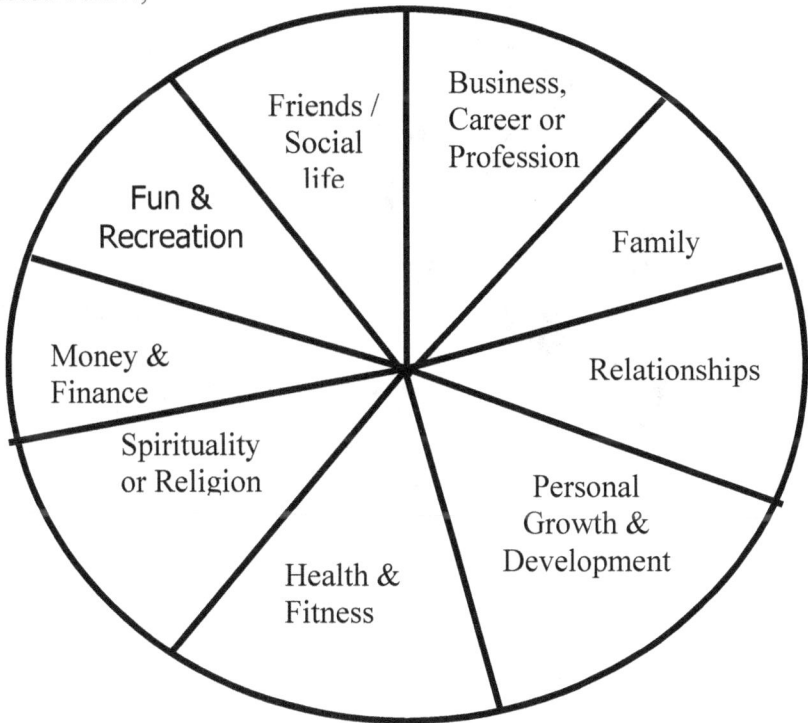

For each of these sections we will have a set of values, all of which will be different in some way. When eliciting values it is important to do it in a specific context, as your values in Fun and Recreation are going to be different to those in Money and Finance. You may find that there are values that run throughout each context; these values can be seen as life values.

The way to use this wheel is;
   a) Elicit your values in each context (segment);
   b) Then mark on a scale of 0 to ten, how much your current, Job, Health & fitness, Relationship meets your values, 10 being completely aligned with your values and 0 being not at all/ not being fulfilled.

For example:

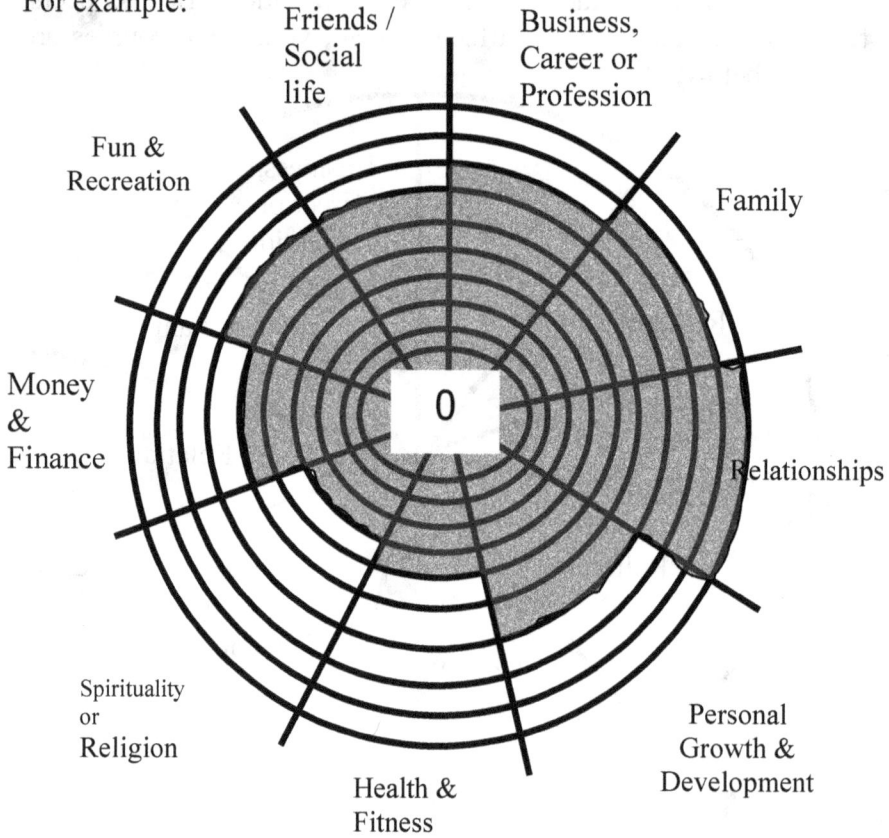

Developmental Periods for Values

As I have just touched upon, we have different influences on our values as we grow older. Sociologist Morris Massey is referenced as providing the theoretical underpinning for personality in "the people puzzle"; where he identified that people are shaped by the events around them and classifies three different developmental phases that an individual experiences in the growth of their personality. His work has been subsequently added to in the form of a later fourth phase by James Williams (psychologist, philosopher and trained as a medical doctor) which takes into consideration that you are forming new or clarifying old values in relation to your work life. Ultimately implying that we test our values in a business context to evaluate and reassess whether their priorities have changed or more drastically whether they still apply.

Moreover think of the changes that occur between the ages of 21-35, what other changes could be occurring during those years? you could still be in education until this later fourth stage and it is not until you commence serious employment that you start to test these values and realise what is important in the real world. During this fourth stage it can be argued that you have finally grown up, with more responsibility and with monumental moments taking place; getting married, buying your first house, starting a family, which cause you to evaluate and reassess your value as your priorities change.

To backtrack, Morris Massey states that young people go through a series of developmental periods in creation of their core values. These developmental periods are also impacted by the significant emotional events in our lives and many of those take place at the transitions on the next page;

Transitions

(0 – 7)   **Imprint Period** – This is the time of laying down our filters. We get our basic programming at this time. This is generally all done at the unconscious level. We are like a sponge, absorbing everything that goes on around us.

(7 – 14)   **Modelling Period** – This is the time when we purposely and unknowingly model basic behaviour. We start by modelling the adults in our life (parents, grandparents etc.) Before age 8, we have little awareness of any differences between ourselves and others. We become aware of the behaviour of friends and family and model them. At that point, we begin to develop heroes (either real or fictional) and then pick up the values of the people we have made into heroes. Our major values on/about life are picked up in this developmental period.

> *"My Grandfather once told me that there were two kinds of people: those who do the work and those who take the credit. He told me to try and be in the first group; there was much less competition."* Indira Gandhi

(14 – 21)   **Socialisation Period** –We start to develop social and relationship values, most of which will be used throughout the rest of our lives. At this stage our values are nearly formed; "you become your own person", you become more independent with a sense of what is important to you. Once formed it takes a significantly emotional experience to change our core values.

> *"Be yourself; everyone else is already taken"* Oscar Wilde

(21 – 35)   **Business Persona (James Williams)** – Our business values take form in this time frame. Up until this process you could still have been in education and now is the time you are in serious employment, testing these values for the first time, and realising what is important in the real world.

Major value groups based on generations (as per Lisa Wake 2008)

It is also important to take into account the (major) events that were taking place as you were growing up and the impact they could have in shaping your values. For example:

1910's - Death of Edward VII, George V comes to throne. British Empire at its height. First World War, Lord Kitchener and the 'Pals' Battalions. Mud trenches, gas shells and rise of aeroplane. Defeat of Germany, break up of Austro-Hungarian Empire. Remembrance Day, the Spanish flu pandemic.

1920's - League of Nations and reparations against Germany. Rise of America and emigration across the Atlantic. Scheduled flights to the 4 corners of the Empire. The Charleston and Flapper Girls, music hall and silent films. Prohibition in America and the Stock Market crash.

1930's - Poverty and despair, start of social awareness to modernise living conditions. America's New Deal, building the Hoover Dam and The Jarrow March. Rise of Hitler and Nazism. Annexing territory and march towards war. Plight of Jews, Spanish Civil War. Edward and Mrs Simpson, Italy invades Abyssinia, Munich crisis and war is declared.

1940's - Churchill steps forward, fall of France and Battle of Britain. Rationing, the Blitz, GI's and 'make do and mend'. Evacuation and separation, collecting shrapnel, keeping an eye out for Fifth Columnists. V for Victory, street parties, new start, NHS and Nationalisation of the railways. Berlin air lift and the start of the Cold War. End of the war – baby booms.

1950's - End of sweet rationing, death of George VI and coronation of Elizabeth. Television for some, homes for others. Rise of affluence. Rock and Roll, Teddy Boys, and

Elvis, the Goon Show, Hancock's Half Hour. Yuri Gagarin and the space race, Suez Canal, jet liners to America and the crash that killed the Busby Babes.

1960's - More affluence and cars, JFK and the Cuban Missile crisis, Berlin Wall and spies, Profumo scandal, satire and swearing on TV. Moonwalk, England win World cup, Flower Power, love and peace, Vietnam war, Summer of love, Beeching closed Railways

1970's - Watergate scandal, use of terrorism, PLO, Black September and the Olympic hostages. Glam rock, punk rock and flares, unions and strikes, 3 day week, power cuts, IMF and the winter of discontent. The IRA, Balcombe Street Siege, the Birmingham 6 and the death of Airey Neave, Decimalization, Margaret Thatcher.

1980's - Unemployment, factories closing and the miners strike. Yuppies and mobile phones. New Age Romantics and AIDS. Computers and Walkmans, Falklands War, Cleveland child abuse enquiries, Yorkshire Ripper.

1990's - Affluence, house price rises and negative equity. Sleaze and Tony Blair, Globalisation, Diana's death, Gulf War.

What effect do you think these events had on your values as you grew up? People always like to categorise one another, labelling someone as "Traditional", "Modern", "Rebellious", "New Age", "Old School", "Revolutionary", "Entrepreneurial", "Pioneering", etc. It can be argued that these events have a strong impact on our values, with us even adopting one of these labels respective to what we have lived through.

How to do it!

Example 1: Values elicitation script;

This is the standard script for the formal values elicitation;

1. The person wishes to work on their values.
2. You establish rapport and the context in which they would like their values eliciting (family, work etc.)
3. Ask them: *"What's important to you about _____?"* or
   "What do you want from a ___?" or
   "What do you look for from/in a _____?"

(Write down the client's Values in their <u>own words</u> in the form of a list, ensuring they are the values the person has <u>now</u>).

4. Simply repeat; *"what else?"* after pauses - normally ask at least 3 times.

N.B If the word/'Value' they give you is of a too low level *(e.g. "Having a tidy desk",* ask: *"What's important to you about having a tidy desk?"*

5. Elicit their Motivation Strategy by asking:

   a) *"Can you remember/think of a specific time when you were really motivated in the context of _____?"*
   (if they answer yes go to point b, if no go to point 6)
   b) *As you remember that time, what was it that caused you to feel really motivated?"* (their answer will be in the form of a story, pick up on key words that will represent values, e.g. worked well as a team,
   c) To which you would ask; *"is working well as a team important to you"* (if the answer is yes add it to the list, if no, don't)

295

6. Elicit the Threshold Values: STAY/GO loop

Show the client the list of values you have so far;

a) Ask the client: "*If all of these values were present, what would have to happen to make you want to leave?*" The answer they give you, add to the list, if they don't move onto 7.

b) Ask the client: "*All these values being present, plus (Value(s) just mentioned in A above) what would have to happen such that would make you stay?*" the answer they give you add to the list, if there is nothing go to 7.

c) Ask the client: "*All these values being present, plus (Value(s) just mentioned in a and b above) what would have to happen such that would make you leave?*" The answer they give you; add to the list, if there is nothing go to 7.

d) Continue with steps a – c until the client repeats words.

7. Hierarchy of importance:

Now ask the client to "*Number the values according to their importance to you*"

- Of these values, "*which is the most important to you*? ("*If you could only have one of these values, which would it be?*")
- "*Assuming you have (value chosen), if you could have one more, which would it be?*"
- Rewrite the values in numerical order/hierarchical structure of importance.

Example 2: You can use your values to make choices, once you have elicited your values within the areas you are trying to make a decision.

1.To compare, say, 3 job offers.
- a.　Elicit and hierarchy Values (say top 5 or 8).
- b.　Consider to what extent each Value or Criterion will be satisfied by each of the options.
- c.　Mark each of them either 'Yes' or 'No', based on whether the Value will be satisfied, or give them marks out of 10 to denote the extent that each Value will be satisfied.
- d.　Remember that the higher the Value, the more weight needs to be placed on it i.e. Value number 1 is more important than Value number 5.

Option = Value	A		B		C	
1 – Job Enjoyment	Y	8	Y	8	N	3
2 – Salary	Y	9	Y	9	N	2
3 – Potential career potential	N	3	Y	7	Y	8
4 – Distance away from home	N	2	Y	10	Y	7
5 – Hours a week	N	2	N	2	N	1

2. To choose what you're looking for from a whole list of Values, e.g. in a partner, rank each Value A, B or C, where
- A is absolutely essential
- B is nice to have but not essential
- C is icing on the cake.

Keep your eyes open for someone with all the A's! This helps you focus on what's really important and avoids wasting your and other people's time.

Exercises

Exercise 1

1. This exercise involves two people – Person A is the 'client', Person B is the NLPer carrying out the exercise.
2. Follow the values elicitation script above, points 1 -7.
3. Change places so Person A has the opportunity to try the technique.

Exercise 2

1. This exercise involves two people – Person A is the 'client', Person B is the NLPer carrying out the exercise.
2. Person A chooses a situation that has multiple options, for example employment, and the three job adverts they are interested in applying for.
3. Person B helps Person A gauge how each option (job advert) fulfils each value they have elicited to be important to them in the previous exercise.
4. Swap places so that each person has the opportunity to try the technique.

Summary

Values are a huge subject area and one could argue it is not right to simply have one chapter on its contents. We have simply focussed on one of the NLP techniques for values and given the relative theory and history around it.

Values are our mental filters, they affect every representation of what we make of the world, moment by moment, consequently they affect all the outcomes that we set for ourselves and the decisions we make. In short they steer our lives completely motivating our actions, determining what we achieve, what we perceive ourselves and how we develop as individuals.

To have your values elicited gives you great insight into what is truly important to you, so that you can evaluate and align the different areas of your life to your values to have all parts of you working towards the same goals.

References

- The origins of attachment theory: John Bowlby and Mary Ainsworth BRETHERTON - Developmental psychology, 1992
- Value Theory" article in the *Stanford Encyclopedia of Philosophy*
- Hartman (1967). *The Structure of Value.*
- Rescher, Nicholas (2005). *Value Matters: Studies in Axiology.* Frankfurt: Ontos Verlag.

299

Chapter 14

Concluding Thoughts

"Taking responsibility for your own results"

Concept

The principal theme throughout this book and all the techniques taught relates to the presupposition; *the mind and body affect each other.* What you believe about yourself, another person or a situation will affect how you perceive things to be. The neurological system regulates how the body functions, language determines how individuals interface and communicate with other people and a person's programming determines the kinds of models of the world they create. All the techniques within this book give you ways to gain insight into your own behaviour, other people's behaviour and your impact upon them, enabling you to act from a more resourceful state, communicate and relate to other people even more effectively, ensuring you get the results that you want. Remember you are responsible for your own results; if you are not getting the results you want then change what you are doing.

Moreover this book is about self development and self empowerment. All the techniques can be used by you on your personal development, enhancing your personal skills; your communication, management and leadership skills. They can be used both personally and professionally, enhancing your relationships at work, allowing you to understand, predict and influence your colleague's behaviour; using values is an example of how. Also by using these techniques you can support your colleagues with their problems, assisting them to gain their own insights into how to resolve their problem.

> *"Everything is practice"*
> Pele

The purpose of Psychobabble is to provide you with a straight-forward, plain English guide to the benefits of NLP at Diploma level. Cutting out all the mumbo jumbo so that you can clearly understand the technique, it's defining principles, the relevant history and science into what makes these techniques work and showing the practical day to day benefits of NLP and how you would use each NLP technique in the real world. The practical exercises to each technique will enable you to practice and learn the technique, as it is not in the reading but in the doing that brings about change.

NLP consistently asks the key question *"What do you want?"* in a personal context. *"What do you want out of life?"* which was one of the big questions asked to you in the goals and well formed outcomes chapter. People tend to focus more easily on the things they don't want (i.e. their problems) which can lead to a great deal of analysis but little actual change. One of the keys to success is to have clear outcomes in all areas of your life. People that are not happy in their professional life, are often not sure what they really want in a career. If your career was an area you worked on in the values section, or in well formed outcomes you will have realised; how just becoming clear on what you want from your work is essential, if that work is going to be fulfilling for you. Equally, within an organisation, having clear outcomes for yourself, your team and the organisation is vital. NLP has been used to great benefit by large and small organisations to make sure that everyone has shared goals and is moving (and pulling!) in the same direction.

Our ability to communicate effectively with others and understand how they are thinking is paramount in today's society. The limits of your language are the limits of your world. Language as you now know is hugely powerful; just by being aware of the impact of your communication will improve your responses immediately. By being able to create and maintain rapport, with anyone at anytime and to notice through using your sensory acuity whether the other person understands, makes your communication congruent. Many organisations pay lip service to the importance of communication skills. Yet, if we think of highly successful colleagues and managers, is it not true that their ability to communicate, influence and motivate is one of the keys to their success?

Through submodalities you learnt how to programme your brain. I am sure that you will appreciate, that it is all too easy to feel the 'victim' of events outside of our control. Taking on board the presuppositions of NLP and Cause and Effect allows you to take more control of your thinking, feeling and emotional processes so that you are in the driving seat. Through understanding how your mind works, you will be able to take more control of your thoughts, emotions and behaviours.

Our values are one of the gateways to our behaviour, as we learnt from the foundations of NLP, subjective experience and logical levels chapters. Our beliefs and values are often 'unconscious' so we are not always aware of the important role they play. By discovering your values within your 'Wheel of life' you can identify your values and beliefs. This represents some of the most powerful tools for personal change available. We all have aspects of our life that we wish to improve. You will be in a better position to change unwanted feelings and behaviours when you understand more of how you, as a human being, work.

NLP seamlessly fits into existing models of change as the majority of the techniques have been modelled on psychologists, hypnotherapists, family therapists and gestalt therapists, adding in a set of practical tools and techniques for quick change management. These can be used in combination with your existing professional background to help people achieve their goals and master their thinking and feeling.

I hope that you have enjoyed this book and found it not only useful but easy to digest and apply. I want to leave you with a few thoughts; What changes do you want to see in your life both personally and professionally? And, What is the difference that would make the difference to you?

1. One day a traveller was walking along a road on his journey from one village to another. As he walked he noticed a monk tending the ground in the fields beside the road. The monk said *"Good day"* to the traveller, and the traveller nodded to the monk. The traveller then turned to the monk and said *"Excuse me, do you mind if I ask you a question?"*.

"Not at all," replied the monk.

"I am travelling from the village in the mountains to the village in the valley and I was wondering if you knew what it is like in the village in the valley?"

"Tell me," said the monk, *"What was your experience of the village in the mountains?"*

"Dreadful," replied the traveller, *"to be honest I am glad to be away from there. I found the people most unwelcoming. When I first arrived I was greeted coldly. I was never made to feel part of the village no matter how hard I tried. The villagers keep very much to themselves, they don't take kindly to strangers. So tell me, what can I expect in the village in the valley?"*

"I am sorry to tell you," said the monk, *"but I think your experience will be much the same there"*. The traveller hung his head despondently and walked on.

A while later another traveller was journeying down the same road and he also came upon the monk.
"I'm going to the village in the valley," said the second traveller, *"Do you know what it is like?"*
"I do," replied the monk *"But first tell me - where have you come from?"*

"I've come from the village in the mountains."

"And how was that?"

"It was a wonderful experience. I would have stayed if I could but I am committed to travelling on. I felt as though I was a member of the family in the village. The elders gave me much advice, the

children laughed and joked with me and people were generally kind and generous. I am sad to have left there. It will always hold special memories for me. And what of the village in the valley?" he asked again.

"I think you will find it much the same" replied the monk, *"Good day to you".*

"Good day and thank you," the traveller replied, smiled, and journeyed on.

---

2.   A man was walking along a beach, reflecting on his life. He had always wanted to make a difference, but no matter how hard he tried, he wound up feeling as though he was spitting in the wind.

Suddenly, the man heard a "crunch" beneath his feet, as he looked down he noticed he had stepped on a star fish, one of thousands that were being washed up by the tide.

The man continued walking, thinking to himself about how cruel the world was, washing up those little starfish, who were now left in the sun to shrivel and die.

As he continued along the beach he came across an old woman standing by the ocean's edge, throwing the stranded star fish back into the sea.

Struck by the futility of the task he asked the woman what she was doing, she said that she had always wanted to make a difference, and that today was a good day to start.

The man stood back, as another wave brought hundreds more starfish to be stranded on the beach shore and declared "for every one you throw back, a thousand more get washed up, how can you be possibly making a difference?!

The old woman looked thoughtful for a second, then bent down, picked up a starfish and chucked him back into the sea. *"Made a difference to that one!!"* she proudly declared.

3.   It was registration day at the university and the young man was preparing to continue the adventure in learning that had been going on so long it seemed to have no beginning and no end. Lost in thought, his mind racing with possibilities for what lay ahead, he barely noticed the old man in front of him until he bumped straight into him.

"I'm sorry, Professor," the young man said, embarrassed.

"Oh, I'm not a professor," the old man replied. *"I'm a new student, just like you."*

"But how old are you?" the young man said in shock.

"I'm seventy-three," the old man said with a twinkle in his eye.

"And what are you studying?" the young man continued.

"Medicine- I've always wanted to be a doctor, and now..." The old man paused as if remembering something from a long time ago. *"Now, I'm finally ready to follow my dreams!"*

The young man seemed quite taken aback. *"No disrespect, sir, but to become a doctor will take at least seven years. In seven years, you'll be eighty years old!"*

The old man put his hand on the young man's shoulder and looked him straight in the eyes.

"God willing," the old man smiled, *"I'll be eighty years old whether I follow my dreams or not."*

Glossary of terms

7 +/- 2	The maximum number of bits of information that people could deal with consciously at any point in time. More than 9 chunks of information overloads the mind at which point conscious awareness gives way to trance.
Accessing Cues	Slight changes in behaviour that help to trigger and indicate which representational or sensory system a person is using to process information internally.
Alignment	An increased state of internal congruence. Having a more directed attention on a particular outcome.
Analogue	Analogue distinctions have discrete variations and are anything that can be changed gradually e.g. in a visual context, light to dark.
Analogue Marking	Marking out certain words non-verbally as you are talking to someone, to give an additional message by using voice tone, gesture, facial expression or touch.
Anchor	Any stimulus that evokes a response. Anchors will change our state.
"As If" Frame	To presuppose something is true and then act upon it. To 'pretend'. Enables us to proceed to a desired mental end without being hung up on imagined difficulties.
Association	You are inside an experience, seeing through your own eyes, fully in your senses. Experiencing something as if you are actually there.
Auditory	The representation system pertaining to hearing, including our own internal

	dialogue and external sounds.
Auditory Digital (Ad)	The representation system dealing with logic using abstract and non-sensory language and the way we talk to ourselves, e.g. our internal dialogue.
Backtrack Frame	Repeating or summarising what a person has said using their key words together with their same vocal tone, tempo and volume.
Behaviour	Human activity, both physical and mental that we engage in, including thought processes. One of six neurological levels as defined by Robert Dilts.
Beliefs	The generalisations that we make about ourselves, others and the world. What we take as true. One of six neurological levels as defined by Robert Dilts.
Body Language	The way we communicate with our body, without words or sounds, e.g. our posture, gestures, facial expressions, breathing and tone of voice.
Break State	Using a movement or distraction to change one's own or another's internal state e.g. changing physiology, cracking a joke. Useful when separating states elicited during anchoring. Also useful if someone is becoming unresourceful.
Breathing	An important indicator of an individual's internal state.
Calibration	The ability to notice and measure changes with respect to a standard. Usually involves the comparison between two different sets of external, non-verbal cues eg eye movements, posture, facial expression and breathing.
Capability	Our ability to successfully perform a

	task. One of six neurological levels as defined by Robert Dilts.
Chunking	The process of grouping and classifying data, perceptions, thinking and experience into chunks of information so it can be easily absorbed. Chunking up occurs when all the smaller parts are tied together and placed in the context of the total subject being considered. Metaphor chunks sideways to a different meaning on the same level. Chunking down involves dropping to a level by asking for specific instances.
Circle of Excellence	Using an imaginary circle on the floor as a spatial anchor to add additional resources relative to any situation where different behaviour or thinking would be helpful.
Comparisons	An element from the Meta Model by the use of words such as 'better', 'worse', 'harder', 'easier.'
Complex Equivalence	Two statements that are considered to mean the same thing, e.g. you are not smiling means that you are unhappy.
Confusion to Understanding	Pattern developed by Richard Bandler using submodalities to change the meaning of internal representations. Basis of "Like" to "Dislike."
Communication	The process of conveying information, ideas or intention, by language, signs, symbols and behaviour.
Congruence	Alignment of identity, beliefs and values, capabilities and behaviour. Being in rapport with oneself. Basis of effective leadership.
Conscious	Anything in the present moment

	awareness.
Content	The details of a story. The history of a client.
Content Reframe	Giving another meaning to a statement by recovering more content, which changes the focus. Also called a meaning reframe.
Context	The particular setting or situation in which the content occurs.
Context Reframing	Giving a statement or action another meaning by changing the context.
Contrastive Analysis	Comparing two or more elements and looking for critical differences between them. Process used to discover critical submodalities.
Conversational Postulate	Hypnotic form of language, a question that can be interpreted as a command e.g. 'I'm wondering if you could begin now ....'
Convincer	The filter used in becoming certain or confident that something is okay.
Criteria	Another word for values, i.e. the determinants of why we do certain things.
Critical Submodalities	Critical submodalities are the difference that makes the difference. Discovered through the process of contrastive analysis, critical submodalities are the difference between two different internal representations. When submodalities are compared through contrastive analysis, critical submodalities are the submodalities that are different.
Cross Over Matching	Matching a person's body movement with a different type of movement, e.g. tapping your foot in time to their speech

	rhythm.
Deletion	Deletion occurs when we exclude part of an experience from thought or speech. One of three major processes on which Meta Model is based.
Digital	Digital is a submodality that has to be one thing or another, e.g. black or white, on or off, associated or dissociated. Language is digital communication
Digital Language	Abstract words or language that have no sensory component.
Dissociated	Being outside an experience, seeing it as an observer rather than as a participant. As if seeing yourself in a film.
Distortion	Changing the meaning of someone else's experience, according to your map of reality. One of three major processes (including deletion and generalisation) on which the Meta Model is based.
Driver	The submodality that makes the most difference in our meaning of an experience. It is so important that it carries all the other submodality differences, the critical submodalities, when we change it.
Ecology	The study of the consequences or results or impact of any change that occurs on the wider system.
Ecology Check	Checking the consequences of any change to ensure that it is something that is desirable for all concerned. A check on the total system implications of any course of action.
Elicitation	Drawing out or evoking some given

	human behaviour such as a state or a strategy.
Embedded Command	An indirect form of giving instructions, by embedding direct commands into a larger sentence structure, e.g. as you begin to relax now you may find it easier to close your eyes.
Embedded Questions	A question that is inside a longer sentence, marked out by voice tone or gesture.
Environment	Context: the where and the when, also the people we are with. One of Robert Dilts' six neurological levels.
Evidence Procedure	The sensory information that will let you know that you have achieved your outcome.
Feedback	The results of your actions to influence your next step.
First Position	This is one of the Perceptual Positions. Perceiving the world from your own reality, your own point of view only. Being aware of your own inner reality.
Frame	The context or particular point of view around a specific experience. For example, what is inside the frame is noticed; whereas what is outside the frame is not attended to.
Future Pace	Mentally rehearsing a future result by projecting a situation into the future so that the desired outcome automatically occurs.
Generalisation	The process by which one specific experience comes to represent a whole class of experiences. One of three major processes on which Meta Model is based.

Gestalt	A collection of memories around a certain topic.
Gustatory (G)	The representational system dealing with taste.
Hallucination	Sensory experience of something that does not exist.
Hypnotism	A relaxed state induced in a person so that change work can be done at an unconscious level.
Identity	Your self image or self concept. Your sense of self. One of Robert Dilts' six neurological levels.
Incongruence	The simultaneous presentation of contradictory signals. Sequential: one action followed by another that contradicts it Simultaneous: agreement in words but with a doubtful voice tone.
Imprinting	An imprint experience that is a significant event in which a strong belief or beliefs are formed. These may be either positive experiences that give rise to resourceful beliefs or negative experiences which lead to limiting beliefs.
Intention	The purpose of a behaviour or its desired outcome.
Internal Representations	The arrangement of information we create and store in our minds in the form of pictures, sounds, feelings, tastes, smells and self talk.
In Time	Having a time line where the past is behind you, and the future in front, with the 'now' passing through your body.
Kinaesthetic	The feeling sense, tactile sensations and internal feelings such as remembered sensations, emotions, and the sense of

	balance.
Law of Requisite Variety	In a given physical system, that part of the system with the greatest flexibility of behaviour will control the system.
Leading	Changing what you do with enough rapport for the other person to follow.
Lead System	The representational system you use to lead you to stored information from your unconscious to your conscious. Watching eye accessing cues discovers the lead system.
Limiting Belief	A belief that reduces and limits the possibility of performing certain actions, adopting certain strategies, being certain ways, or conceiving of oneself in more complete and fulfilling ways.
Limiting Decision	The decision that preceded the adoption of a limiting belief.
Logical Levels	Different levels of experience: environment, behaviour, capability, beliefs and values, identity, spiritual. Also called neurological levels.
Map of Reality	Each person's unique representation of the world built from his or her individual perceptions and experiences. Also referred to as 'Model of the World'.
Mapping Across	Following contrastive analysis, mapping across is the submodality process of actually changing the set of submodalities of a certain internal representation to change its meaning.
Matching	Doing the same, copying or approximating aspects of another person's behaviour, skills, beliefs or values for the purpose of enhancing

	rapport.
Meaning Reframe	Giving another meaning to a statement by recovering more content, which changes the focus. Sometimes called a Content Reframe.
Meta	From the Greek meaning 'above or beyond'.
Meta Model	A set of language patterns and questions that links and reunites language with experience.
Metaphor	Indirect communication by a story or figure of speech implying a comparison. In NLP metaphor covers similes, stories and parables. Allows us to bypass the conscious resistance of the client and to have the client make connections at a deeper level.
Meta Position	A location outside a situation enabling you to view the situation in a more objective way. A dissociated position not involved with the content of the event or the person. Similar to Third Position.
Meta Programs	Unconscious content free filters which filter our experience.
Milton Model	The inverse of the Meta Model, using artfully vague language patterns to pace another person's experience and access unconscious resources.
Mirroring	Reflecting the behaviour or the physiology of the client as if looking into a mirror.
Mismatching	Deliberately breaking rapport by the use of contradictory behaviour patterns for the purpose of redirecting or severing communication.
Modality	Any one of five senses: VAKOG

Modal Operators	Modal Operators of Necessity relates to words which form the rules in our lives (should, must, have to). Modal Operators of Possibility relates to words that denote that which is considered possible (can, want, will) etc.
Model of the World	A person's values, beliefs and attitudes as well as their internal representations, states and physiology, that all relate to and create their belief system of how the world operates.
Model	A description of how something works, with the intention of putting it to practical use.
Modelling	The process of discerning the sequence of ideas and behaviour that enables someone to accomplish a task. The basis of NLP.
Multiple Description	Having different points of view of the same event using a number of different perceptual positions. Having first, second, and third positions together is called a 'triple description'.
Neuro-Linguistic Programming	NLP is the study of excellence and how the language of the mind produces our behaviour – a model of how individuals structure their experience, and the study of the structure of subjective experience.
Nominalisation	Linguistic term for the process of turning a verb into an abstract noun, e.g. 'relating' becomes 'the relationship', a process has become a thing.
Olfactory	The sense of smell.
Outcome	A specific sensory based desired goal, with evidence procedure.

Overlapping	Moving from one sensory modality to another by a phased transition.
Pacing	Gaining and maintaining rapport with another person over a period of time by meeting them in their model of the world by matching or mirroring their external behaviour.
Parts	Parts are a portion of the unconscious mind, often having conflicting beliefs and values that are different from the whole of the system.
Parts Integration	A technique which allows us to integrate parts at the unconscious level by assisting each one to traverse logical levels by chunking up and to go beyond the boundaries of each to find a higher level of intention and wholeness.
Pattern Interrupt	Changing a person's state rather abruptly, often by mismatching them.
Perceptual Position	Describes our point of view in a specific situation: First Position is our own point of view; Second Position is usually someone else's point of view; Third position is the point of view of a dissociated observer i.e. the relationship between the two.
Personal Edit	Being aware of and aligning conscious and unconscious processes. Left and Right brain integration.
Phobia	An extreme negative kinaesthetic experience that is involuntarily triggered by the person experiencing it.
Phonological Ambiguity	This occurs when there are two words which sound the same but have different meanings.
Physiology	The way we breathe, our posture and body language, our facial expressions

	and skin tone.
Physiology of Excellence	Modelling excellence in others and utilising it in yourself and others.
Positive Intention	The positive purpose underlying any action or belief. The real desire that is driving the particular behaviour. NLP presupposes that every behaviour has a positive intention, even though the behaviour may seem to be self-defeating.
Predicates	Sensory based words that indicate the use of one or more representational systems.
Preferred Representational System	The representational system that an individual typically uses most to think consciously and organise their experience.
Presuppositions	The assumptions that a person makes to support their model of the world.
Presuppositions of NLP	Assumptions or convenient beliefs, which are not necessarily "true", but which if accepted and believed will change our thinking and improve our results.
Primary Representational System	This is how we represent our internal processing externally. Most people tend to favour one representational system over another and process most communication in that manner.
Projection	To attribute one's ideas or feelings to other people or to another model of the world.
Rapport	A relationship of trust and responsiveness with self or others. The naturally occurring 'dance' that happens when people meet. A harmonising of values, energies and natural rhythms

	that creates a sense of mutual acknowledgement.
Reference Experience	A significant experience that is the basis of learning, and to which you can refer thereafter.
Reference System	The base against which we calibrate. How we organise information so that we know what we know.
Reframing	The process of making a shift in the nature of a problem, or changing the structure or context of a statement to give it another meaning.
Relevancy Challenge	An intervention used to keep people focused on a specific outcome, especially during the course of a meeting.
Representational Systems	The different channels whereby we re-present information on the inside, using our senses; visual (sight), auditory (hearing), kinaesthetic (feelings), olfactory (smell), gustatory (taste).
Resources	Anything that can help one achieve an outcome, e.g. physiology, states, thoughts, beliefs, strategies, experiences, people, events, places, possessions, procedures, techniques, stories etc.
Resourceful State	This refers to any state where a person has positive helpful emotions and strategies available to him or her, and is operating from them behaviourally. Obviously the state implies a successful outcome.
Secondary Gain	The reason/reward the person has or receives for not changing from a presenting problem.
Second Position	Relating to Perceptual Positions. The

	second perceptual position relates to perceiving things from another person's point of view, putting yourself in their shoes.
Sensory Acuity	The ability to notice and gain awareness of another person's conscious and unconscious responses through their physiology.
Sensory Based Description	The use of words to describe, but not diagnose, an observation or experience directly verified by the senses, e.g. his jaw is clenched tightly provides a sensory-based description.
State	The sum of our thoughts, feelings, emotions, physical and mental energy. In NLP, our internal representations, plus our state and our physiology results in our behaviour.
Strategy	A sequence of behaviour patterns intended to produce a specific outcome; the way we organise our ideas and behaviour in order to perform a specific task.
Submodalities	The components that make up each modality or representational system, enabling our brains to sort and code our experience.
Third Position	Relating to Perceptual Positions. Looking at a situation from a place of non-involvement.
Through Time	Having a time line where both past, present and future are in front of you. For example time can be spatially represented as a year planner.
Time Code	The way we store our memories into the past, present and future.
Time Line	A metaphorical line that connects your

	past with your future. The way we store pictures, sounds and feelings of our past, present and future.
Trance	An altered state resulting from a temporarily fixed, narrowed and inward focus of attention.
Triple Description	Seeing an event from first, second and third position.
Unconscious	Everything that is not in your present moment awareness.
Unconscious Mind	The part of your mind that you are not consciously aware of.
Universal	An experience that is so well known that it is assumed.
Universal Quantifiers	Words such as 'all', 'every', 'never' that admit no exception.
Unspecified nouns	Nouns that do not clearly state who or what they refer to, e.g. 'they.'
Utilisation	Pacing someone's reality by simply describing their ongoing sensory experience of what they must be feeling, hearing, or seeing.
Values	High level generalisations that describe that which is important to you. In NLP sometimes called criteria.
Visual	The representational system dealing with the sense of sight.
Well-formedness Conditions	The well-formedness conditions allow us to specify outcomes that are more achievable, because the language conforms to certain rules.

Index

<u>Training Courses</u>

Inspirational Solutions offers in house tailored training programs specifically for your organization to precisely achieve the outcomes you desire. We are a leading Neuro Linguistic Programming (NLP) training and consultancy organisation based in Mid Wales who work in partnership with other top UK NLP team and leadership trainers, including Jeremy Lazarus, and Lisa Wake, the only recognised trainer-trainers of NLP who are accredited by Kingston University.

Inspirational Solutions specialises in training and coaching the application of NLP in Business, Health care and on a specific one to one, personal level, working with our clients continuously to ensure the practices we are teaching are being understood and utilized correctly, but above all to ensure that we are giving high quality teachings and good customer service.

<u>What has NLP got to offer to Businesses?</u>

Success requires courage, commitment and focus. When applied appropriately to the needs of your organisation NLP can significantly contribute to your success through:

- Increased sales and revenue.
- Improved personal performance.
- Improved leadership and coaching abilities.
- More focused & effective change initiatives.
- Better personal communication and influencing skills.
- Greater team work, creativity and problem solving skills.
- Enhanced staff motivation.

<u>Your Training Course</u>- *wherever you are in your career, there is an Inspirational course for you*

Inspirational Solutions offers a range of training courses specifically tailored to your business, for a free consultation please contact us via our details on page 337. These courses can be carried out in house, at a mutual training venue, or at our training facilities here in Rhydymain. We also offer pre-structured courses accredited by Kingston University outlined below:

NLP Diploma
A four day Diploma giving candidates a deep and broad understanding of the key skills and techniques of NLP. This course is both unique and practical as you will be able to go away and immediately use these techniques in your personal and professional environments due to the modular program schedule and practical exercises.

Inspirational Management
This three day Management course is underpinned by Neuro linguistic programming, providing a range of tools and techniques to understand the behaviour of others and teaching the user how to use language to empower and motivate their staff.

Inspirational Leadership
A two day NLP course; teaching a range of personal and leadership development tools for professionals who are in or entering into a leadership position.

Introduction to NLP for Business Professionals
An inside view to the techniques and practices of NLP. During this 1 day course, you will be experiencing and learning an approach to applying NLP in business which is both unique and practical, as you will have many opportunities to explore the application of NLP in your own professional environment.

Inspirational Communication
A one day course touching on some of the aspects of NLP, taking the theory that there is no such thing as bad listeners, only poor communicators. By taking responsibility for your communication and changing the way you communicate to your colleagues and

clients; you will learn how to communicate more effectively, achieving your aim's and desires whilst understanding the other parties' point of view.

Inspirational Presentations
This short half day course draws upon NLP theory and techniques, teaching you how to capture, engage and inspire your audience while remaining in a calm, confident and relaxed state.

NLP Communication Course

The meaning of communication to another individual is the response it elicits in them, regardless of your intention. Everybody is 100% responsible for their communication; people respond to what they think you have said. If your communication is poor then the other person may not fully understand/grasp what you have said. There is no such thing as bad listeners, just inflexible communicators. By taking responsibility for your communication and changing the way you communicate to different people, you will get more of what you want and less of what you don't.

Who is the course for?
The course is for anyone who wants to improve themselves and learn new skills. This course is available for all business professionals, being of particular value for team leaders or professionals looking to improve in this area of expertise.

What will be covered?
- A brief history of NLP.
- The principles of NLP.
- The communication model.
- Rapport, what it is and how to really use it.
- Sensory acuity.
- Giving and receiving feedback.

What will you get out of the course?

- An increased self awareness that will make you even more effective in your communication.
- The ability to get what you need from who you communicate to.
- The ability to inspire and motivate others.
- Understanding of rapport and how to use it to build rapport with colleagues & clients.
- To understand your role and impact on others and why they are different.

NLP Diploma Course

The NLP Business Diploma covers; leadership, sales, training and strategic change as well as learning and development, creativity and problem solving. This 4 day NLP diploma will provide your business with a variety of strategies for maximising both efficiency and future profit potential.

How is the Diploma Structured?
From day one you will be learning the theory behind each technique followed by a demonstration of how and when this technique would be used. Each candidate will then carry-out an exercise on the technique so that each delegate gets the opportunity to learn and practice the technique in a teaching environment. The delegates will be consistently assessed on the competencies to follow the techniques and the understanding of how and when the techniques would be used.

Who is this Course For?
This course is for anyone who wants to learn new skills and have immediate results in both their personal and professional life. This course is excellent for candidates working in the fields of; Management, HR, Sales, Training & Business Development.

What Will Be Covered?
During this program, you will be experiencing and learning an approach to applying NLP in business which is both unique and practical as it is based on many years of real world experience. You

will have many opportunities to explore the application of NLP in your own professional environment due to the modular program schedule and practical exercises. Please contact us for further information on specific modules.

Why Attend This Course?

On attending this diploma you receive hands on experience of the powerful techniques of NLP. This will not only be an amazing learning and development course for your own personal development, but also for the development and success of your business. By the end of the diploma not only will you have learnt how to use the techniques of NLP, but you will know which technique to use to achieve the desired solution to a problem.

What will You Obtain from Attending this Diploma ?

Leadership Skills

1. Develop peak performance & motivation - understand how people 'tick'.
2. Increase your flexibility to work with a variety of contrasting personalities.
3. Experience greater well being even under very stressful conditions.
4. Elicit valuable unconscious information to help colleagues transform.

Sales & Marketing Skills

1. Apply advanced communication, rapport and influence.
2. Sharpen your negotiation, sales & presentation skills.
3. Understand, model & replicate success strategies.
4. Lead, persuade and motivate colleagues to accomplish greater goals.

Management Skills

1. Enhance abilities to respond to a variety of challenges & situations.
2. Create dynamic, personal and stronger relationships.
3. Enhance risk management abilities by eliciting better quality information.

4. Facilitate change & create greater acceptance, co-operation & involvement.

Creativity, Invention and Problem Solving Skills
1. Develop new problem solving skills that generate innovation & new insight.
2. Generate deep states of 'FLOW' and accelerate creativity & accomplishment.
3. Apply Walt Disney's creativity model and learn to "imaginer" invention.
4. Improve outcomes by understanding how to transform your perspective.

NLP Management Course

Within this course you will learn a range of tools and techniques that will help staff understand the behaviour of their colleagues and clients. By understanding why people behave the way they do, you will be able to pre-empt and influence them. You will learn how to use language to empower and motivate your staff and how to communicate even more effectively. This 3 day course will give you the tools to understand yourself and your behaviours, which in turn allows you to develop the qualities of a great manager.

Who is the course for?
The course is for anyone who wants to improve themselves and learn new skills. This course is of particular value for business professionals who are in, or entering into a managerial position. This course is excellent for candidates in HR, recruitment and managerial positions.

What will be covered?
· A brief history of NLP and the principles of NLP.
· Rapport, what it is and how to really use it.
· Giving and receiving feedback.
· Insight into how other people perceive you.
· The communication model.

· The structure of experience.
· Managing state.
· Understanding patterns of behaviour.
· Reframing techniques.
· Creative problem solving techniques.
· Logical Levels of Change and development.

What will you get out of the course?
· Gain insight into your own management style.
· Know what makes a good manager.
· Learn how people communicate.
· Understand your colleagues by learning the 15 personality traits.
· Learn how to motivate and influence colleagues.
· Learn how to gain insight into someone else's point of view.

NLP Leadership Course

This 2 day course teaches a range of personal and leadership development tools to assist people who are in or entering into a leadership position. The course will give you the tools to understand yourself and appreciate the behaviour of others. This in turn allows you to develop the qualities of a great leader.

Who is the course for?
The course is for anyone who wants to improve themselves and learn new skills. This course is of particular value for team leaders and managers, especially those who are in or entering into a leadership position.

What will be covered?
· A brief history of NLP.
· The principles of NLP.
· The communication model.
· Rapport, what it is and how to really use it.
· Giving and receiving feedback.
· Goals and well formed outcomes.
· Perceptual positions - insight into how other people perceive you.

· To be able to feel how you want to feel, not how you're made.
· Anchoring.
· Logical Levels of learning and communicating.
· Motivational Traits.

What will you get out of the course?

· Gain insight into your own leadership style.
· Understand & know what makes a good leader.
· Strategies leaders use to unite people behind their vision.
· Understand what makes people tick and how to motivate and influence them.
· Confidence in your abilities as a leader.
· The ability to empower and motivate your staff
· How to make effective and achievable goals.

Introduction to NLP Course

An inside view to the techniques and practices of NLP. During this 1 day course you will be experiencing and learning an approach to applying NLP in business which is both unique and practical as you will have many opportunities to explore the application of NLP in your own professional environment.

NLP is the way forward for businesses; it provides excellent communication, leadership, management, sales and facilitation skills, enabling strategic change, creativity and problem solving as well as the effective learning and development for all staff members.

Who is the course for?
The course is for anyone who wants to improve themselves and learn new skills. This course is available for all business professionals, being of particular value for business professionals in managerial positions, HR and sales.

What will be covered?
· Communication and unconscious communication.
· The structure of experience.
· Managing state.
· Rapport, Pacing and Leading.
· Understanding patterns of behaviour.
· Creative problem solving techniques.

What will you get out of the course?
· An increased self awareness that will make you even more effective in your communication.
· The ability to inspire and motivate others.
· How to build rapport with colleagues & clients.
· Understand your role and impact on others.
· To be able to manage your state regardless of current situation.
· Easy and effective problem solving techniques that can be utilised in all areas of your business.

NLP Presentation Course

This 1/2 day presentation course will not only teach you how do give inspirational presentations but also to enjoy them. Teaching you how to structure a presentation/interview to capture, engage and inspire your audience, while remaining in a calm, confident and relaxed state.

Who is the course for?
The course is for anyone who wants to improve themselves and learn new skills. This course is of particular value for business professionals looking to improve in this area of expertise, whether for job interviews, or simply giving presentations to whatever size audience. The tools and techniques taught can be applied to all areas from teaching of junior staff to management & client meetings.

What will be covered?
· A brief history & principles of NLP
· The use of metaphors.
· Content sequencing.
· Anchors - spatial, visual, physical, tonal.
· The 4 - Mat content system.
· The use of humour.

What will you get out of the course?
· Excellent presentation skills.
· The ability to control your emotional state, replacing anxiety and distress with confidence in your abilities and yourself.
· Increased self awareness.
· The ability to inspire and motivate others.

Clients & Testimonials

"The training was clear and easy to understand"

Alan Smith, Aberystwyth.

"I have really enjoyed this course, (Inspirational Management) I have gained so many insights into myself and can't wait to start putting these techniques into practice"

Mandy Strudwick, Chester.

"I have worked with Donna Blinston over a period of around 6 months and found her manner of practice to be both sympathetic and commanding. As an experienced business coach I have come across few people who can maintain the client in a space that is both comfortable and highly challenging and Donna manages to do this in a quiet yet authoritative manner.

I have no hesitation in saying that some of the work she has done with me has been life changing and the remainder was always highly competent and professional."

Richard Clark. Business consultant, London

"Donna is an excellent Master Practitioner. She has both confidence and sensitivity, her years as a nurse has given her a "bedside" manner that adds to the feeling that she knows what she is doing and can support you getting the results and changes you want, and usually more too. I would be equally happy recommending her to my Mum or my Boss!"

Bhavesh Patel, Management Trainer, People Potential, Malaysia

Telephone/Fax: 01341450663

Email: info@inspirationalsolutions-nlp.co.uk

Website: www.inspirationalsolutions-nlp.co.uk

Also from MX Publishing

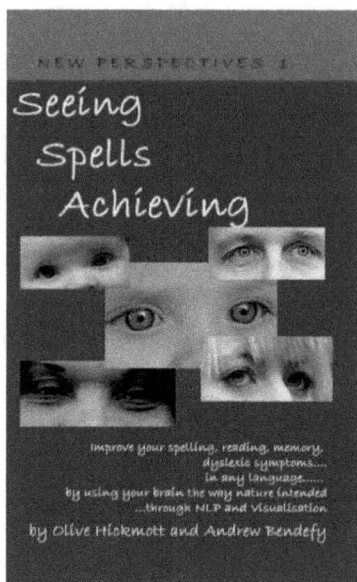

Seeing Spells Achieving

The UK's leading NLP book for
learning difficulties including dyslexia

More NLP books at www.mxpublishing.co.uk

Also from MX Publishing

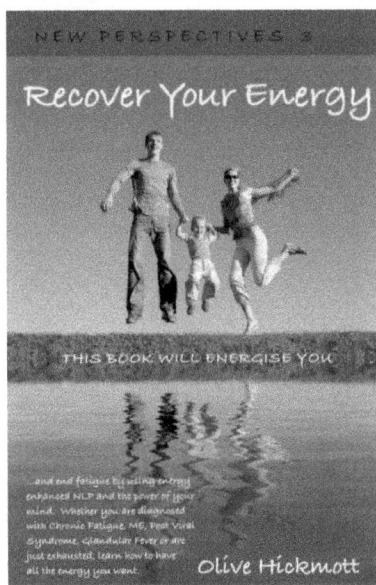

Recover Your Energy

NLP for Chronic Fatigue, ME and tiredness

More NLP books at www.mxpublishing.co.uk

340